D0057848

Slavery in American Society

Slavery in American Society

Third Edition

Edited and with an introduction by

Lawrence B. Goodheart
University of Connecticut, Hartford

Richard D. Brown
University of Connecticut, Storrs

Stephen G. Rabe
University of Texas, Dallas

D. C. HEATH AND COMPANY
Lexington, Massachusetts   Toronto

Address editorial correspondence to:

D. C. Heath
125 Spring Street
Lexington, MA 02173

Cover: The cover illustration is a detail of a stereograph taken by James F. Gibson in Cumberland Landing, Virginia, on May 14, 1862. It depicts a group of "contrabands," fugitive slaves who sought sanctuary behind Union Army lines. As large numbers of slaves—men, women, and children—fled, they acted to subvert the system of bondage and the power of the Confederacy. They left perplexed and outraged slavemasters, who had assumed that their slaves were loyal and obedient. The pressing issue of "contrabands"—who were legally neither slave nor free—also compelled the Lincoln administration toward the military necessity and moral imperative of emancipation. (Archive Photos.)

Published simultaneously in Canada.

Printed in the United States of America.

International Standard Book Number: 0-669-24446-5

Library of Congress Catalog Number: 91-77241

9-CW-06 05 04 03 02

For Clarence, Carol, and Jamie

The Editors

Lawrence B. Goodheart

Born in Washington, D.C., Lawrence B. Goodheart was educated at the University of Rochester, State University of New York at Albany, and the University of Connecticut, where he earned his Ph.D. He taught social studies in the Rochester, New York, public schools and later taught history at Vanderbilt University and Nichols College. Goodheart is now assistant professor of history at the University of Connecticut, Hartford. He has written *Abolitionist, Actuary, Atheist: Elizur Wright and the Reform Impulse* (1990) and coedited, with Richard O. Curry, *American Chameleon: Essays on Individualism in Trans-National Context* (1991). His essays have appeared in the *Journal of the Early Republic, Civil War History, Canadian Review of American Studies,* and the *Historian.* He has served on the editorial board of the *Journal of the Early Republic* and is director of the University of Connecticut Academy, a teacher training institute funded by the U.S. Department of Education.

Richard D. Brown

Richard D. Brown, professor of history at the University of Connecticut, earned his B.A. at Oberlin College and his Ph.D. at Harvard University, where he was a student of Bernard Bailyn. He is the author of four books: *Knowledge Is Power: The Diffusion of Information in Early America, 1700–1865* (1989); *Massachusetts: A Bicentennial History* (1978); *Modernization: The Transformation of American Life, 1600–1865* (1976); and *Revolutionary Politics in Massachusetts: The Boston Committee of Correspondence and the Towns, 1772–1774* (1970). Brown also has edited two volumes in addition to *Slavery in American Society,* and he has authored numerous articles.

Brown's research has been supported by the National Endowment for the Humanities (NEH), the American Philosophical Society, and the Social Science Research Council. He has been a fellow of the Charles Warren Center at Harvard University, the American Antiquarian Society, and the Center for the History of Freedom at Washington University in St. Louis. He has twice joined University of Connecticut colleagues in leading NEH-sponsored seminars for college and university teachers on the subject of classic texts in early American history. Brown also has taught at Oberlin College, the Harvard University Summer School, and at the University of Toulouse (France) as a Fulbright lecturer. Brown is a past president of the New England Historical Association, a regional affiliate of the American Historical Association.

Stephen G. Rabe

Born in Hartford, Connecticut, Stephen G. Rabe received a B.A. from Hamilton College and a Ph.D. from the University of Connecticut. He is now professor of history at the University of Texas, Dallas. He has written two books: *Eisenhower and Latin America: The Foreign Policy of Anticommunism* (1988), which won the Stuart L. Bernath Memorial Book Award of the Society for Historians of American Foreign Relations, and *The Road to OPEC: United States Relations with Venezuela, 1919–1976* (1982). With Thomas G. Paterson he has edited *Imperial Surge: The United States Abroad, The 1890s–Early 1900s* (1992). Rabe's articles have appeared in *Diplomatic History, Latin American Research Review, Peace and Change,* and *Mid-America,* among others. He has contributed chapters on U.S. relations with Latin America to Richard Immerman, ed., *John Foster Dulles and the Diplomacy of the Cold War* (1989) and Thomas G. Paterson, ed., *Kennedy's Quest for Victory* (1989). Rabe's research and writing have been supported by the National Endowment for the Humanities, the Rockefeller Archive Center, and the Lyndon Baines Johnson Foundation, among others. In 1988 the Society for Historians of American Foreign Relations honored him with its Stuart L. Bernath Lecture Prize, and in 1990–1992 he served on the Executive Council of that organization. The winner of outstanding teaching awards, he was Mary Ball Washington Professor of American History at University College, Dublin, Ireland, in 1990–1991.

Preface

Since the publication of the second edition of this book, the writing on slavery has been extensive and innovative, including some of the most important studies in all of American history. Historians now emphasize that slavery in the transatlantic world was a phenomenon involving the interactions of peoples and cultures in Europe, Africa, and the Americas over four centuries. In addition to new questions and new techniques, recent interpretations have focused on the life and values of the Africans and African-Americans whom Europeans and their descendants in the New World subjected to bondage. Moreover, scholars generally agree that slavery was an integral part of American history and has shaped our society to the present day. This third edition makes the exciting, current literature readily available for classroom use.

Virtually everything about this edition is new. The introduction has been substantially rewritten, and a chronology has been added to mark the dates of pivotal events mentioned in the readings. The illustrations, paintings, and photographs provide a fascinating visual record that we hope will enhance readers' understanding of slavery. Of the eighteen selections, only one has been retained from previous editions. The revised format features six sections that consider issues from the origins of slavery to emancipation. Parts I and II define slavery and discuss its emergence. Parts III and IV deal with slave life, family, and gender. Parts V and VI explore the relationship of slavery to society in the United States and compare U.S. slavery with bondage in South Africa, Russia, and the rest of the Americas. A headnote introduces each selection as well as identifies important themes and places the reading in a historical context. The updated, expanded bibliography is organized topically so that faculty and students can further investigate specific issues raised in this volume.

We thank the authors and publishers whose work is included in this anthology for permission to reprint their writings. *Slavery in*

American Society was greatly improved by the constructive criticism of the anonymous reviewers engaged by D. C. Heath while the book was in preliminary form. They include John B. Boles, Rice University; Lorin Lee Cary, University of Toledo; Franklin W. Knight, The Johns Hopkins University; Peter Kolchin, University of Delaware; and Robert L. Paquette, Hamilton College. James Miller and Sylvia Mallory of D. C. Heath skillfully oversaw the development of the manuscript. Sylvia deserves credit for much of the work on the illustrations, as well as for her expert editorship.

Lawrence B. Goodheart
Richard D. Brown
Stephen G. Rabe

Contents

III. Slave Life and Culture

IV. Family and Gender

V. United States Slavery in Comparative Perspective

VI. Slavery and Society

Introduction

Slavery and the resulting pattern of race relations have long exercised a decisive role in shaping the society of the United States. Although more than a century separates us from slavery as an established institution, its heritage remains a dynamic force of immense proportions. Our own attitudes, behavior, and institutions continue to reflect impulses generated in a system that has long since vanished. As a result this defunct social institution retains a profound continuity with our own times, possessing a special immediacy for contemporary society.

No one planned the creation of black slavery on the mainland of British North America. Like many other innovations in the New World, it was a synthesis produced by interaction between the colonists and their environment. Ironically, the Englishmen who introduced slavery to the British North American mainland and who molded most colonial institutions came from a nation that boasted that it knew no law of slavery and that English soil was synonymous with personal and political freedom. Nevertheless, social arrangements resembling a racial caste system emerged during the seventeenth century as a central feature of Anglo-American society.

The first challenge to English social conventions came from Native Americans. After meager efforts at assimilation, English colonists responded to the problems of ethnic heterogeneity by displacing or destroying the native peoples, ultimately rejecting them as alien enemies. This solution seemed to permit the development of a purely Christian society. But the ethnic homogeneity of European society in North America was never actually established. At the same time that Native Americans were disappearing from English settlements, European slave ships brought Africans. Their entry—first in small numbers, later by the thousands—posed a variety of social and religious challenges to the scattered English settlements. The colonists' solutions were not entirely uniform, except that everywhere they established the supremacy of Europeans and the subjection of Africans.

By the early eighteenth century, white supremacy had made chattel slavery the normal status of African immigrants in every colony. As chattels, Africans became articles of movable property, devoid of the minimum rights of English subjects. For any person with at least one black parent or grandparent, hereditary, lifelong servitude became a fixed condition unless written proof of free status was provided. In short, a servant caste was emerging. Even though this caste was intimately connected with many phases of colonial life, it was regarded with disdain and fear and was excluded from sharing the social and economic mobility that was an essential condition of whites in a developing society. Blacks lived in the dynamic, exploitative society of the thirteen colonies as oppressed, often hostile, servants. They never were, however, simply passive victims of a brutal institution but responded in a variety of ways to lessen their degradation.

The existence of white supremacy and black subjection has been so much a part of American life that it was long seen as inevitable. For many years historians believed that, given the intensive colonial demand for labor, the physical and ethnic characteristics of the Europeans and Africans necessarily established whites as masters over black slaves. But since the end of World War II, a new, consciously antiracist attitude has characterized inquiry into the development of American race relations. Now the particular pattern of white subjection of blacks—however natural and necessary it may have seemed to generations of Americans—demands explanation. Historians wonder why the English imposed a slave status and why they attached it to Africans. Moreover, they ask why slavery in the Americas and South Africa—as well as serfdom in Russia—produced different forms of subjection. Important questions arise, too, about the nature of slave life and culture, the family and women, and accommodation and resistance. Historians are probing the answers to such questions by examining the processes whereby captive Africans were transformed into African-American slaves.

During the last three decades, the historiography of slavery has been not only extensive but also extremely innovative. No less than a revolution has taken place in the assessment of slavery. New questions, new approaches, and new interpretations have expanded the dimensions of the subject, especially the consideration of slave life and culture.

Historians not longer view slavery as static, monolithic, or benign. Instead, they regard it as a harsh institution based on racial discrimination and class exploitation that varied according to time and place. Slavery did not suddenly appear full blown with the arrival in 1619 at Jamestown of nineteen Africans aboard a Dutch slave ship, the first such event on the mainland of British North America. The initial status of these blacks in Virginia remains unclear. What is certain, however, is that the institution of slavery emerged gradually over the course of the seventeenth century in the Chesapeake Bay region (the tidewater area of Virginia and Maryland), the major slaveholding settlement in what would become the United States.

Change and diversity, irony and paradox characterized slavery until its abolition by the Thirteenth Amendment to the United States Constitution in 1865. After 1820, King Cotton reigned in the Old South, producing an expansive planter-dominated society. Yet more acreage was devoted in the antebellum South to corn, a vital staple crop, than to the profit-making export of cotton. In addition, there were powerful planters whose wealth came from tobacco in the Chesapeake, rice in coastal South Carolina and Georgia, and sugar cane in Louisiana. Slave populations predominated in the low country and fertile black belt of Alabama and Mississippi, but slaves were absent from some of the upcountry of Appalachia, an area peopled by a white yeomanry.

Tara, the fictional plantation of Margaret Mitchell's romantic novel of the Old South, *Gone with the Wind* (1936), was the exception rather than the rule. At the zenith of plantation slavery in the mid-nineteenth century, 75 percent of southern white families owned no slaves at all. Half of all slaveholders owned a modest five slaves or fewer and worked their small farms side by side with their bondsmen and bondswomen. (Black women, unlike white women, regularly performed field labor.) Nevertheless, on the eve of the Civil War, a majority of the South's 4 million slaves belonged to owners of twenty slaves or more. Most slaves therefore lived on large farms and plantations and toiled as fieldhands. A minority of their fellow slaves served as slave drivers, overseers, artisans, and house servants. Other slaves, about 10 percent of the total, lived in cities and were hired out in a variety of occupations including working in iron mills and coal mines and as boatmen.

Contradiction and complexity further describe the portrait of slavery drawn by modern historians. Slaves were legally categorized as chattel, movable property like horses and wagons. They were also, of course, flesh-and-blood men, women, and children who expressed their frustrations and hopes in various ways that served to influence the institution of slavery and lessen their degradation. Their distinctive African-American culture combined African traditions with the American experience. Music, family life, religion, and a variety of folkways set slaves apart from their masters. Yet at the same time, blacks and whites shared some similar patterns of thought and behavior; slave culture could not be autonomous, given the superior authority of the master. Still, life within the slave quarters provided blacks with the resilience to assert and define their humanity within the confines of bondage. Historians also recognize that slave personality usually was not overtly rebellious or utterly resigned but that slaves engaged in a range of behaviors between those two extremes, depending on the circumstances. Acting servile in front of whites was expected behavior, but slaves hardly adopted that role in all situations.

Slavery is furthermore an integral part of the history of the United States, a nation that has long praised the ideals of liberty and equality. American revolutionaries, including large slaveholders such as Thomas Jefferson, declared that "all men are created equal," yet one-sixth of the new nation's inhabitants remained enslaved, an inconsistency apparent even in the late eighteenth century. Indeed, nine of the first twelve presidents of the United States owned slaves.

It is also ironic that the rapid growth of cotton production could flourish alongside the rise of factory-based capitalism and the emergence of bourgeois democracy in the Anglo-American world. Yet the slaveholders' equation of freedom with the absolute right to own slave property prompted bitter contention, first over the extension of slavery into the western territories and then over secession from the Union. The contradiction between slavery and freedom was resolved only through a civil war. With the exception of Haiti, where an earlier slave revolution had occurred, the United States was the only modern nation in which a violent confrontation accompanied emancipation. The Civil War and Reconstruction marked, however, an incomplete revolution for 4 million former slaves. The effort to achieve black equality in the postbellum South failed just as it had faltered in the post-Revolutionary North.

Historians have not always found slavery such a complex and contradictory institution. In *American Negro Slavery* (1918), Ulrich B. Phillips formulated a fundamentally different interpretation that dominated historical thought for nearly forty years. Born in 1877 at the end of Reconstruction, Phillips learned during his Georgia boyhood to revere the ideals of the planter class. As a historian trained at Columbia University, and later as a faculty member at Yale University, he drew on plantation records in his writing on slavery and distinguished himself as the nation's leading authority on the subject.

According to Phillips and his followers, slavery was a benign and paternalistic system in which genial planters socially uplifted their backward and childlike slaves. Phillips concluded that slave labor was inefficient and that plantation slavery was unprofitable, findings that historians accepted for decades as self-evident truths. Slavery would have withered away without war, Phillips maintained, if abolitionists, with their fanatical demands for racial equality, had not provoked hostilities. His belief in the innate and inherited inferiority of blacks—an attitude of white supremacy that was pervasive during the first decades of the twentieth century—precluded not only concern with the American dilemma of slavery and freedom but also interest in the subject of slave life and culture in its own right. The pioneering scholarship on African-Americans by early black historians W. E. B. Du Bois and G. Carter Woodson (both of whom held Ph.D. degrees from Harvard University) was largely ignored by white Americans, given the racial mores of the time.

The first major revision of Phillips and his school came with the publication in 1956 of *The Peculiar Institution: Slavery in the AnteBellum South* by Kenneth Stampp, a historian at the University of California, Berkeley. Strongly influenced by the antiracist values that had emerged during and after World War II, Stampp had different assumptions and a different perspective from those of Phillips. "I have simply found no convincing evidence," Stampp declared in neoabolitionist tones, "that there are any significant differences between the innate emotional traits and intellectual capacities of Ne-

groes and whites" (ix, footnote). Stampp responded within the
framework of Phillips's argument but overturned his thesis. Slavery,
he argued, was a brutal system of racial oppression and labor exploitation. He used original sources even more thoroughly than did
Phillips and found that slavery was profitable in the 1850s. Economic self-interest alone dictated that planters in 1860 would defend
their peculiar institution militantly. War, Stampp argued, was necessary to remove the blatant contradiction of bondage from American society.

Stampp revised Phillips on his own terms, but Stanley Elkins's
Slavery: A Problem in American Institutional and Intellectual Life
(1959) redirected scholarship, although in a way that this Smith
College historian did not anticipate. Elkins desired to move the historiography beyond the moral debate in which Stampp had answered Phillips, much as abolitionists had disputed proslavery ideologues a century earlier. The old discussion of the moral issue, Elkins
asserted, had reached a point of diminishing return because slavery
was morally indefensible. Elkins's innovation was the use of social
psychology and comparative history to advance a provocative thesis.
Relying largely on secondary sources, Elkins theorized that the stereotype of "Sambo"—the image of the compliant, fawning slave—
was a reality in the antebellum South. Lacking the institutional restraints of church and state that mitigated the severity of slavery in
Latin America, Elkins claimed that unopposed capitalism in the
United States gave the planter absolute power to reduce his slaves
to childlike dependence. Slaves were emotionally infantilized in a
manner analogous to the psychological degradation that occurred to
inmates in Nazi death camps. Sambo was thus the product of racial
victimization but not of any genetic deficiencies as Phillips had assumed.

A scholarly furor engulfed Elkins's book during the late 1960s
and early 1970s. Critics lambasted his misuse of social psychology,
his inaccurate reading of slavery in the Americas and of the Nazi
death camp experience, and above all his failure to understand the
complexity of the slave personality. Elkins ironically had accepted an
essential part of Phillips's racist assumption—the reality of Sambo as
a dominant type—and it was an untenable position. The sharp dichotomy that Elkins drew between slavery in the Americas was too
simple at best and inaccurate at worst. Slavery was not a closed sys-

tem like a Nazi death camp, nor was Sambo an internalized persona, but only one of a number of roles that slaves purposefully played. Although critics demolished his thesis, Elkins had led historians to reassess the nature of slave life and culture, which are now seen to have constituted a creative and dynamic response to oppression. The historiography of slavery has moved irreversibly beyond Phillips's paradigm.

Additional factors contributed to the recent reassessment of slavery. National and international events after World War II provided an altered perception of racial relations. The momentous civil rights and black power movements in the United States were part of a challenge to white supremacy and European colonialism throughout Africa and its diaspora. There was also change within the white-dominated historical profession, which had undervalued the pioneering work of early black historians such as W. E. B. Du Bois and G. Carter Woodson. By the 1970s black studies courses were instituted at many colleges and universities, and February was widely observed as Black History Month. The eminent historian John Hope Franklin was elected president of the American Historical Association and the Organization of American Historians, the first African-American to hold such positions.

Change in the social character of the historical profession coincided with fresh perspectives on the past and the use of innovative research techniques. The emergence of the new social history stressed the importance of studying neglected groups such as slaves, whose experience was as integral to a comprehensive understanding of the past as that of slavemasters. Black historians and Marxist historians, who became influential in the last generation, endorsed such assumptions. Indeed, historians writing on slavery today tend to have liberal, radical, or black nationalist politics. The study of slavery as "history from the bottom up" has thus taken on its own special momentum.

Recovering the past of a people who were relatively inarticulate, invisible, and illiterate has required creativity in the use of sources. Historians have used slave narratives, folk traditions, oral history, genealogy, and local records resourcefully. Statistical techniques and the computer have allowed the mining of census data, agricultural production figures, and other quantifiable information. The interdisciplinary reliance on anthropology, economics, psychology, and sociology and the use of comparative history are now commonplace. Compared to their counterparts of only a generation ago, historians of slavery are employing theory more explicitly, just as they are more systematic in defining problems, more aware of procedures, and more exacting about proof.

Intellectual boldness characterizes the study of slavery today. Historians concur that slavery and race relations were integral forces shaping the general nature of American society. Slavery, therefore, should not be examined in isolation. Throughout its history the institution and its internal attributes always were enmeshed in larger social patterns. The traditional conception of the United States as a free society has put slavery and its patterns of behavior among blacks and whites conveniently outside the mainstream. They have been seen as anomalies to be dealt with as special cases, because slavery ultimately did not become the general way of American life and was extinguished after 1865. But if patterns of behavior between whites and blacks, as between ethnic groups, are part of the mainstream of American history, then slavery must be included. Examining slavery's origins and evolution becomes necessary for an understanding of American society. A comparative approach supplies conceptual leverage and enables us to determine what was common to slavery as a system of labor exploitation and what were the cultural influences that gave the institution its variety.

Chronology

1450s	The Portuguese establish trading posts along the west coast of Africa and shortly thereafter began making large purchases of black slaves.
1492	By the time Columbus set out on his first voyage, about 25,000 black slaves had been imported into Europe.
1500–1650	England's population expanded from about 3 million to 4.5 million, a demographic incentive for colonization in the New World.
1502	Customary date of the beginning of the New World slave trade, because the first references to blacks appeared in the records of the Spanish colonial administrators.
1619	First Africans arrived in Virginia and mainland British North America.
1641	Massachusetts was the first British colony in mainland North America to recognize slavery in its legal code.
1660s	Formal development of slave law codes in the Chesapeake, where slaves could not claim freedom by professing Christianity.
1676	Bacon's Rebellion in Virginia.
1700	After this date, leading white southerners irrevocably were committed to black slavery as a major source of labor. Slaves now composed close to a majority of Virginia's labor force.
1712	New York City slave revolt.
1720	By this date the annual rate of natural increase of the enslaved population in mainland British North America was greater than the annual increase owing to imports.
1730–1760	Deaths outnumbered births among blacks in the rice coast from North Carolina to Georgia.

1734–
1754   Blacks composed a third of all immigrants to New York.
1739   Stono slave rebellion in South Carolina.
1740   By this date, slaves born in the New World made up the majority of the slave population in mainland British North America.
1741   Slave revolt scare in New York City.
1750   By the mid-eighteenth century a distinctive African-American life cycle had developed in the Chesapeake. Black freemen composed probably no more than 5 percent of the black population in the Chesapeake.
1770   Blacks made up 22 percent of the population of mainland British North America and 40 percent of the population in the southern colonies.
1775   Lord Dunmore's proclamation offered freedom to slaves who would support the crown.
1776   Declaration of Independence.
1780–
1804   Northern states enacted abolition laws.
1810   The African-born component of the slave population in mainland British North America was about 20 percent.
1787   Northwest Ordinance.
1788   Federal Constitution ratified.
1793   Mulattos and blacks on Saint Domingue (Haiti) under the leadership of Toussaint L'Ouverture overthrew French rule. Eli Whitney invented the cotton gin.
1800   Gabriel Prosser's conspiracy in Richmond. There were 1 million blacks in the United States.
1808   The United States ended the legal importation of slaves.
1810–
1820   Some 137,000 slaves were forced to move westward across the Appalachian Mountains.
1811   The largest slave revolt ever in the United States took place in Louisiana.
1820   Missouri Compromise.
1820–
1860   Some 2 million blacks were sold to meet the demand for slave labor. Perhaps one slave family out of four experienced the sale of a family member.

1820s	New England textile mills expanded.
1822	Denmark Vesey's slave conspiracy in Charleston.
1825	The South was the world's major exporter of cotton. There were 1.75 million slaves in the southern United States, representing about 36 percent of all slaves in the New World at this time.
1830s	Blacks who merged with the Seminole Indians resisted white encroachment in Florida.
1831	Abolitionist William Lloyd Garrison, financed in part by Northern blacks, began publication of the *Liberator* in Boston. Nat Turner's slave rebellion in Southampton County, Virginia.
1832–	
1833	Nullification crisis.
1840	The proportion of native-born blacks in the United States stood at about 96 percent and would reach almost 100 percent by 1860.
1845	Publication of the *Narrative of the Life of Frederick Douglass: An American Slave* by Frederick Douglass.
1846	War with Mexico; Wilmot Proviso.
1848	Free Soil party formed.
1850	Compromise of 1850. In the South, about 75 percent of slaveholders owned fewer than ten slaves, and about 75 percent of slaves resided in units that had ten or more slaves. One-half of all slaves lived on plantations with more than twenty slaves.
1852	Publication of *Uncle Tom's Cabin* by Harriet Beecher Stowe.
1854	Kansas-Nebraska Act. Republican party formed.
1856	Civil war in "Bleeding Kansas."
1857	*Dred Scot* v. *Sanford*.
1858	Lincoln-Douglas debates.
1859	John Brown's raid at Harpers Ferry, Virginia.
1860	Lincoln elected president; South Carolina secedes from the Union. Nearly a quarter of a million free blacks resided in the South, where the slave population stood at about 4 million.

Among white southern families, three-quarters did not own any slaves.

In the Deep South, one-third of slaves lived on plantations with more than fifty slaves.

1860s   End of the transatlantic slave trade, during which about 9 million Africans were forcibly transported to the New World.

1861   Confederate States of America established; Fort Sumter attacked.

Czar Alexander II of Russia declared serfdom abolished.

1861–

1865   Civil War in the United States.

1862   Preliminary Emancipation Proclamation.

Black soldiers joined the Union Army.

1863   Emancipation Proclamation.

1865   Thirteenth Amendment, ending slavery and involuntary servitude, ratified.

1888   Brazil abolished slavery.

1970   Slavery was outlawed in the Arabian peninsula, its last bastion.

I

What Is Slavery?

Orlando Patterson

SLAVERY AND SOCIAL DEATH

The practice of slavery has endured throughout human history, existing in a variety of societies into the twentieth century. In the most comprehensive current analysis of different slave systems, Orlando Patterson, professor of sociology at Harvard University, discusses the common characteristics of slavery over the ages. His twelve-year-long project involved the comparison of sixty-six slaveholding societies.

Slavery is an extreme form of domination of one person by another that is, Patterson argues, a form of social parasitism. It originated as a substitute for certain death, such as sparing condemned prisoners of war, and was maintained through brutality. "Slavery," he writes, "is the permanent, violent domination of natally alienated and generally dishonored persons." By natal alienation, Patterson means that the slave lost a birthright to his or her own cultural existence beyond what the master permitted, thus experiencing a kind of social death. Slaves still formed strong personal ties, but masters did not recognize these relations as legitimate. Slaves in the United States, for example, had consensual marriage, but the institution did not carry the weight of law. The lack of power and the inability to create an independent social existence made the slave a dishonored figure without public worth in the master's society.

All human relationships are structured and defined by the relative power of the interacting persons. Power, in Max Weber's terms, is "that opportunity existing within a social relationship which permits one to carry out one's will even against resistance and regardless of the basis on which this opportunity rests." Relations of inequality or domination, which exist whenever one person has more power than another, range on a continuum from those of marginal asymmetry to those in which one person is capable of exercising, with impunity, total power over another. Power relationships differ from one another not only in degree, but in kind. Qualitative differences result

Reprinted by permission of the publishers from *Slavery and Social Death: A Comparative Study*, pp. 1–7, 10–13, by Orlando Patterson, Cambridge, Mass.: Harvard University Press, Copyright © 1982 by the President and Fellows of Harvard College.

from the fact that power is a complex human faculty, although perhaps not as "sociologically amorphous" as Weber thought.

Slavery is one of the most extreme forms of the relation of domination, approaching the limits of total power from the viewpoint of the master, and of total powerlessness from the viewpoint of the slave. Yet it differs from other forms of extreme domination in very special ways. If we are to understand how slavery is distinctive, we must first clarify the concept of power.

The power relation has three facets. The first is social and involves the use or threat of violence in the control of one person by another. The second is the psychological facet of influence, the capacity to persuade another person to change the way he perceives his interests and his circumstances. And third is the cultural facet of authority, "the means of transforming force into right, and obedience into duty" which, according to Jean Jacques Rousseau, the powerful find necessary "to ensure them continual mastership." Rousseau felt that the source of "legitimate powers" lay in those "conventions" which today we would call culture. But he did not specify the area of this vast human domain in which the source of authority was to be found. Nor for that matter, did Weber, the leading modern student of the subject. . . . Authority rests on the control of those private and public symbols and ritual processes that induce (and seduce) people to obey because they feel satisfied and dutiful when they do so.

With this brief anatomy of power in mind we may now ask how slavery is distinctive as a relation of domination. The relation has three sets of constituent features corresponding to the three facets of power. It is unusual, first, both in the extremity of power involved, and all that immediately implies, and in the qualities of coercion that brought the relation into being and sustained it. As Georg Hegel realized, total personal power taken to its extreme contradicts itself by its very existence, for total domination can become a form of extreme dependence on the object of one's power, and total powerlessness can become the secret path to control of the subject that attempts to exercise such power. Even though such a sublation is usually only a potential, the possibility of its realization influences the normal course of the relation in profound ways. . . .

The coercion underlying the relation of slavery is also distinctive in its etiology and its composition. In one of the liveliest passages of the *Grundrisse,* Karl Marx, while discussing the attitudes of former masters and slaves in postemancipation Jamaica, not only shows clearly that he understood slavery to be first and foremost "a relation of domination" (his term and a point worth emphasizing in view of what has been written by some recent "Marxists" on the subject) but identifies the peculiar role of violence in creating and maintaining that domination. Commenting on the fact that the Jamaican ex-slaves refused to work beyond what was necessary for their own subsistence, he notes: "They have ceased to be slaves, . . . not in order to become wage labourers, but, instead, self-sustaining peasants working for their own consumption. As far as they are concerned, capital does not exist as capital, because autonomous wealth as such can exist only either on the basis of *direct* forced labour, slavery, or *indirect* forced labour, *wage labour.* Wealth confronts direct forced labour not as capital, but rather as *relation of domination*" (emphasis in original). It is important to stress that Marx was not saying that the master interprets the relationship this way, that the master is in any way necessarily precapitalist. Indeed, the comment was provoked by a November 1857 letter to the *Times* of London from a West Indian planter who, in what Marx calls "an utterly delightful cry of outrage," was advocating the reimposition of slavery in Jamaica as the only means of getting the Jamaicans to generate surplus in a capitalistic manner once again.

Elisabeth Welskopf, the late East German scholar who was one of the leading Marxist students of slavery, discussed at great length the critical role of direct violence in creating and maintaining slavery. Force, she argued, is essential for all class societies. Naked might—violence, in Georges Sorel's terminology—is essential for the creation of all such systems. However, organized force and authority—what Welskopf calls "spiritual force"—usually obviated the need to use violence in most developed class societies where nonslaves made up the dominated class. The problem in a slaveholding society, however, was that it was usually necessary to introduce new persons to the status of slaves because the former slaves either died out or were manumitted. The worker who is fired remains a worker, to be hired elsewhere. The slave who was freed was no longer a slave. Thus it was necessary continually to repeat the original, violent act of transforming free man into slave. This act of violence constitutes the prehistory of all stratified societies, Welskopf argued, but it determines both "the prehistory and (concurrent) history of slavery." To be sure, there is the exceptional case of the Old South in the United States, where the low incidence of manumission and the high rate of reproduction obviated the need continually to repeat the violent "original accumulation" of slaves. While Welskopf does not consider this case (her concern is primarily with the ancient world), her analysis is nonetheless relevant, for she goes on to note that the continuous use of violence in the slave order was also made necessary by the low motivation of the slave to work—by the need to reinforce reward with the threat and actuality of punishment. Thus George P. Rawick has written of the antebellum South: "Whipping was not only a method of punishment. It was a conscious device to impress upon the slaves that they were slaves; it was a crucial form of social control particularly if we remember that it was very difficult for slaves to run away successfully."

But Marx and the Marxists were not the first to recognize fully the necessity or the threat of naked force as the basis of the master-slave relationship. It was a North Carolina judge, Thomas Ruffin, who in his 1829 decision that the intentional wounding of a hired slave by his hirer did not constitute a crime, articulated better than any other commentator before or after, the view that the master-slave relationship originated in and was maintained by brute force. He wrote:

> With slavery . . . the end is the profit of the master, his security and the public safety; the subject, one doomed in his own person, and his posterity, to live without knowledge, and without the capacity to make anything his own, and to toil that another may reap his fruits. What moral considerations such as a father might give to a son shall be addressed to such a being, to convince him what it is impossible but that the most stupid must feel and know can never be true—that he is thus to labour upon a principle of natural duty, or for the sake of his own personal happiness. Such services can only be expected from one who has no will of his own; who surrenders his will in implicit obedience in the consequence only of uncontrolled authority over the body. There is nothing else which can operate to produce the effect. The power of the master must be absolute, to render the submission of the slave perfect.

Justice Ruffin may have gone a little too far in what Robert M. Cover describes as "his eagerness to confront the reality of the unpleasant iron fist beneath the law's polite, neutral language." He certainly underestimated the role of "moral considerations," to use his term, in the relationship. But his opinion did penetrate to the heart of what was most fundamental in the relation of slavery. . . . There is no known slaveholding society where the whip was not considered an indispensable instrument.

Another feature of the coercive aspect of slavery is its individualized condition: the slave was usually powerless in relation to another individual. We may conveniently neglect those cases where the slave formally belonged to a corporation such as a temple, since there was always an agent in the form of a specific individual who effectively exercised the power of a master. In his powerlessness the slave became an extension of his master's power. He was a human surrogate, recreated by his master with god-like power in his behalf. Nothing in Hegel or Friedrich Nietzsche more frighteningly captures the audacity of power and ego expansion than the view of the Ahaggar Tuaregs of the Sahara that "without the master the slave does not exist, and he is socializable only through his master." And they came as close to blasphemy as their Islamic creed allowed in the popular saying of the Kel Gress group: "All persons are created by God, the slave is created by the Tuareg."

These Tuareg sayings are not only extraordinarily reminiscent of Ruffin's opinion but of what Henri Wallon, in his classic study, wrote of the meaning of slavery in ancient Greece:

> The slave was a dominated thing, an animated instrument, a body with natural movements, but without its own reason, an existence entirely absorbed in another. The proprietor of this thing, the mover of this instrument, the soul and the reason of this body, the source of this life, was the master. The master was everything for him: his father and his god, which is to say, his authority and his duty. . . . Thus, god, fatherland, family, existence, are all, for the slave, identified with the same being; there was nothing which made for the social person, nothing which made for the moral person, that was not the same as his personality and his individuality.

Perhaps the most distinctive attribute of the slave's powerlessness was that it always originated (or was conceived of as having originated) as a substitute for death, usually violent death. Ali Abd Elwahed, in an unjustly neglected comparative work, found that "all the situations which created slavery were those which commonly would have resulted, either from natural or social laws, in the death of the individual." Archetypically, slavery was a substitute for death in war. But almost as frequently, the death commuted was punishment for some capital offense, or death from exposure or starvation.

The condition of slavery did not absolve or erase the prospect of death. Slavery was not a pardon; it was, peculiarly, a conditional commutation. The execution was suspended only as long as the slave acquiesced in his powerlessness. The master was essentially a ransomer. What he bought or acquired was the slave's life, and restraints on the master's capacity wantonly to destroy his slave did not undermine his claim on that life. Because the slave had no socially recognized existence outside of his master, he became a social nonperson.

This brings us to the second constituent element of the slave relation: the slave's natal alienation. Here we move to the cultural aspect of the relation, to that aspect of it which rests on authority, on the control of symbolic instruments. This is achieved in a unique way in the relation of slavery: the definition of the slave, however recruited, as a socially dead person. Alienated from all "rights" or claims of birth, he ceased to belong in his own right to any legitimate social order. All slaves experienced, at the very least, a secular excommunication.

Not only was the slave denied all claims on, and obligations to, his parents and living blood relations but, by extension, all such claims and obligations on his more remote ancestors and on his descendants. He was truly a genealogical isolate. Formally isolated in his social relations with those who lived, he also was culturally isolated from the social heritage of his ancestors. He had a past, to be sure. But a past is not a heritage. Everything has a history, including sticks and stones. Slaves differed from other human beings in that they were not allowed freely to integrate the experience of these ancestors into their lives, to inform their understanding of social reality with the inherited meanings of their natural forebears, or to anchor the living present in any conscious community of memory. That they reached back for the past, as they reached out for the related living, there can be no doubt. Unlike other persons, doing so meant struggling with and penetrating the iron curtain of the master, his community, his laws, his policemen or patrollers, and his heritage.

In the struggle to reclaim the past the odds were stacked even more heavily in favor of the master than in the attempt to maintain links with living relatives. One of the most significant findings of Michael Craton's study of the oral history of the descendants of the Worthy Park plantation slaves of Jamaica was the extraordinary shallowness of their genealogical and historical memory. The same is attested by the recorded interviews with American ex-slaves.

When we say that the slave was natally alienated and ceased to belong independently to any formally recognized community, this does not mean that he or she did not experience or share informal social relations. A large number of works have demonstrated that slaves in both ancient and modern times had strong social ties among themselves. The important point, however, is that these relationships were never recognized as legitimate or binding. Thus American slaves, like their ancient Greco-Roman counterparts, had regular sexual unions, but such unions were never recognized as marriages; both groups were attached to their local communities, but such attachments had no binding force; both sets of parents were deeply attached to their children, but the parental bond had no social support.

The refusal formally to recognize the social relations of the slave had profound emotional and social implications. In all slaveholding societies slave couples could be and were forcibly separated and the consensual "wives" of slaves were obliged to submit sexually to their masters; slaves had no custodial claims or powers over their children, and children inherited no claims or obligations to their parents. And the master had the power to remove a slave from the local community in which he or she was brought up.

Even if such forcible separations occurred only infrequently, the fact that they were possible and that from time to time they did take place was enough to strike terror in the hearts of all slaves and to transform significantly the way they behaved and conceived of themselves. Nothing comes across more dramatically from the hundreds of interviews with American ex-slaves than the fear of separation. Peter Clifton, an eighty-nine-year-old ex-slave from South Carolina, was typical when he said: "Master Biggers believe in whippin' and workin' his slaves long and hard; then a man was scared all de time of being sold away from his wife and chillun. His bark was worse than his bite tho', for I never knowed him to do a wicked thing lak dat."

Isaiah Butler, another South Carolina ex-slave, observed: "Dey didn't have a jail in dem times. Dey'd whip em, and dey'd sell 'em. Every slave know what 'I'll put you in my pocket, Sir' mean."

The independent constituent role of natal alienation in the emergence of slavery is vividly illustrated by the early history of slavery in America. Winthrop D. Jordan has shown that in the early decades of the seventeenth century there were few marked differences in the conception of black and white servitude, the terms "slave" and "servant" being used synonymously. The power of the master over both black and white servants was near total: both could be whipped and sold.

Gradually there emerged, however, something new in the conception of the black servant: the view that he did not belong to the same community of Christian, civilized Europeans. The focus of this "we-they" distinction was at first religious, later racial. "Enslavement was captivity, the loser's lot in a contest of power. Slaves were infidels or heathens." But as Jordan argues, although the focus may have changed, there was really a fusion of race, religion, and nationality in a generalized conception of "us"—white, English, free—and "them"—black, heathen, slave. "From the first, then, vis-à-vis the Negro the concept embedded in the term Christian seems to have conveyed much of the idea and feeling of *we* as against *they:* to be Christian was to be civilized rather than barbarous, English rather than African, white rather than black." The strangeness and seeming savagery of the Africans, reinforced by traditional attitudes and the context of early contact, "were major components in that sense of *difference* which provided the mental margin absolutely requisite for placing the European on the deck of the slave ship and the Negro in the hold." . . .

I prefer the term "natal alienation," because it goes directly to the heart of what is critical in the slave's forced alienation, the loss of ties of birth in both ascending and descending generations. It also has the important nuance of a loss of native status, of deracination. It was this alienation of the slave from all formal, legally enforceable ties of "blood," and from any attachment to groups or localities other than those chosen for him by the master, that gave the relation of slavery its peculiar value to the master. The slave was the ultimate human tool, as imprintable and as disposable as the master wished. . . .

The peculiar character of violence and the natal alienation of the slave generates the third constituent element of slavery: the fact that slaves were always persons who had been dishonored in a generalized way. Here we move to the sociopsychological aspect of this unusual power relationship. The slave could have no honor because of the origin of his status, the indignity and all-pervasiveness of his indebtedness, his absence of any independent social existence, but most of all because he was without power except through another.

Honor and power are intimately linked. No one understood this more than Thomas Hobbes. In the chapter of *Leviathan* in which he sets out to define his central concept—power—and related conditions, Hobbes devotes more than two-thirds of his effort to a detailed disquisition on the nature of honor. Fully recognizing that honor is a social-psychological issue, Hobbes wrote: "The manifestation of the Value we set on one another, is that which is commonly called *Honouring*, and *Dishonouring*. To Value a man at a high rate, is to *Honour* him; at a low rate, is to *Dishonour* him. But high, and low, in this case, is to be understood by comparison to the rate that each man setteth on himself." The link between honor and power is direct: "To obey, is to Honour; because no man obeys them, whom they think have no power to help, or hurt them. And consequently to disobey, is to Dishonour." Somewhat cynically, Hobbes observes that it really does not matter "whether an action . . . be just or unjust: for Honour consisteth onely in the opinion of Power." . . .

The slave, as we have already indicated, could have no honor because he had no power and no independent social existence, hence no public worth. He had no name of his own to defend. He could only defend his master's worth and his master's name. That the dishonor was a generalized condition must be emphasized, since the free and honorable person, ever alive to slights and insults, occasionally experiences specific acts of dishonor to which, of course, he or she responds by taking appropriate action. The slave, as we shall see, usually stood outside the game of honor. . . .

The counterpart of the master's sense of honor is the slave's experience of its loss. The so-called servile personality is merely the outward expression of this loss of honor. . . .

It was in the interaction between master and slave that such feelings were expressed and played out. Clearly, no authentic human relationship was possible where violence was the ultimate sanction.

There could have been no trust, no genuine sympathy; and while a kind of love may sometimes have triumphed over this most perverse form of interaction, intimacy was usually calculating and sadomasochistic.

Occasionally we get a glimpse of the relationship in action from incidents recalled by American ex-slaves. This is how Grace Gibson from South Carolina described the moment when she was given as a present to her young mistress:

> I was called up on one of her [Miss Ada's] birthdays, and Marster Bob sorta looked out of de corner of his eyes, first at me and then at Miss Ada, and then he make a little speech. He took my hand, put it in Miss Ada's hand, and say: "Dis your birthday present, darlin'." I make a curtsy and Miss Ada's eyes twinkle like a star and she take me in her room and took on powerful over me.

Frederick Douglass, undoubtedly the most articulate former slave who ever lived, repeatedly emphasized as the central feature of slavery the loss of honor and its relation to the loss of power. After physically resisting a brutal white who had been hired by his exasperated master to break him, Douglass, whose spirit had nearly broken and who had run the risk of being executed for his resistance, recalls that he felt "a sense of my own manhood. . . . I was nothing before, I was a man now." And he adds in a passage for which this chapter may be read as an extended exegesis: "A man without force is without the essential dignity of humanity. Human nature is so constituted that it cannot honor a helpless man, although it can pity him; and even that it cannot do long, if the signs of power do not arise."

At this point we may offer a preliminary definition of slavery on the level of personal relations: *slavery is the permanent, violent domination of natally alienated and generally dishonored persons.*

Eugene D. Genovese

ON PATERNALISM

Eugene D. Genovese has played a central role in the modern interpretation of slavery. During the 1960s his writing focused on the economics and ideology of southern slaveholders. His *Roll*, Jordan, Roll: The World the Slaves Made (1974), from which this excerpt is taken, is a major analysis of plantation slavery in the Old South, especially of the African-American community. It stated an explicit definition of slavery that was influenced by the neo-Marxist theory of Antonio Gramsci, an Italian communist who sought to understand the mass appeal of fascism.

Gramsci accepted class struggle as the dominant reality of the economic exploitation of capitalism. Similarly, Genovese defines slavery as "class power in racial form." Gramsci's intellectual innovation was to propose that a ruling class not only controls wealth and power but also seeks cultural hegemony—the spontaneous acceptance of its moral legitimacy by the entire society. Cultural conflict over whose ideas and values are sanctioned is thus an essential aspect of class struggle. Genovese's application of Gramscian theory is seen in the concept of "paternalism"—the particular form that planter hegemony took—and in the cultural resistance of slaves, notably through their religion. Genovese offers a different frame of reference for defining slavery than the previous selection by Orlando Patterson but one that is compatible with Patterson's idea of social death. A professor of history, Genovese holds multiple appointments at the University of Georgia, Georgia Institute of Technology, and Georgia State University.

Cruel, unjust, exploitative, oppressive, slavery bound two peoples together in bitter antagonism while creating an organic relationship so complex and ambivalent that neither could express the simplest human feelings without reference to the other. Slavery rested on the principle of property in man—of one man's appropriation of another's person as well as of the fruits of his labor. By definition and in essence it was a system of class rule, in which some people lived off the labor of others. American slavery subordinated one race to another and thereby rendered its fundamental class relationships more

From *Roll, Jordan, Roll: The World the Slaves Made* by Eugene D. Genovese, pp. 3–7, 587–598. Copyright © 1972, 1974 by Eugene D. Genovese. Reprinted by permission of Pantheon Books, a division of Random House, Inc.

complex and ambiguous; but they remained class relationships. The racism that developed from racial subordination influenced every aspect of American life and remains powerful. But slavery as a system of class rule predated racism and racial subordination in world history and once existed without them. Racial subordination, as postbellum American developments and the history of modern colonialism demonstrate, need not rest on slavery. Wherever racial subordination exists, racism exists; therefore, southern slave society and its racist ideology had much in common with other systems and societies. But southern slave society was not merely one more manifestation of some abstraction called racist society. Its history was essentially determined by particular relationships of class power in racial form.

The Old South, black and white, created a historically unique kind of paternalist society. To insist upon the centrality of class relations as manifested in paternalism is not to slight the inherent racism or to deny the intolerable contradictions at the heart of paternalism itself. Imamu Amiri Baraka captures the tragic irony of paternalist social relations when he writes that slavery "was, most of all, a paternal institution" and yet refers to "the filthy paternalism and cruelty of slavery." Southern paternalism, like every other paternalism, had little to do with Ole Massa's ostensible benevolence, kindness, and good cheer. It grew out of the necessity to discipline and morally justify a system of exploitation. It did encourage kindness and affection, but it simultaneously encouraged cruelty and hatred. The racial distinction between master and slave heightened the tension inherent in an unjust social order.

Southern slave society grew out of the same general historical conditions that produced the other slave regimes of the modern world. The rise of a world market—the development of new tastes and of manufactures dependent upon non-European sources of raw materials—encouraged the rationalization of colonial agriculture under the ferocious domination of a few Europeans. African labor provided the human power to fuel the new system of production in all the New World slave societies, which, however, had roots in different European experiences and emerged in different geographical, economic, and cultural conditions. They had much in common, but each was unique.

Theoretically, modern slavery rested, as had ancient slavery, on the idea of a slave as *instrumentum vocale*—a chattel, a possession, a thing, a mere extension of his master's will. But the vacuousness of such pretensions had been exposed long before the growth of New World slave societies. The closing of the ancient slave trade, the political crisis of ancient civilization, and the subtle moral pressure of an ascendant Christianity, had converged in the early centuries of the new era to shape a seigneurial world in which lords and serfs (not slaves) faced each other with reciprocal demands and expectations. This land-oriented world of medieval Europe slowly forged the traditional paternalist ideology to which the southern slaveholders fell heir.

The slaveholders of the South, unlike those of the Caribbean, increasingly resided on their plantations and by the end of the eighteenth century had become an entrenched regional ruling class. The paternalism encouraged by the close living of masters and slaves was enormously reinforced by the closing of the African slave trade, which compelled masters to pay greater attention to the reproduction of their labor force. Of all the slave societies in the New World, that of the Old South alone maintained a slave force that reproduced itself. Less than 400,000 imported Africans had, by 1860, become an American black population of more than 4,000,000.

A paternalism accepted by both masters and slaves—but with radically different interpretations—afforded a fragile bridge across the intolerable contradictions inherent in a society based on racism, slavery, and class exploitation that had to depend on the willing reproduction and productivity of its victims. For the slaveholders paternalism represented an attempt to overcome the fundamental contradiction in slavery: the impossibility of the slaves' ever becoming the things they were supposed to be. Paternalism defined the involuntary labor of the slaves as a legitimate return to their masters for protection and direction. But, the masters' need to see their slaves as acquiescent human beings constituted a moral victory for the slaves themselves. Paternalism's insistence upon mutual obligations—duties, responsibilities, and ultimately even rights—implicitly recognized the slaves' humanity.

Wherever paternalism exists, it undermines solidarity among the oppressed by linking them as individuals to their oppressors. A lord (master, *padrone, patron, padrón, patrão*) functions as a direct provider and protector to each individual or family, as well as to the community as a whole. The slaves of the Old South displayed impressive solidarity and collective resistance to their masters, but in a web of paternalistic relationships their action tended to become defensive and to aim at protecting the individuals against aggression and abuse; it could not readily pass into an effective weapon for liberation. Black leaders, especially the preachers, won loyalty and respect and fought heroically to defend their people. But despite their will and considerable ability, they could not lead their people over to the attack against the paternalist ideology itself.

In the Old South the tendencies inherent in all paternalistic class systems intersected with and acquired enormous reinforcement from the tendencies inherent in an analytically distinct system of racial subordination. The two appeared to be a single system. Paternalism created a tendency for the slaves to identify with a particular community through identification with its master; it reduced the possibilities for their identification with each other as a class. Racism undermined the slaves' sense of worth as black people and reinforced their dependence on white masters. But these were tendencies, not absolute laws, and the slaves forged weapons of defense, the most important of which was a religion that taught them to love and value each other, to take a critical view of their masters, and to reject the ideological rationales for their own enslavement.

The slaveholders had to establish a stable regime with which their slaves could live. Slaves remained slaves. They could be bought and sold like any other property and were subject to despotic personal power. And blacks remained rigidly subordinated to whites. But masters and slaves, whites and blacks, lived as well as worked together. The existence of the community required that all find some measure of self-interest and self-respect. Southern paternalism developed as a way of mediating irreconcilable class and racial conflicts; it was an anomaly even at the moment of its greatest apparent strength. But, for about a century, it protected both masters and slaves from the worst tendencies inherent in their respective conditions. It mediated, however unfairly and even cruelly, between masters and slaves, and it disguised, however imperfectly, the appropriation of one man's labor power by another. Paternalism in any historical setting defines relations of superordination and subordination. Its strength as a prevailing ethos increases as the members of the community accept—or feel compelled to accept—these relations as legitimate. Brutality lies inherent in this acceptance of patronage and dependence, no matter how organic the paternalistic order. But southern paternalism necessarily recognized the slaves' humanity— not only their free will but the very talent and ability without which their acceptance of a doctrine of reciprocal obligations would have made no sense. Thus, the slaves found an opportunity to translate paternalism itself into a doctrine different from that understood by their masters and to forge it into a weapon of resistance to assertions that slavery was a natural condition for blacks, that blacks were racially inferior, and that black slaves had no rights or legitimate claims of their own.

Thus, the slaves, by accepting a paternalistic ethos and legitimizing class rule, developed their most powerful defense against the dehumanization implicit in slavery. Southern paternalism may have reinforced racism as well as class exploitation, but it also unwittingly invited its victims to fashion their own interpretation of the social order it was intended to justify. And the slaves, drawing on a religion that was supposed to assure their compliance and docility, rejected the essence of slavery by projecting their own rights and value as human beings.

II

The Emergence of Slavery

Robert Fogel

SLAVERY IN THE NEW WORLD

In 1974 economic historians Robert Fogel and Stanley L. Engerman published *Time on the Cross.* The controversial study was intended to be a model of quantitative analysis applied to slavery. The authors emphasized in precise numerical terms that slavery was a highly efficient and productive institution in which slaves, responding to a system of punishment and especially rewards, exhibited a more diligent work ethic than their free white counterparts in the North. Although the authors condemned slavery as morally abhorrent, they found less overt brutality in the slave system than had historians Kenneth Stampp in *The Peculiar Institution* (1956) and Stanley Elkins in *Slavery* (1959). Among other conclusions in their wide-ranging study, Fogel and Engerman downplayed the frequency of whipping and the rate at which the slave family was separated through sale, and they found the slaves' sexual life prudish. Critics, however, faulted their statistics as narrowly based and their generalizations as sweeping, in so doing largely discrediting the work. Nonetheless, *Time on the Cross* stimulated historians to produce new scholarship, as well as to use greater care in their methodology.

The following selection is taken from Robert Fogel's recent ambitious study of slavery in the New World, which is partly a response to his earlier critics. Based on extensive research and quantitative analysis contained in three volumes in addition to the main text, the project was a group effort that Fogel directed over the course of twenty-four years. In this excerpt he discusses the origins of the Atlantic slave trade and the general characteristics of slavery in the Americas, focusing on the special aspects of the evolution of slavery in the United States. Professor Fogel is director of the Center of Population Economics at the University of Chicago.

Slavery is not only one of the most ancient but also one of the most long-lived forms of economic and social organization. It came into being at the dawn of civilization, when mankind passed from hunting and nomadic pastoral life into primitive agriculture. And although legally sanctioned slavery was outlawed in its last bastion—

Selections are reprinted from *Without Consent or Contract: The Rise and Fall of American Slavery,* by Robert William Fogel, pp. 17–23, 29–34, with the permission of W. W. Norton & Company, Inc. Copyright © 1989 by Robert W. Fogel.

the Arabian peninsula—in 1970, slavery is still practiced covertly in parts of Asia, Africa, and South America.

The Origins of the Atlantic Slave Trade

Over the ages the incidence of slavery has waxed and waned. One high-water mark was reached during the first two centuries of the Roman Empire when, according to some estimates, three out of every four residents of the Italian peninsula—21 million people— lived in bondage. Eventually, Roman slavery was transformed into serfdom, a form of servitude that mitigated some of the harsher features of the older system.

While serfdom was the most characteristic condition of labor in Europe during the Middle Ages, slavery was never fully eradicated. The Italians imported slaves from the area of the Black Sea during the thirteenth century. And the Moors captured during the interminable religious wars were enslaved on the Iberian peninsula along with Slavs and captives from the Levant.

Black slaves were imported into Europe during the Middle Ages through the Moslem countries of North Africa. Until the Portuguese exploration of the west coast of Africa, however, such imports were quite small. About the middle of the fifteenth century, the Portuguese established trading posts along the west coast of Africa below the Sahara and shortly thereafter began to make relatively large purchases of black slaves. Soon the average imports of slaves into the Iberian peninsula and the Iberian-controlled islands off the coast of Africa (the Canaries, the Madeiras, and São Thomé) rose to about 1,000 per year. By the time Columbus set sail on his first expedition across the Atlantic, accumulated imports of black slaves into the Old World were probably in excess of 25,000. Although blacks continued to be imported into the Old World until the beginning of the eighteenth century, it was the New World that became the great market for slaves.

It is customary to date the beginning of the New World traffic in Africans to the year 1502, when the first references to blacks appear in the documents of Spanish colonial administrators. The end of this trade did not come until the 1860s. Over the three and a half centuries between these dates about 9,900,000 Africans were forcibly transported across the Atlantic. Brazil was by far the largest single participant in the traffic, accounting for 41 percent of the total. British- and French-owned colonies in the Caribbean and the far-flung Spanish-American empire were the destination of 47 percent. Dutch, Danish, and Swedish colonies took another 5 percent. The remaining 7 percent represent the share of the United States (or the colonies that eventually became the United States) in the Atlantic slave trade.

To those who identify slavery with cotton and tobacco, the small size of the U.S. share in the slave trade may seem surprising. The temporal pattern of slave imports, however, clearly reveals that the course of the Atlantic slave trade cannot be explained by the demand for these crops. Over 75 percent of all slaves were imported between 1451 and 1810. This fact clearly rules out cotton as a dominant factor in the traffic since the production of cotton was still in its infancy in 1810. There was also an enormous increase in the extent of the Atlantic slave trade during the eighteenth century. This fact rules out the possibility of a major role for tobacco: During the eighteenth century, tobacco imports into Europe increased at an average annual rate of about 350 tons per annum. Since an average slave hand could produce about a ton of tobacco yearly, the total increase in the tobacco trade over the century required an increase of about 70,000 hands, a minuscule fraction of the 5.7 million slaves imported during the same period.

It was Europe's sweet tooth, rather than its addiction to tobacco or its infatuation with cotton cloth, that determined the extent of the Atlantic slave trade (see the map on page 24). Sugar was the greatest of the slave crops. Between 60 and 70 percent of all the Africans who survived the Atlantic voyages ended up in one or another of Europe's sugar colonies.

The first of these colonies was in the Mediterranean. Sugar was introduced into the Levant in the seventh century by the Arabs. Europeans became familiar with it during the Crusades. Prior to that time honey was the only sweetening agent available to them. After taking over the Arab sugar industry in Palestine, the Normans and Venetians promoted the production of sugar in the Mediterranean islands of Cyprus, Crete, and Sicily. From the twelfth to the fifteenth centuries these colonies shipped sugar to all parts of Europe. Moreover, the sugar produced there was grown on plantations that uti-

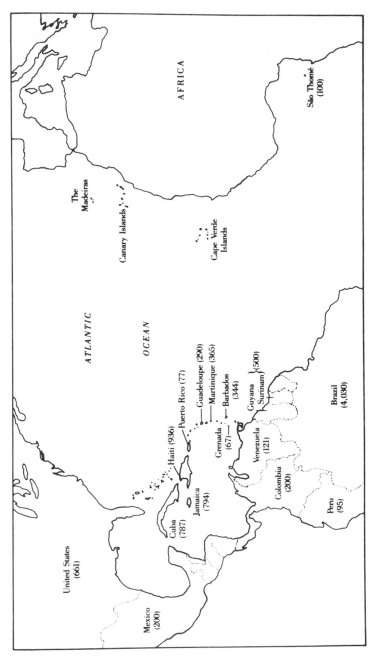

The principal importers of black slaves, 1451–1870 (imports in thousands).

AFRICA

São Thomé
(100)

The
Madeiras

Canary Islands

Cape Verde
Islands

ATLANTIC

OCEAN

Puerto Rico (77)

Guadeloupe (290)

Martinique (365)

Barbados
(344)

Grenada
(67)

Guyana
Surinam (500)

Venezuela
(121)

Brazil
(4,030)

Haiti (936)

Jamaica
(794)

Cuba
(787)

Colombia
(200)

Peru
(95)

United States
(661)

Mexico
(200)

lized slave labor. While the slaves were primarily white, in these islands Europeans developed the institutional apparatus that was
eventually applied to blacks.

The rapid growth of European demand for sugar led the Spanish and Portuguese to extend sugar cultivation to the Iberian peninsula and to the Iberian-owned Atlantic islands off the coast of Africa. Here, as in the Mediterranean, slaves on plantations provided
the labor for the new industry. While some of these bondsmen were
natives of the newly conquered islands, as in the Cape Verde archi-
pelago, most were blacks imported from Africa. For the first century
of the Atlantic slave trade, the scope of imports was determined almost exclusively by the needs of the sugar planters in the Canaries,
the Madeiras, and São Thomé. Of the 130,000 blacks imported between 1451 and 1559, 90 percent were sent to these islands and only
10 percent to the New World.

During the last half of the sixteenth century, the center of sugar
production and of black slavery shifted across the Atlantic to the
Western Hemisphere. By 1600 Brazil had emerged as Europe's leading supplier of sugar. Cane was also grown in substantial quantities
in Mexico, Peru, Cuba, and Haiti. Although the Old World colonies
continued to plant the crop, their absolute and relative shares of the
European market declined rapidly. By the close of the seventeenth
century sugar production all but disappeared from the Madeiras, the
Cape Verde Islands, the Canaries, and São Thomé. The end of sugar
production also marked the end of slaves imported into these territories.

The sugar monopoly of the Spanish and Portuguese was broken during the seventeenth century when the British, French, and
Dutch became major powers in the Caribbean. The British venture
into sugar production began in Barbados during the second quarter
of the seventeenth century. In 1655 the British seized Jamaica from
the Spanish and shortly thereafter began developing sugar plantations on that island. During the eighteenth century the output of
sugar grew rapidly, not only in these colonies but throughout the
British West Indies. It has been estimated that the annual export of
the sugar crop in the British West Indies in 1787 stood at 106,000
tons, more than five times as much as the exports of Brazil in the
same year. The British continued to expand their grip on sugar production, partly by acquiring additional territory during the Napo-

leonic Wars, so that by 1806 its West Indian colonies accounted for 55 percent of the sugar trade.

The development of the sugar culture in French Caribbean possessions was also spectacular. Haiti (then called Saint Domingue) was the principal sugar colony of the French. The French promoted plantations in that territory from the early seventeenth century until the Haitians revolted against their rule in 1794. By 1787 Haiti was shipping about 86,000 tons and production elsewhere brought the sugar trade of French Caribbean possessions to 125,000 tons. In contrast to Britain and France, Spain had been largely squeezed out of the international sugar trade, ranking a poor fourth in 1787 with slightly over 6 percent of exports. However, its colonies reemerged as a major sugar supplier in the nineteenth century, after the development of extensive plantations in Cuba and Puerto Rico. Sugar was also an important crop in Dutch Guiana (located on the north-central coast of South America, in terrain that embraces the modern nations of Guyana and Surinam), and in the Danish island of St. Croix. Together they contributed slightly more to the sugar trade in 1787 than the Spanish colonies.

The great majority of the slaves brought into the British, French, and Dutch Caribbean colonies were engaged in sugar production and its ancillary industries. In the 1820s in the British West Indies between two-thirds and three-quarters of the slaves were directly or indirectly engaged in sugar production. In Brazil, perhaps 40 percent of the slaves imported were involved in sugar culture, and in Spanish America the share was probably between 30 and 50 percent. Mining, which probably stood second to sugar in the demand for labor, claimed about 20 percent of the slaves in Brazil. The balance of the blacks brought to the New World were utilized in the production of such diverse crops as coffee, cocoa, tobacco, indigo, hemp, cotton, and rice. Of the relatively small percentage of Africans engaged in urban pursuits, most were usually servants or manual laborers, although some became artisans. However, it is probable that by the mid-eighteenth century most of the urban occupations were held by creoles, slaves born in the New World, rather than by recent arrivals.

Some General Characteristics of New World Slavery

Between 1600 and 1800, New World slaves represented less than a fifth of the population of the Western Hemisphere and less than 1 percent of the world's population. Yet, during this long period and extending into the nineteenth century as well, slave-produced commodities dominated the channels of world trade. Sugar was the single most important of the internationally traded commodities, dwarfing in value the trade in grain, meat, fish, tobacco, cattle, spices, cloth, or metals. Shortly before the American Revolution sugar by itself accounted for about a fifth of all English imports and with the addition of tobacco, coffee, cotton, and rum, the share of slave-produced commodities in England's imports was about 30 percent. The impact of slavery on world trade did not end there. Much of England's shipping was engaged in transporting either sugar to Europe, slaves from Africa to the New World, or manufactured goods from England to the slave colonies. Toward the end of the eighteenth century more than half of Britain's exports were bound for one or another of the slave colonies. It was not just Britain but also France, Spain, Portugal, Holland, and Denmark that thrived on buying from or selling to slave colonies. "The whole of western France—the great ports of Bordeaux and Nantes, the cordage and sail-making industries of Brittany, the textile manufacture of Cholet, the seaport and inland refineries—all developed in great part on sugar and its derived demand."

This intimate connection with trade, especially long-distance trade, differentiates New World slavery from the general form of slavery of the ancient world, or that in Africa and the Middle East in more recent times. Slaves in these societies were usually part of household economies, producing goods or services that would be consumed mainly by themselves and their families, by their masters, or by other members of their masters' households. The same was true of the European serfs. The fruits of their labor were usually consumed on the manors to which they were tied. Indeed, whether bound or free, less than 20 percent of the output of most European agriculturalists during the seventeenth or eighteenth centuries was destined to be exchanged on the market. But about 80 percent of the output of sugar plantations was sold on the world markets. Some New World slave societies grew so little besides sugar that they had to depend on imports, often produced by free farmers or fishermen, to feed their slaves. And so on the eve of the American Revolution most of the corn exports of the thirteen colonies and over 90 percent of livestock, dairy, and vegetable exports were sold to the West Indies.

Another feature of New World slavery was the large scale of the enterprises on which slaves labored. In the beginning—before 1650 in the British West Indies or before 1725 in the Chesapeake Bay region—most slaves lived and worked on fairly small farms. In Barbados prior to 1650, for example, more than three-quarters of the island's population was white. These early colonists were usually Englishmen of modest means. Most were indentured servants but some were landowners whose farms were fairly small, generally under 50 acres. Most of the landowners employed only a few laborers each—at first English indentured servants and later on, also African slaves. But whether farmers, indentured servants, or slaves, those who labored in the fields generally did so in traditional ways, each working on a multitude of tasks, with little supervision, and at a traditional pace. The early pattern in the Chesapeake region was similar. As late as 1725 the *median* slave plantation in the Chesapeake had about 10 slaves.

The advent of the sugar culture, beginning in Barbados about 1640, transformed the British West Indies. The replacement of tobacco by sugar not only changed the main market crop but also the lives of the agriculturalists. Small farms were rapidly consolidated into plantations. White and black hands who had farmed in traditional ways were replaced by large gangs of slaves, working in lock step, and moving methodically across vast fields. As early as 1680, the median size of a plantation in Barbados had increased to about 60 slaves. Over the decades the typical plantation in the West Indies became larger and larger. In Jamaica in 1832, on the eve of the abolition of British slavery, the median plantation contained about 150 slaves, and nearly one out of every four bondsmen lived on units containing at least 250 slaves. . . .

Some Special Aspects of the Evolution of Slavery in the United States

The United States stood apart from the other slave-importing territories, not only because of its comparatively small share in the Atlantic slave trade, but also because of the minor role played by its sugar industry in the growth of U.S. slavery. The commercial production of sugar in Louisiana did not begin until 1795, barely a decade before the United States withdrew from the international slave trade. At the time of the U.S. annexation of Louisiana, annual sugar production was a mere 5,000 tons. Even at its antebellum peak, sugar was never more than a minor southern crop that utilized less than 10 percent of the slave labor force.

The absence of the sugar culture had a profound effect on the development of slavery in the U.S. colonies. For one thing, it affected the rate at which the slave labor force grew, both in absolute numbers and in relative importance. While African labor was introduced into Virginia earlier than in Barbados, there were six times as many blacks in the British Caribbean in 1700 as there were in all of the North American colonies. Some 80 years after the first group of slaves landed in Virginia, the black population of that colony was just 16,000, while all the other North American colonies contained a mere 11,000 blacks. In the British Caribbean the slave population climbed to 60,000 within 30 years after the beginning of the British presence. It took her North American colonies 110 years to reach the same absolute level, despite the higher rate of natural increase of slaves in North America and the high mortality rate in the Caribbean.

As late as 1680 the relatively few slaves in Britain's North American colonies (under 7,000) were widely distributed in general farming and domestic occupations, but a concentration of slave labor in tobacco had already begun to develop in the Chesapeake. By the middle of the 1730s, the slave population had risen to about 120,000 with tobacco production requiring the concentrated effort of perhaps a third of the hands and rice another tenth. Thus, the majority of slaves were still employed mainly in general farming, in domestic service, in crafts, or in other non-farm occupations. This basic pattern continued for the next three decades, although by the mid-1760s the share of the labor of slave hands claimed by the three principal plantation crops—tobacco, rice, and indigo—had risen to a bit over 50 percent and there were rapidly growing slave populations in the Carolinas and Georgia. Allowing for the slaves engaged in crafts, domestic service, and secondary-market products, plantations specializing in these three crops may have accounted for two-thirds of the slave labor.

Cotton did not emerge as a major southern crop until the beginning of the nineteenth century, after the cotton gin lowered the cost of fiber (see the graph on page 30). At the beginning of the nineteenth century about 11 percent of all slaves lived on cotton

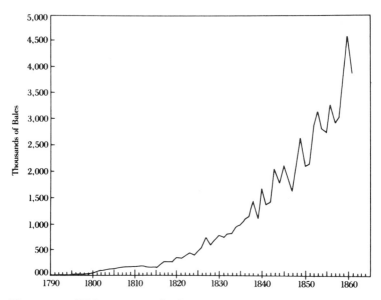

The course of U.S. cotton production, 1791–1861.

plantations. With the swelling demand, production rose so rapidly that by 1850 the proportion engaged on cotton plantations had risen to about 64 percent. The tobacco share had dwindled to 12 percent; sugar was next with 5 percent; rice had about 4 percent; and indigo was no longer commercially produced in the South.

The differences in the U.S. and West Indian patterns of crop specialization led to striking differences in the ratios of blacks to total population. As early as 1650, blacks formed 25 percent of the population in the British Caribbean. In 1770 the ratio stood at 91 percent. The experience in the French Caribbean was similar. By contrast, blacks formed only 4 percent of the population of the North American colonies in 1650 and rose to a pre-Revolutionary peak of 22 percent in 1770. In the southern U.S. colonies the percentages for 1650 and 1770 were 3 and 40, respectively. Thus, while blacks were the overwhelming majority of the population and labor force of the Caribbean during most of the colonial era, they were generally a minority of the population of the U.S. colonies and for most of the colonial period a relatively small minority, even in the South. It was only toward the middle of the eighteenth century, after slaves became geographically concentrated, that they emerged as the majority of the population in certain counties.

The U.S. pattern of crop specialization also affected the size of the units on which slaves lived and had far-reaching effects on the development of slave culture. During the colonial era, the median size of tobacco plantations remained below 20 slaves, and it increased only slightly thereafter. Slaves who labored in tobacco typically worked on plantations consisting of a white family and a few slave families; even large tobacco plantations were usually organized as a series of small units. Cotton plantations were not much larger; the median in 1860 was 35 slaves. The biggest plantations in the United States were in rice and sugar. There were about 100 slaves on the typical Louisiana sugar plantation in 1860. Although this figure exceeds the averages for tobacco, cotton, and even rice, it falls below the averages of sugar estates in the Caribbean or Brazil. And so, U.S. slave plantations were dwarfed by those of the West Indies. Blacks in these islands, particularly in Jamaica, had relatively little contact with the European culture of the white slave owner both because of the small percentage of whites who lived there and because of the enormous size of the typical plantation. But blacks in the U.S. colonies were usually a minority of the population and, even toward the end of the antebellum era, lived on relatively small units (generally fewer than seven or eight families), which brought them into continuous contact with their white masters.

U.S. slaves were not only in closer contact with European culture, they were also more removed from their African origins than were slaves in the Caribbean. Down through the end of the eighteenth century and into the nineteenth century, the majority of the slave populations of the British and French Caribbean islands and of Brazil were born in Africa because Africans were continually imported to offset the high death rates there. Indeed, as late as 1800, one-quarter of the population of Jamaica consisted of Africans who had arrived in the New World within the previous decade. On the other hand, creoles (slaves born in the New World) made up the majority of the slave population in the U.S. colonies as early as 1740 (see the graph on page 32). By the time of Washington's presidency, the African-born component of the black population had shrunk to a bit over 20 percent. It hovered close to this share from 1780 to

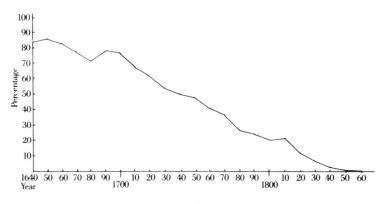

Foreign-born blacks as a percentage of all U.S. blacks, 1640–1860.

1810 and then rapidly headed toward zero. By 1850 all but a minute fraction of U.S. slaves were native born, and most of them were third-, fourth-, or fifth-generation Americans. This finding does not contradict the view that African heritage played a large role in shaping the culture of blacks, but it does serve to emphasize the extent to which black culture had, by 1860, been exposed to indigenous American influences.

The rapid decline in the relative share of Africans in the U.S. black population during the last half of the eighteenth century was not due to a decline in imports (see the graph on page 33). With the exception of the decade of the American Revolution, which brought with it a sharp decline in all international commerce, the trend in imports of slaves into the United States was strongly upward from 1620 until the end of legal U.S. involvement in the international slave trade in 1808. It has been frequently asserted that slavery was dying in the United States from the end of the Revolution until 1810 and that if it had not been for the rise of the cotton culture, slavery would have passed from existence long before the Civil War. This proposition rests partly on erroneous but widely cited estimates of slave imports for the period from 1790 to 1810 put forward by Henry Carey. Revised estimates show that far from declining, slave imports were higher in this period than in any previous 20-year period of U.S. history. There were, in fact, almost as many Africans brought into the United States during the 30 years from 1780 to 1810 as during the previous 160 years.

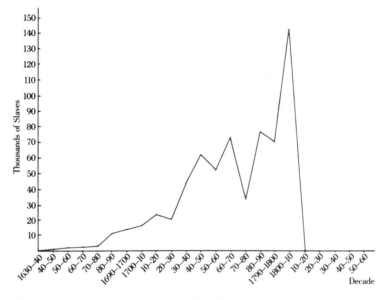

U.S. imports of slaves per decade, 1630–1860.

While the imports of Africans certainly contributed to the growth in the slave population of the U.S. colonies, they were of secondary importance in explaining that growth after 1720. Natural increase was by far the more significant factor during the eighteenth and nineteenth centuries—another respect in which the U.S. experience differed from that of Latin America. In the British and French West Indies, in Dutch Guiana, and in Brazil, the death rate of slaves was so high and the birth rate so low that these territories could not sustain their population levels without large and continuous importations of Africans.

Whatever the factors responsible for the high rate of natural increase experienced by U.S. slaves, its consequences were clear. Despite their low rates of importations, which initially caused the growth of the U.S. slave population to lag behind that of the Caribbean, the U.S. colonies not only overtook but far exceeded the rate of growth of the slave populations elsewhere in the hemisphere. By 1720, the annual rate of natural increase in the United States was greater than the annual increase due to importations. And although the absolute level of importations was high after the Revolution, importations contributed only half as much to the growth of the black population as did natural increase. Even these statements underestimate the impact of the favorable demographic experience for they fail to take into account the unfavorable demographic experience elsewhere. In 1800 there were 1,002,000 blacks in the United States. But if the United States had duplicated the demographic experience of the West Indies, its black population in 1800 would have been only 186,000.

Thus, the United States became the leading user of slave labor in the New World, not because it participated heavily in the slave trade but because of the unusually high rate of natural increase. By 1825 there were about 1,750,000 slaves in the southern United States. This represented 36 percent of all of the slaves in the New World in that year. Despite its peripheral role in the Atlantic slave trade, the size of its slave population and the success of its plantation system during the three decades preceding the Civil War made the South the greatest center of slavery in the New World and the bulwark of resistance to the abolition of slavery.

Ira Berlin

TIME, SPACE, AND THE EVOLUTION OF AFRICAN-AMERICAN SOCIETY

In this selection, Ira Berlin, director of the Freedmen and Southern Society Project at the University of Maryland, shows that slavery originated differently on the mainland of British North America, depending on the time and the place. During the colonial period, three distinct slave systems emerged: a northern nonplantation system and two southern plantation systems, one centered around the Chesapeake Bay and the other in the low country of the Carolinas and Georgia. Berlin's essay is important not only for its comprehensive analysis of the emergence and development of slavery in the thirteen colonies but also in its challenge to

From "Time, Space, and the Evolution of Afro-American Society on British Mainland North America," by Ira Berlin from *American Historical Review*, 85, Feb. 1980, pp. 44–78. Reprinted by permission of the author.

historians not to view slavery and African-American society as static phenomena or as singular types. The evolution of black culture was a complex process that involved a universal tension between freedom and bondage, as well as a dependence on particular social circumstances that varied from place to place and from one period to another.

Time and space are the usual boundaries of historical inquiry. The last generation of slavery studies in the United States has largely ignored these critical dimensions, but has, instead, been preoccupied with defining the nature of American slavery, especially as compared with racial bondage elsewhere in the Americas. These studies have been extraordinarily valuable not only in revealing much about slave society but also in telling a good deal about free society. They have been essential to the development of a new understanding of American life centered on social transformation: the emergence of bourgeois society in the North with an upward-striving middle class and an increasingly self-conscious working class and the development of a plantocracy in the South with a segmented social order and ideals of interdependence, stability, and hierarchy. But viewing Southern slavery from the point of maturity, dissecting it into component parts, comparing it to other slave societies, and juxtaposing it to free society have produced an essentially static vision of slave culture. . . .

Recent interest in the beginnings of slavery on the mainland of British North America, however, has revealed a striking diversity in Afro-American life. During the seventeenth and eighteenth centuries, three distinct slave systems evolved: a Northern nonplantation system and two Southern plantation systems, one around Chesapeake Bay and the other in the Carolina and Georgia low country. Slavery took shape differently in each with important consequences for the growth of black culture and society. The development of these slave societies depended upon the nature of the slave trade and the demographic configurations of blacks and whites as well as upon the diverse character of colonial economy. Thus, while cultural differences between newly arrived Africans and second and third generation Afro-Americans or creoles* everywhere provided the basis for social stratification within black society, African-creole differ-

---

*In the United States, "creole" has also been specifically applied to people of mixed but usually non-African origins in Louisiana.

ences emerged at different times with different force and even different meaning in the North, the Chesapeake region, and the lowcountry. A careful examination of the diverse development of Afro-American culture in the colonial era yields important clues for an understanding of the full complexity of black society in the centuries that followed.

The nature of slavery and the demographic balance of whites and blacks during the seventeenth and first decades of the eighteenth centuries tended to incorporate Northern blacks into the emerging Euro-American culture, even as whites denied them a place in Northern society. But changes in the character of the slave trade during the middle third of the eighteenth century gave new impetus to African culture and institutions in the Northern colonies. By the American Revolution, Afro-American culture had been integrated into the larger Euro-American one, but black people remained acutely conscious of their African inheritance and freely drew on it in shaping their lives.

Throughout the colonial years, blacks composed a small fraction of the population of New England and the Middle Colonies. Only in New York and Rhode Island did they reach 15 percent of the population. In most Northern colonies the proportion was considerably smaller. At its height, the black population totaled 8 percent of the population of New Jersey and less than 4 percent in Massachusetts and Connecticut. But these colony-wide enumerations dilute the presence of blacks and underestimate the importance of slave labor. In some of the most productive agricultural regions and in the cities, blacks composed a larger share of the population, sometimes constituting as much as one-third of the whole and perhaps one-half of the work force. Although many Northern whites never saw a black slave, others had daily, intimate contact with them. And, although some blacks found it difficult to join together with their former countrymen, others lived in close contact.

The vast majority of Northern blacks lived and worked in the countryside. A few labored in highly capitalized rural industries—tanneries, salt works, and iron furnaces—where they often composed the bulk of the work force, skilled and unskilled. Iron masters, the largest employers of industrial slaves, also were often the largest slaveholders in the North. Pennsylvania iron masters manifested their dependence on slave labor when, in 1727, they petitioned for a reduction in the tariff on slaves so they might keep their furnaces in operation. Bloomeries and forges in other colonies similarly relied on slave labor. But in an overwhelmingly agrarian society only a small proportion of the slave population engaged in industrial labor.

Like most rural whites, most rural blacks toiled as agricultural workers. In southern New England, on Long Island, and in northern New Jersey, which contained the North's densest black populations, slaves tended stock and raised crops for export to the sugar islands. Farmers engaged in provisioning the West Indies with draft animals and foodstuffs were familiar with slavery and had easy access to slaves. Some, like the Barbadian émigrés in northern New Jersey, had migrated from the sugar islands. Others, particularly those around Narragansett Bay, styled themselves planters in the West Indian manner. They built great houses, bred race horses, and accumulated slaves, sometimes holding twenty or more bondsmen. But, whatever the aspirations of this commercial gentry, the provisioning trade could not support a plantation regime. Most slaves lived on farms (not plantations), worked at a variety of tasks, and never labored in large gangs. No one in the North suggested that agricultural labor could be done only by black people, a common assertion in the sugar islands and the Carolina lowcountry. In northern New England, the Hudson Valley, and Pennsylvania, the seasonal demands of cereal farming undermined the viability of slavery. For most wheat farmers, as Peter Kalm shrewdly observed, "a Negro or black slave requires too much money at one time," and they relied instead on white indentured servants and free workers to supplement their own labor. Throughout the North's bread basket, even those members of the gentry who could afford the larger capital investment and the concomitant risk that slave ownership entailed generally depended on the labor of indentured servants more than on that of slaves. Fully two-thirds of the bond servants held by the wealthiest farmers in Lancaster and Chester counties, Pennsylvania, were indentured whites rather than chattel blacks. These farmers tended to view their slaves more as status symbols than as agricultural workers. While slaves labored in the fields part of the year, as did nearly everyone, they also spent a large portion of their time working in and around their masters' houses as domestic servants, stable keepers, and gardeners. Significantly, the wills and inventories of Northern slaveholders listed their slaves with other high status objects like clocks and carriages rather than with land or agricultural implements.

The distinct demands of Northern agriculture shaped black life in the countryside. Where the provisioning trade predominated, black men worked as stock minders and herdsmen while black women labored as dairy maids as well as domestics of various kinds. The large number of slaves demanded by the provisioning trade and the ready access to horses and mules it allowed placed black companionship within easy reach of most bondsmen. Such was not always true in the cereal region. Living scattered throughout the countryside on the largest farms and working in the house as often as in the field, blacks enjoyed neither the mobility nor the autonomy of slaves employed in the provisioning trade. But, if the demands of Northern agriculture affected black life in different ways, almost all rural blacks lived and worked in close proximity to whites. Slaves quickly learned the rudiments of the English language, the Christian religion, the white man's ways. In the North, few rural blacks remained untouched by the larger forces of Euro-American life.

Northern slaves were also disproportionately urban. During the eighteenth century, a fifth to a quarter of the blacks in New York lived in New York City. Portsmouth and Boston contained fully a third of the blacks in New Hampshire and Massachusetts, and nearly half of Rhode Island's black population resided in Newport. Ownership of slaves was almost universal among the urban elite and commonplace among the middling classes as well. On the eve of the Revolution, nearly three-fourths of Boston's wealthiest quartile of propertyholders ranked in the slaveholding class. Fragmentary evidence from earlier in the century suggests that urban slave-ownership had been even more widespread but contracted with the growth of a free working class. Viewed from the top of colonial society, the observation of one visitor that there was "not a house in Boston" that did "not have one or two" slaves might be applied to every Northern city with but slight exaggeration.

Urban slaves generally worked as house servants—cooking, cleaning, tending gardens and stables, and running errands. They lived in back rooms, lofts, closets, and, occasionally, makeshift alley shacks. Under these cramped conditions, few masters held more than one or two slaves. However they might cherish a large retinue of retainers, urban slaveholders rarely had the room to lodge them. Because of the general shortage of space, masters discouraged their slaves from establishing families in the cities. Women with reputations for fecundity found few buyers, and some slaveholders sold their domestics at the first sign of pregnancy. A New York master candidly announced the sale of his cook "because she breeds too fast for her owners to put up with such inconvenience," and others gave away children because they were an unwarranted expense. As a result, black women had few children, and their fertility ratio was generally lower than that of whites. The inability or unwillingness of urban masters to support large households placed a severe strain on black family life. But it also encouraged masters to allow their slaves to live out, hire their own time, and thereby gain a measure of independence and freedom.

Slave hirelings along with those bondsmen owned by merchants, warehouse keepers, and ship chandlers kept Northern cities moving. Working outside their masters' houses, these bondsmen found employment as teamsters, wagoners, and stockmen on the docks and drays and in the warehouses and shops that composed the essential core of the mercantile economy. In addition, many slaves labored in the maritime trades not only as sailors on coasting vessels, but also in the rope walks, shipyards, and sail factories that supported the colonial maritime industry. Generally, the importance of these slaves to the growth of Northern cities increased during the eighteenth century. Urban slavery moved steadily away from the household to the docks, warehouses, and shops, as demonstrated by the growing disproportion of slave men in the urban North. Aside from those skills associated with the maritime trades, however, few slaves entered artisan work. Only a handful could be found in the carriage trades that enjoyed higher status and that offered greater opportunity for an independent livelihood and perhaps the chance to buy freedom.

In the cities as in the countryside, blacks tended to live and work in close proximity to whites. Northern slaves not only gained first-hand knowledge of their masters' world, but they also rubbed elbows with lower-class whites in taverns, cock fights, and fairs where poor people of varying status mingled. If urban life allowed slaves to meet more frequently and enjoy a larger degree of social autonomy than did slavery in the countryside, the cosmopolitan nature of cities speeded the transformation of Africans to Afro-Americans. Acculturation in the cities of the North was a matter of years, not generations.

For many blacks, the process of cultural transformation was well under way before they stepped off the boat. During the first century of American settlement, few blacks arrived in the North directly from Africa. Although American slavers generally originated in the North, few gave priority to Northern ports. The markets to the south were simply too large and too lucrative. Slaves dribbled into the Northern colonies from the West Indies or the mainland South singly, in twos and threes, or by the score but rarely by the boatload. Some came on special order from merchants or farmers with connections to the West Indian trade. Others arrived on consignment, since few Northern merchants specialized in selling slaves. Many of these were the unsalable "refuse" (as traders contemptuously called them) of larger shipments. Northern slaveholders generally disliked these scourings of the transatlantic trade who, the governor of Massachusetts observed, were "usually the worst servants they have"; they feared that the West Indian re-exports had records of recalcitrance and criminality as well as physical defects. In time, some masters may have come to prefer seasoned slaves because of their knowledge of English, familiarity with work routines, or resistance to New World diseases. But, whatever their preference, Northern colonies could not compete with the wealthier staple-producing colonies for prime African field hands. Before the 1740s, Africans appear to have arrived in the North only when a temporary glut made sale impossible in the West Indies and the mainland South. Even then they did not always remain in the North. When conditions in the plantation colonies changed, merchants re-exported them for a quick profit. The absence of direct importation during the early years and the slow, random, haphazard entry of West Indian creoles shaped the development of black culture in the Northern colonies. While the nature of the slave trade prevented the survival of tribal or even shipboard ties that figured so prominently in Afro-American life in the West Indies and the Lower South, it better prepared blacks to take advantage of the special circumstances of their captivity.

Newly arrived blacks, most already experienced in the New World and familiar with their proscribed status, turned Northern bondage to their advantage where they could. They quickly established a stable family life and, unlike newly imported Africans elsewhere on the continent, increased their numbers by natural means during the first generation. By 1708, the governor of Rhode Island observed that the colony's slaves were "supplied by the offspring of those they have already, which increase daily. . . ." The transplanted creoles also seized the opportunities provided by the complex Northern economy, the relatively close ties of master and slave, and, for many, the independence afforded by urban life. In New Amsterdam, for example, the diverse needs of the Dutch mercantile economy induced the West India Company, the largest slaveholder in the colony, to allow its slaves to live out and work on their own in return for a stipulated amount of labor and an annual tribute. "Half-freedom," as this system came to be called, enlarged black opportunities and allowed for the development of a strong black community. When the West India Company refused to make these privileges hereditary, "half-free" slaves organized and protested, demanding that they be allowed to pass their rights to their children. Failing that, New Amsterdam slaves pressed their masters in other ways to elevate their children's status. Some, hearing rumors that baptism meant freedom, tried to gain church membership. A Dutch prelate complained that these blacks "wanted nothing else than to deliver their children from bodily slavery, without striving for piety and Christian virtues." Even after the conquering English abolished "half-freedom" and instituted a more rigorous system of racial servitude, blacks continued to use the leverage gained by their prominent role in the city's economy to set standards of treatment well above those in the plantation colonies. Into the eighteenth century, New York slaves informally enjoyed the rights of an earlier era, including the right to hold property of their own. "The Custome of this Country," bristled a frustrated New York master to a West Indian friend, "will not allow us to use our Negroes as you doe in Barbados."

Throughout the North, the same factors that mitigated the harshest features of bondage in New York strengthened the position of slaves in dealing with their masters. Small holdings, close living conditions, and the absence of gang labor drew masters and slaves together. A visitor to Connecticut noted in disgust that slaveowners were "too Indulgent (especially the farmers) to their Slaves, suffering too great a familiarity from them, permitting them to sit at Table and eat with them (as they say to save time) and into the dish goes the black hoof as freely as the white hand." Slaves used knowledge gained at their masters' tables to press for additional privileges: the right to visit friends, live with their families, or hire their own time. One slaveholder reluctantly cancelled the sale of his slaves because of "an invariable indulgence here to permit Slaves of any kind of worth or Character who must change Masters, to choose those Masters," and he could not persuade his slaves "to leave their Country (if I may call it so), their acquaintances & friends." Such indulgences originated not only in the ability of slaves to manipulate their masters to their own benefit, but also from the confidence of slaveholders in their own hegemony. Surety of white dominance, derived from white numerical superiority, complemented the blacks' understanding of how best to bend bondage to their own advantage and to maximize black opportunities within slavery.

During the middle decades of the eighteenth century, the nature of Northern slavery changed dramatically. Growing demand for labor, especially when European wars limited the supply of white indentured servants and when depression sent free workers west in search of new opportunities, increased the importance of slaves in the work force. Between 1732 and 1754, blacks composed fully a third of the immigrants (forced and voluntary) arriving in New York. The new importance of slave labor changed the nature of the slave trade. Merchants who previously took black slaves only on consignment now began to import them directly from Africa, often in large numbers. Before 1741, for example, 70 percent of the slaves arriving in New York originated in the West Indies and other mainland sources and only 30 percent came directly from Africa. After that date, the proportions were reversed. Specializing in the slave trade, African slavers carried many times more slaves than did West Indian traders. Whereas slaves had earlier arrived in small parcels rarely numbering more than a half-dozen, direct shipments from Africa at times now totaled over a hundred and, occasionally, several times that. Slaves increasingly replaced white indentured servants as the chief source of unfree labor not only in the areas that had produced for the provisioning trade, where their pre-eminence had been established earlier in the century, but in the cities as well. In the 1760s, when slave importation into Pennsylvania peaked, blacks composed more than three-quarters of Philadelphia's servant population.

Northern whites generally viewed this new wave of slaves as substitutes for indentured labor. White indentured servants had come as young men without families, and slaves were now imported in much the same way. "For this market they must be young, the younger the better if not quite children," declared a New York merchant. "Males are best." As a result, the sex ratio of the black population, which earlier in the century had been roughly balanced, suddenly swung heavily in favor of men. In Massachusetts, black men outnumbered black women nearly two to one. Elsewhere sex ratios of 130 or more became commonplace. Such sexual imbalance and the proscription of interracial marriage made it increasingly difficult for blacks to enjoy normal family lives. As the birth rate slipped, mortality rates soared, especially in the cities where newly arrived blacks appeared to be concentrated. Since most slaves came without any previous exposure to New World diseases, the harsh Northern winters took an ever higher toll. Blacks died by the score; the crude death rate of Philadelphia and Boston blacks in the 1750s and 1760s was well over sixty per thousand, almost double that of whites. In its demographic outline, Northern slavery at mid-century often bore a closer resemblance to the horrors of the West Indies during the height of a sugar boom than to the relatively benign bondage of the earlier years.

Whites easily recovered from this demographic disaster by again switching to European indentured servants and then to free labor as supplies became available, and, as the influx of slaves subsided, black life also regained its balance. But the transformation of Northern slavery had a lasting influence on the development of Afro-American culture. Although the Northern black population remained predominantly Afro-American after nearly a century of slow importation from the West Indies and steady natural increase, the direct entry of Africans into Northern society reoriented black culture.

Even before the redirection of the Northern slave trade, those few Africans in the Northern colonies often stood apart from the creole majority. While Afro-American slaves established precedents and customs, which they then drew upon to improve their condition, Africans tended to stake all to recapture the world they had lost. Significantly, Africans, many of whom did not yet speak English and still carried tribal names, composed the majority of the participants in the New York slave insurrection of 1712, even though most of the city's blacks were creoles. The division between Africans and Afro-Americans became more visible as the number of Africans increased after mid-century. Not only did creoles and Africans evince different aspirations, but their life-chances—as reflected in their resistance to disease and their likelihood of establishing a family—also diverged sharply. Greater visibility may have sharpened differences between creoles and Africans, but Africans were too few in number to stand apart for long. Whatever conflicts different life-chances and beliefs created, whites paid such distinctions little heed in incorporating the African minority into their slaveholdings. The propensity of Northern whites to lump blacks together mitigated intraracial differences. Rather than permanently dividing blacks, the entry of Africans into Northern society gave a new direction to Afro-American culture.

Newly arrived Africans reawakened Afro-Americans to their African past by providing direct knowledge of West African society. Creole blacks began to combine their African inheritance into their own evolving culture. In some measure, the easy confidence of Northern whites in their own dominance speeded the syncretization of African and creole culture by allowing blacks to act far more openly than slaves in the plantation colonies. Northern blacks incorporated African culture into their own Afro-American culture not only in the common-place and unconscious way that generally characterizes the transit of culture but also with a high degree of consciousness and deliberateness. They designated their churches "African," and they called themselves "Sons of Africa." They adopted African forms to maximize their freedom, to choose their leaders, and, in general, to give shape to their lives. This new African influence was manifested most fully in Negro election day, a ritual festival of role reversal common throughout West Africa and celebrated openly by blacks in New England and a scattering of places in the Middle Colonies.

The celebration of Negro election day took a variety of forms, but everywhere it was a day of great merrymaking that drew blacks from all over the countryside. "All the various languages of Africa, mixed with broken and ludicrous English, filled the air, accompanied with the music of the fiddle, tambourine, the banjo, [and] drum," recalled an observer of the festival in Newport. Negro election day culminated with the selection of black kings, governors, and judges. These officials sometimes held symbolic power over the whole community and real power over the black community. While the black governors held court, adjudicating minor disputes, the blacks paraded and partied, dressed in their masters' clothes and mounted on their masters' horses. Such role reversal, like similar status inversions in Africa and elsewhere, confirmed rather than challenged the existing order, but it also gave blacks an opportunity to express themselves more fully than the narrow boundaries of slavery ordinarily allowed. Negro election day permitted a seeming release from bondage, and it also provided a mechanism for blacks to recognize and honor their own notables. Most important, it established a framework for the development of black politics. In the places where Negro election day survived into the nineteenth century, its politics shaped the politics within the black community and merged with partisan divisions of American society. Slaves elsewhere in the New World also celebrated this holiday, but whites in the plantation colonies found the implications of role reversal too frightening to allow even symbolically. Northern whites, on the other hand, not only aided election day materially, but sometimes joined in themselves. Still, white cooperation was an important but not the crucial element in the rise of Negro election day. Its origin in the 1740s and 1750s suggests how the entry of Africans reoriented Afro-American culture at a formative point in its development.

African acculturation in the Northern colonies at once incorporated blacks into American society and sharpened the memory of their African past and their desire to preserve it. While small numbers and close proximity to whites forced blacks to conform to the forms of the dominant Euro-American culture, the confidence of whites in their own hegemony allowed black slaves a good measure of autonomy. In this context it is not surprising that a black New England sea captain established the first back-to-Africa movement in mainland North America.

Unlike African acculturation in the Northern colonies, the transformation of Africans into Afro-Americans in the Carolina and Georgia low country was a slow, halting process whose effects resonated differently within black society. While creolization created a unified Afro-American population in the North, it left low-country blacks deeply divided. A minority lived and worked in close proximity to whites in the cities that lined the rice coast, fully conversant with the most cosmopolitan sector of low land society. A portion of this urban elite, increasingly light-skinned, pressed for further incorporation into white society, confident they could compete as equals. The mass of black people, however, remained physically separated and psychologically estranged from the Anglo-American world and culturally closer to Africa than any other blacks on continental North America.

The sharp division was not immediately apparent. At first it seemed that African acculturation in the Lower South would follow the Northern pattern. The first blacks arrived in the low country in small groups from the West Indies. Often they accompanied their owners and, like them, frequently immigrated in small family groups. Many had already spent considerable time on the sugar islands, and some had doubtless been born there. Most spoke English, understood European customs and manners, and, as their language skills and family ties suggest, had made the difficult adjustment to the conditions of black life in the New World.

As in the Northern colonies, whites dominated the population of the pioneer Carolina settlement. Until the end of the seventeenth century, they composed better than two-thirds of the settlers. During this period and into the first years of the eighteenth century, most white slaveholders engaged in mixed farming and stock raising for export to the West Indian islands where they had originated. Generally, they lived on small farms, held few slaves, and worked closely with their bond servants. Even when they hated and feared blacks and yearned for the prerogatives of West Indian slave masters, the demands of the primitive, labor-scarce economy frequently placed master and slave face-to-face on opposite sides of a sawbuck. Such direct, equalitarian confrontations tempered white domination and curbed slavery's harshest features.

White dependence on blacks to defend their valuable low land beachhead reinforced this "sawbuck equality." The threat of invasion by the Spanish and French to the south and Indians to the west hung ominously over the low country during its formative years. To bolster colonial defenses, officials not only drafted slaves in time of war but also regularly enlisted them into the militia. In 1710 Thomas Nairne, a knowledgeable Carolina Indian agent, observed that "enrolled in our Militia [are] a considerable Number of active, able, Negro Slaves; and Law gives every one of those his freedom, who in Time of an Invasion kills an Enemy." Between the settlement of the Carolinas and the conclusion of the Yamasee War almost fifty years later, black soldiers helped fend off every military threat to the colony. Although only a handful of slaves won their freedom through military service, the continued presence of armed, militarily experienced slaves weighed heavily on whites. During the Yamasee War, when the governor of Virginia demanded one Negro woman in return for each Virginia soldier sent to defend South Carolina, the beleaguered Carolinians rejected the offer, observing that it was "impracticable to Send Negro Women in their Roomes by reason of the Discontent such Usage would have given their husbands to have their wives taken from them which might have occasioned a Revolt."

The unsettled conditions that made the low country vulnerable to external enemies strengthened the slave's hand in other ways. Confronted by an overbearing master or a particularly onerous assignment, many blacks took to the woods. Truancy was an easy alternative in the thinly settled, heavily forested low country. Forest dangers generally sent truant slaves back to their owners, but the possibility of another fight induced slaveholders to accept them with few questions asked. Some bondsmen, however, took advantage of these circumstances to escape permanently. Maroon [fugitive slave] colonies existed throughout the low land swamps and into the backcountry. Maroons lived a hard life, perhaps more difficult than slaves, and few blacks chose to join these outlaw bands. But the ease of escape and the existence of a maroon alternative made masters chary about abusing their slaves.

The transplanted African's intimate knowledge of the subtropical low land environment—especially when compared to the Englishman's dense ignorance—magnified white dependence on blacks and enlarged black opportunities within the slave regime. Since the geography, climate, and topography of the low country more closely resembled the West African than the English countryside, African not European technology and agronomy often guided lowland development. From the first, whites depended on blacks to identify useful flora and fauna and to define the appropriate methods of production. Blacks, adapting African techniques to the circumstances of the Carolina wilderness, shaped the lowland cattle industry and played a central role in the introduction and development of the region's leading staple. In short, transplanted Englishmen learned as much or more from transplanted Africans as did the former Africans from them. While whites eventually appropriated this knowledge and turned it against black people to rivet tighter the bonds of servitude, white dependence on African know-how operated during those first years to place blacks in managerial as well as menial positions and thereby permitted blacks to gain a larger share of the fruits of the new land than whites might otherwise allow. In such circumstances, white domination made itself felt, but both whites and blacks incorporated much of West African culture into their new way of life.

The structure of the fledgling low land economy and the demands of stock raising, with deerskins as the dominant "crop" during the initial years of settlement, allowed blacks to stretch white military and economic dependence into generous grants of autonomy. On the small farms and isolated cowpens (hardly plantations by even the most latitudinous definition), rude frontier conditions permitted only perfunctory supervision and the most elementary division of labor. Most units were simply too small to employ overseers, single out specialists, or benefit from the economies of gang labor. White, red, and black laborers of varying legal status worked shoulder to shoulder, participating in the dullest drudgery as well as the most sophisticated undertakings. Rather than skilled artisans or prime field hands, most blacks could best be characterized as jacks-of-all-trades. Since cattle roamed freely through the woods until fattened for market, moreover, black cowboys—suggestively called "cattle chasers"—moved with equal freedom through the countryside, gaining full familiarity with the terrain. The autonomy of the isolated cowpen and the freedom of movement stock raising allowed made a mockery of the total dominance that chattel bondage implied. Slaves set the pace of work, defined standards of workmanship, and divided labor among themselves, doubtless leaving a good measure of time for their own use. The insistence of many hard-pressed frontier slaveowners that their slaves raise their own provisions legitimated this autonomy. By law, slaves had Sunday to themselves. Time allowed for gardening, hunting, and fishing both affirmed slave independence and supplemented the slave diet. It also enabled some industrious blacks to produce a small surplus and to participate in the colony's internal economy, establishing an important precedent for black life in the low country.

Such independence burdened whites. They complained bitterly and frequently about blacks traveling unsupervised through the countryside, congregating in the woods, and visiting Charles Town [South Carolina] to carouse, conspire, or worse. Yet knowledge of the countryside and a willingness to take the initiative in hunting down cattle or standing up to Spaniards were precisely the characteristics that whites valued in their slaves. They complained but they accepted. Indeed, to resolve internal disputes within their own community, whites sometimes promoted black participation in the affairs of the colony far beyond the bounds later permitted slaves or even black freemen. "For this last election," grumbled several petitioners in 1706, "Jews, Strangers, Sailors, Servants, Negroes, & almost every French Man in Craven & Berkly County came down to elect, & their votes were taken." Such breaches of what became an iron law of Southern racial policy suggest how the circumstances of the pioneer lowcountry life shrank the social as well as the cultural distance between transplanted Africans and the mélange of European settlers. During the first generations of settlement, Afro-American and Anglo-American culture and society developed along parallel lines with a large degree of overlap.

If the distinction between white and black culture remained small in the low country, so too did differences within black society. The absence of direct importation of African slaves prevented the emergence of African-creole differences; and, since few blacks gained their liberty during those years, differences in status within the black community were almost nonexistent. The small radius of settlement and the ease of water transportation, moreover, placed most blacks within easy reach of Charles Town. A "city" of several dozen rude buildings where the colonial legislature met in a tavern could hardly have impressed slaves as radically different from their own primitive quarters. Town slaves, for their part, doubtless had first-hand familiarity with farm work as few masters could afford the luxury of placing their slaves in livery.

Thus, during the first years of settlement, black life in the low country, like black life in the North, evolved toward a unified Afro-American culture. Although their numbers combined with other circumstances to allow Carolina blacks a larger role in shaping their culture than that enjoyed by blacks in the North, there remained striking similarities in the early development of Afro-American life in both regions. During the last few years of the seventeenth century, however, changes in economy and society undermined these com-

monalities and set the development of lowcountry Afro-American
life on a distinctive course.

The discovery of exportable staples, first naval stores and then
rice and indigo, transformed the low country as surely as the sugar
revolution transformed the West Indies. Under the pressure of the
riches that staple production provided, planters banished the white
yeomanry to the hinterland, consolidated small farms into large plantations, and carved new plantations out of the malaria-ridden
swamps. Before long, black slaves began pouring into the region
and, sometime during the first decade of the eighteenth century,
white numerical superiority gave way to the lowcountry's distinguishing demographic characteristic: the black majority.

Black numerical dominance grew rapidly during the eighteenth
century. By the 1720s, blacks outnumbered whites by more than two
to one in South Carolina. In the heavily settled plantation parishes
surrounding Charles Town, blacks enjoyed a three to one majority.
That margin grew steadily until the disruptions of the Revolutionary
era, but it again increased thereafter. Georgia, where metropolitan
policies reined planter ambition, remained slaveless until mid-century. Once restrictions on slavery were removed, planters imported
blacks in large numbers, giving lowland Georgia counties considerable black majorities.

Direct importation of slaves from Africa provided the impetus
to the growth of the black majority. Some West Indian Afro-Americans continued to enter the low country, but they shrank to a small
fraction of the whole. As African importation increased, Charles
Town took its place as the largest mainland slave mart and the center
of the low land slave trade. Almost all of the slaves in Carolina and
later in Georgia—indeed, fully 40 percent of all pre-Revolutionary
black arrivals in mainland North America—entered at Charles Town.
The enormous number of slaves allowed slave masters a wide range
of choices. Low-country planters developed preferences far beyond
the usual demands for healthy adult and adolescent males and concerned themselves with the regional and tribal origins of their purchases. Some planters may have based their choices on long experience and a considered understanding of the physical and social
character of various African nations. But, for the most part, these
preferences were shallow ethnic stereotypes. Coromantees revolted;
Angolans ran away; Iboes destroyed themselves. At other times,

lowland planters apparently preferred just those slaves they did not get, perhaps because all Africans made unsatisfactory slaves and the unobtainable ones looked better at a distance. Although low-country slave masters desired Gambian people above all others, Angolans composed a far larger proportion of the African arrivals. But, however confused or mistaken in their beliefs, planters held them firmly and, in some measure, put them into practice. "Gold Coast and Gambia's are the best, next to them the Windward Coast are prefer'd to Angola's," observed a Charles Town merchant in describing the most salable mixture. "There must not be a Callabar amongst them." Planter preferences informed low-country slave traders and, to a considerable degree, determined the tribal origins of low land blacks.

Whatever their origins, rice cultivation shaped the destiny of African people arriving at Charles Town. Although the production of pitch and tar played a pivotal role in the early development of the staple-based economy in South Carolina, rice quickly became the dominant plantation crop. Rice cultivation evolved slowly during the late seventeenth and early eighteenth centuries as planters, aided by knowledgeable blacks, mastered the complex techniques necessary for commercial production. During the first half of the eighteenth century, rice culture was limited to the inland swamps, where slave-built dikes controlled the irrigation of low-lying rice fields. But by mid-century planters had discovered how to regulate the tidal floods to irrigate and drain their fields. Rice production moved to the tidal swamps that lined the region's many rivers and expanded greatly. By the beginning of the nineteenth century, the rice coast stretched from Cape Fear in North Carolina to the Satilla River in Georgia. Throughout the low country, rice was king.

The relatively mild slave regime of the pioneer years disappeared as rice cultivation expanded. Slaves increasingly lived in large units, and they worked in field gangs rather than at a variety of tasks. The strict requirements of rice production set the course of their work. And rice was a hard master. For a large portion of the year, slaves labored knee deep in brackish muck under the hot tropical sun; and, even after the fields were drained, the crops laid-by, and the grain threshed, there were canals to clear and dams to repair. By mid-century planters had also begun to grow indigo on the upland sections of their estates. Indigo complemented rice in its seasonal requirements, and it made even heavier labor demands. The ready availability of African imports compounded the new harsh realities of plantation slavery by cheapening black life in the eyes of many masters. As long as the slave trade remained open, they skimped on food, clothing, and medical attention for their slaves, knowing full well that substitutes could be easily had. With the planters' reliance on male African imports, slaves found it increasingly difficult to establish and maintain a normal family life. Brutal working conditions, the disease-ridden, low land environment, and the open slave trade made for a deadly combination. Slave birth rates fell steadily during the middle years of the eighteenth century and mortality rates rose sharply. Between 1730 and 1760, deaths outnumbered births among blacks and only African importation allowed for continued population growth. Not until the eve of the Revolution did the black population begin again to reproduce naturally.

As the low country plantation system took shape, the great slave masters retreated to the cities of the region; their evacuation of the countryside was but another manifestation of the growing social and cultural distance between them and their slaves. The streets of Charles Town, and, later, of Beaufort, Georgetown, Savannah, Darien, and Wilmington sprouted great new mansions as planters fled the malarial lowlands and the black majority. By the 1740s, urban life in the low country had become attractive enough that men who made their fortunes in rice and slaves no longer returned home to England in the West Indian tradition. Instead, through intermarriage and business connections, they began to weave their disparate social relations into a close-knit ruling class, whose self-consciousness and pride of place became legendary. Charles Town, as the capital of this new elite, grew rapidly. Between 1720 and 1740 its population doubled, and it nearly doubled again by the eve of the Revolution to stand at about twelve thousand. With its many fine houses, its great churches, its shops packed with luxury goods, Charles Town's prosperity bespoke the maturation of the low land plantation system and the rise of the planter class.

Planters, ensconced in their new urban mansions, their pockets lined with the riches rice produced, ruled their low country domains through a long chain of command: stewards located in the smaller rice ports, overseers stationed near or on their plantations, and plantation-based black drivers. But their removal from the plantation did not breed the callous indifference of West Indian absenteeism. For one thing, they were no more than a day's boat ride away from their estates. Generally, they resided on their plantations during the non-malarial season. Their physical removal from the direct supervision of slave labor and the leisure their urban residences afforded appear to have sharpened their concern for "their people" and bred a pater-nalist ideology that at once legitimated their rule and informed all social relations.

The low country plantation system with its urban centers, its black majority, its dependence on "salt-water" slaves transformed black culture and society just as it reshaped the white world. The unified Afro-American culture and society that had evolved during the pioneer years disappeared as rice cultivation spread. In its place a sharp division developed between an increasingly urban creole and a plantation-based African population. The growth of plantation slavery not only set blacks further apart from whites, it also sharply divided blacks.

One branch of black society took shape within the bounds of the region's cities and towns. If planters lived removed from most slaves, they maintained close, intimate relations with some. The mas-ters' great wealth, transient life, and seasonal urban residence placed them in close contact with house servants who kept their estates, boatmen who carried messages and supplies back and forth to their plantations, and urban artisans who made city life not only possible but comfortable. In addition, coastal cities needed large numbers of workers to transport and process the plantation staples, to serve the hundreds of ships that annually visited the low country, and to sat-isfy the planters' newly acquired taste for luxury goods. Blacks did most of this work. Throughout the eighteenth century they com-posed more than half the population of Charles Town and other lowcountry ports. Probably nothing arrived or left these cities with-out some black handling it. Black artisans also played a large role in urban life. Master craftsmen employed them in every variety of work. A visitor to Charles Town found that even barbers "are sup-ported in idleness & ease by their negroes . . . ; & in fact many of the mechaniks bear nothing more of their trade than the name." Al-though most black artisans labored along the waterfront as ship-wrights, ropemakers, and coopers, low country blacks—unlike blacks in Northern cities—also entered the higher trades, working as gold beaters, silversmiths, and cabinetmakers. In addition, black women gained control over much of the marketing in the low country ports, mediating between slave-grown produce in the countryside and urban consumption. White tradesmen and journeymen periodically protested against slave competition, but planters, master craftsmen, and urban consumers who benefited from black labor and services easily brushed aside these objections.

Mobile, often skilled, and occasionally literate, urban slaves understood the white world. They used their knowledge to improve their position within low country society even while the condition of the mass of black people deteriorated in the wake of the rice revolution. Many urban creoles not only retained the independence of the earlier years but enlarged upon it. They hired their own time, earned wages from "overwork," kept market stalls, and sometimes even opened shops. Some lived apart from their masters and rented houses of their own, paying their owners a portion of their earnings in return for *de facto* freedom. Such liberty enabled a few black people to keep their families intact and perhaps even accumulate property for themselves. The small black communities that developed below the Bluff in Savannah and in Charles Town's Neck confirm the growing independence of urban creoles.

The incongruous prosperity of urban bondsmen jarred whites. By hiring their own time, living apart from their masters, and controlling their own family life, these blacks forcibly and visibly claimed the white man's privileges. Perhaps no aspect of their behavior was as obvious and, hence, as galling as their elaborate dress. While plantation slaves—men and women—worked stripped to the waist wearing no more than loin cloths (thereby confirming the white man's image of savagery), urban slaves appropriated their masters' taste for fine clothes and often the clothes themselves. Low country legislators enacted various sumptuary regulations to restrain the slaves' penchant for dressing above their station. The South Carolina Assembly once even considered prohibiting masters from giving their old clothes to their slaves. But hand-me-downs were clearly not the problem as long as slaves earned wages and had easy access to the urban marketplace. Frustrated by the realities of urban slavery, lawmakers passed and repassed the old regulations to little effect. On the eve of the Revolution, a Charles Town Grand Jury continued to bemoan the fact that the "Law for preventing the excessive and costly Apparel of Negroes and other Slaves in this province (especially in *Charles Town*) [was] not being put into Force."

Most of these privileged bondsmen appear to have been creoles with long experience in the New World. Although some Africans entered urban society, the language skills and the mastery of the complex interpersonal relations needed in the cities gave creoles a clear advantage over Africans in securing elevated positions within the growing urban enclaves. To be sure, their special status was far from "equal." No matter how essential their function or intimate their interaction, their relations with whites no longer smacked of the earlier "sawbuck equality." Instead, these relations might better be characterized as paternal, sometimes literally so.

Increasingly during the eighteenth century, blacks gained privileged positions within low country society as a result of intimate, usually sexual, relations with white slave masters. Like slaveholders everywhere, low land planters assumed that sexual access to slave women was simply another of the master's prerogatives. Perhaps because their origin was West Indian or perhaps because their dual residence separated them from their white wives part of the year, white men established sexual liaisons with black women frequently and openly. Some white men and black women formed stable, long-lasting unions, legitimate in everything but law. More often than other slaveholders on continental British North America, low country planters recognized and provided for their mulatto offspring, and, occasionally, extended legal freedom. South Carolina's small free Negro population, almost totally confined to Charles Town, was largely the product of such relations. Light-skinned people of color enjoyed special standing in the low country ports, as they did in the West Indies, and whites occasionally looked the other way when such creoles passed into the dominant caste. But even when the planters did not grant legal freedom, they usually assured the elevated standing of their mulatto scions by training them for artisan trades or placing them in household positions. If the countryside was "blackened" by African imports, Charles Town and the other low country ports exhibited a mélange of "colored" peoples.

While one branch of black society stood so close to whites that its members sometimes disappeared into the white population, most plantation slaves remained alienated from the world of their masters, physically and culturally. Living in large units often numbering in the hundreds on plantations that they had carved out of the malarial swamps and working under the direction of black drivers, the black majority gained only fleeting knowledge of Anglo-American culture.

What they knew did not encourage them to learn more. Instead, they strove to widen the distance between themselves and their captors. In doing so, they too built upon the large degree of autonomy black people had earlier enjoyed.

In the pioneer period, many masters required slaves to raise their own provisions. Slaves regularly kept small gardens and tended barnyard fowl to maintain themselves, and they often marketed their surplus. Blacks kept these prerogatives with the development of the plantation system. In fact, the growth of low country towns, the increasing specialization in staple production, and the comparative absence of nonslaveholding whites enlarged the market for slave-grown produce. Planters, of course, disliked the independence truck gardening afforded plantation blacks and the tendency of slaves to confuse their owners' produce with their own, but the ease of water transportation and the absence of white supervision made it difficult to prevent.

To keep their slaves on the plantation, some planters traded directly with their bondsmen, bartering manufactured goods for slave produce. Henry Laurens, a planter who described himself as a "factor" for his slaves, exchanged some "very gay Wastcoats which some of the Negro Men may want" for grain at "10 Bushels per Wastcoat." Later, learning that a plantation under his supervision was short of provisions, he authorized the overseer "to purchase of your own Negroes all that you know Lawfully belongs to themselves at the lowest price they will sell it for." As Laurens's notation suggests, planters found benefits in slave participation in the low country's internal economy, but the small profits gained by bartering with their bondsmen only strengthened the slaves' customary right to their garden and barnyard fowl. Early in the nineteenth century, when Charles C. Pinckney decided to produce his own provisions, he purchased breeding stock from his slaves. By the Civil War, low land slaves controlled considerable personal property—flocks of ducks, pigs, milch cows, and occasionally horses—often the product of stock that had been in their families for generations. For the most part, slave propertyholding remained small during the eighteenth century. But it helped insulate plantation blacks from the harsh conditions of primitive rice production and provided social distance from their masters' domination.

The task system, a mode of work organization peculiar to the low country, further strengthened black autonomy. Under the task system, a slave's daily routine was sharply defined: so many rows of rice to be sowed, so much grain to be threshed, or so many lines of canal to be cleared. Such a precise definition of work suggests that city-bound planters found it almost impossible to keep their slaves in the fields from sunup to sundown. With little direct white supervision, slaves and their black foremen conspired to preserve a large portion of the day for their own use, while meeting their masters' minimum work requirements. Struggle over the definition of a task doubtless continued throughout the formative years of the low country plantation system and after, but by the end of the century certain lines had been drawn. Slaves generally left the field sometime in the early afternoon, a practice that protected them from the harsh afternoon sun and allowed them time to tend their own gardens and stock. Like participation in the low country's internal economy, the task system provided slaves with a large measure of control over their own lives.

The autonomy generated by both the task system and truck gardening provided the material basis for low land black culture. Within the confines of the overwhelmingly black countryside, African culture survived well. The continual arrival of Africans into the low country renewed and refreshed slave knowledge of West African life. In such a setting blacks could hardly lose their past. The distinctive pattern of the low land slave trade, moreover, heightened the impact of the newly arrived Africans on the evolution of black culture. While slaves dribbled into the North through a multiplicity of ports, they poured into the low country through a single city. The large, unicentered slave trade and the large slaveholding units assured the survival not only of the common denominators of West African culture but also many of its particular tribal and national forms. Planter preferences or perhaps the chance ascendancy of one group sometimes allowed specific African cultures to reconstitute themselves within the plantation setting. To be sure, Africans changed in the low country. Even where blacks enjoyed numerical superiority and a considerable degree of autonomy, they could no more transport their culture unchanged than could their masters. But low country blacks incorporated more of West African culture—as reflected in their language, religion, work patterns, and much else—into their new lives than did other black Americans. Throughout the seventeenth century and into the nineteenth, low country blacks continued to work the land, name their children, and communicate through word and song in a manner that openly combined African traditions with the circumstances of plantation life.

The new pattern of creolization that developed following the rice revolution smashed the emerging homogeneity of black life in the first years of settlement and left low country blacks deeply divided. One branch of black culture evolved in close proximity to whites. Urban, often skilled, well-traveled, and increasingly American-born, creoles knew white society well, and they used their knowledge to better themselves. Some, clearly a well-connected minority, pressed for incorporation into the white world. They urged missionary groups to admit their children to school and later petitioned lawmakers to allow their testimony in court, carefully adding that they did not expect full equality with whites. Plantation slaves shared few of the assimilationist aspirations of urban creoles. By their dress, language, and work routine, they lived in a world apart. Rather than demand incorporation into white society, they yearned only to be left alone. Within the quarter, aided by their numerical dominance, their plantation-based social hierarchy, and their continued contact with Africa, they developed their own distinctive culture, different not only from that of whites but also from the cosmopolitan world of their Afro-American brethren. To be sure, there were connections between the black majority and the urban creoles. Many—market women, jobbing artisans, and boatmen—moved easily between these two worlds, and most blacks undoubtedly learned something of the other world through chance encounters, occasional visits, and word of mouth. Common white oppression continually shrank the social distance that the distinctive experience created, but by the eve of the Revolution, deep cultural differences separated those blacks who sought to improve their lives through incorporation into the white world and those who determined to disregard the white man's ways. If the movement from African to creole obliterated cultural differences among Northern blacks, creolization fractured black society in the lowcountry.

Cultural distinctions between Africans and Afro-Americans developed in the Chesapeake as well, although the dimension of differences between African and creole tended to be time rather than space. Unlike in the low country, white planters did not promote the creation of a distinctive group whose origins, function, and physical appearance distinguished them from the mass of plantation slaves and offered them hope, however faint, of eventual incorporation into white society. And, compared to the North, African immigration into the Chesapeake came relatively early in the process of cultural transformation. As a result, African-creole differences disappeared with time and a single, unified Afro-American culture slowly emerged in the Chesapeake.

As in the low country, little distinguished black and white laborers during the early years of settlement. Most of the first blacks brought into the Chesapeake region were West Indian creoles who bore English or Spanish surnames and carried records of baptism. Along the James, as along the Cooper, the demands of pioneer life at times operated to strengthen the slaves' bargaining position. Some blacks set the condition of their labor, secured their family life, participated in the region's internal economy, and occasionally bartered for their liberty. This, of course, did not save most black people from the brutal exploitation that almost all propertyless men and women faced as planters squeezed the last pound of profit from the tobacco economy. The blacks' treatment at the hands of planters differed little from that of white bound labor in large measure because it was difficult to treat people more brutally. While the advantages of this peculiar brand of equality may have been lost on its beneficiaries, those blacks who were able to complete their terms of servitude quickly joined whites in the mad scramble for land, servants, and status.

Many did well. During the seventeenth century, black freemen could be found throughout the region owning land, holding servants, and occasionally attaining minor offices. Like whites, they accumulated property, sued their neighbors, and passed their estates to their children. In 1651, Anthony Johnson, the best known of these early Negro freemen, received a two-hundred-and-fifty-acre headright for importing five persons into Virginia. John Johnson, a neighbor and probably a relative, did even better, earning five hundred and fifty acres for bringing eleven persons into the colony. Both men owned substantial farms on the Eastern Shore, held servants, and left their heirs sizable estates. As established members of their communities, they enjoyed the rights of citizens. When a servant claiming his freedom fled Anthony Johnson's plantation and took refuge with a nearby white farmer, Johnson took his neighbor to court and won the return of his servant along with damages against the white man.

The class rather than racial basis of early Chesapeake society enabled many black men to compete successfully for that scarcest of all New World commodities: the affection of white women. Bastardy lists indicate that white female servants ignored the strictures against what white lawmakers labeled "shameful" and "unnatural" acts and joined together with men of their own condition regardless of color. Fragmentary evidence from various parts of seventeenth-century Virginia reveals that approximately one-quarter to one-third of the bastard children born to white women were mulattoes. The commonplace nature of these interracial unions might have been the reason why one justice legally sanctioned the marriage of Hester, an English servant woman, to James Tate, a black slave. Some successful, property-owning whites and blacks also intermarried. In Virginia's Northampton County, Francis Payne, a Negro freeman, married a white woman, who later remarried a white man after Payne's death. William Greensted, a white attorney who represented Elizabeth Key, a mulatto woman, in her successful suit for her freedom, later married her. In 1691, when the Virginia General Assembly finally ruled against the practice, some propertied whites found the legislation novel and obnoxious enough to muster a protest.

By the middle of the seventeenth century, Negro freemen sharing and fulfilling the same ideals and aspirations that whites held were no anomaly in the Chesapeake region. An Eastern Shore tax list of 1668 counted nearly a third of black tithables free. If most blacks did not escape the tightening noose of enslavement, they continued to live and work under conditions not much different from white servants. Throughout the seventeenth and into the first decades of the eighteenth century, black and white servants ran away together, slept together, and, upon occasion, stood shoulder to shoulder against the weighty champions of established authority. Thus viewed from the first years of settlement—the relatively small number of blacks, their creole origins, and the initial success of some in establishing a place in society—black acculturation in the Chesapeake appeared to be following the nonplantation pattern of the Northern colonies and the pioneer low country.

The emergence of a planter class and its consolidation of power during a series of political crises in the middle years of the seventeenth century transformed black life in the Chesapeake and threatened this pattern of cultural change. Following the legalization of slavery in the 1660s, black slaves slowly but steadily replaced white indentured servants as the main source of plantation labor. By 1700, blacks made up more than half the agricultural work force in Virginia and, since the great planters could best afford to purchase slaves, blacks composed an even larger share of the workers on the largest estates. Increased reliance on slave labor quickly outstripped West Indian supplies. Beginning in the 1680s, Africans entered the region in increasingly large numbers. The proportion of blacks born in Africa grew steadily throughout the waning years of the seventeenth century, so that by the first decade of the eighteenth century, Africans composed some three-quarters of the region's blacks. Unlike the lowcountry, African imports never threatened the Chesapeake's overall white numerical superiority, but by the beginning of the eighteenth century they dominated black society. Some eighty years after the first blacks arrived at Jamestown and some forty years after the legalization of slavery, African importation profoundly transformed black life.

Slave conditions deteriorated as their numbers increased. With an eye for a quick profit, planters in the Chesapeake imported males disproportionately. Generally men outnumbered women more than two to one on Chesapeake slavers. Wildly imbalanced sex ratios undermined black family life. Physically spent and emotionally drained by the rigors of the Middle Passage, African women had few children. Thus, as in the North and the Carolina low lands, the black birth rate fell and mortality rate surged upward with the commencement of direct African importation.

The hard facts of life and death in the Chesapeake region distinguished creoles and Africans at the beginning of the eighteenth century. The demands of the tobacco economy enlarged these differences in several ways. Generally, planters placed little trust in newly arrived Africans with their strange tongues and alien customs. While they assigned creoles to artisanal duties on their plantations and to service within their households, they sent Africans to the distant, upland quarters where the slaves did the dull, backbreaking work of clearing the land and tending tobacco. The small size of these specialized upcountry units, their isolation from the mainstream of Chesapeake life, and their rude frontier conditions made these largely male compounds lonely, unhealthy places that narrowed men's vision. The dynamics of creole life, however, broadened black understanding of life in the New World. Traveling freely through the countryside as artisans, watermen, and domestic servants, creoles gained in confidence as they mastered the terrain, perfected their English, and learned about Christianity and other cultural modes that whites equated with civilization. Knowledge of the white world enabled black creoles to manipulate their masters to their own advantage. If Afro-Americans became increasingly knowledgeable about their circumstances and confident in their ability to deal with them, Africans remained provincials, limited by the narrow alternatives of plantation life.

As in the low country and the Northern colonies, Africans in the Chesapeake strove to escape whites, while creoles used their knowledge of white society for their own benefit. These cultural differences, which were reflected in all aspects of black life, can be seen most clearly in the diverse patterns of resistance. Africans ran away toward the back country and isolated swamps. They generally moved in groups that included women and children, despite the hazards such groups entailed for a successful escape. Their purpose was to recreate the only society they knew free from white domination. In 1727, Governor William Gooch of Virginia reported that about a dozen slaves had left a new plantation near the falls of the James River. They headed west and settled near Lexington, built houses, and planted a crop before being retaken. But Afro-Americans ran away alone, usually with the hope of escaping into American society. Moving toward the areas of heaviest settlement, they found refuge in the thick network of black kinship that covered the countryside and sold their labor to white yeomen with few questions asked. While the possibility of passing as free remained small in the years before the Revolution, the creoles' obvious confidence in their ability to integrate themselves into American society stands in stark contrast to that of Africans, who sought first to flee it.

As reflected in the mode of resistance, place of residence, occupation, and much else, Africans and creoles developed distinctive patterns of behavior and belief. To a degree, whites recognized these differences. They stigmatized Africans as "outlandish" and noted how creoles "affect our language, habits, and customs." They played on African-creole differences to divide blacks from each other, and they utilized creole skills to maximize the benefits of slave labor. But this recognition did not elevate creoles over Africans in any lasting

way. Over the course of the century following legal enslavement, it
had precisely the opposite effect. Chesapeake planters consolidated
their class position by asserting white racial unity. In this context,
the entry of large numbers of African—as opposed to creole—blacks
into the region enlarged racial differences and helped secure planter
domination. Thus, as reliance on black labor increased, the opportunities for any black—no matter how fluent in English or conversant with the countryside—to escape bondage and join the scramble
for land, servants, and status diminished steadily.

By the middle of the eighteenth century, the size and character
of the free Negro population had been significantly altered. Instead
of a large minority of the black population, Negro freemen now
composed just a small proportion of all blacks, probably not more
than 5 percent. Many were cripples and old folks whom planters
discarded when they could no longer wring a profit from their labor.
While most were of mixed racial origins, few of these free mulattoes
of the Chesapeake, in contrast to those of the low country, traced
their ancestry to the planter class. Instead, they descended from
white servants, frequently women. These impoverished people had
little status to offer their children. Indeed, planter-inspired legislation further compromised their liberty by requiring that the offspring of white women and black men serve their mother's master
for thirty-one years. Those who survived the term could scarcely
hope for the opportunities an earlier generation of Negro freemen
had enjoyed. The transformation of the free Negro caste in the century between 1660 and 1760 measured the change in Chesapeake
society as its organizing principle changed from class to race.

The free Negro's decline reveals how the racial imperatives of
Chesapeake society operated to lump all black people together, free
and slave, creole and African. In the Chesapeake, planters dared not
grant creoles special status at the expense of Africans. Since the Africans would shortly be creoles and since creoles shared so much with
whites, distinctions among blacks threatened the racial division that
underlay planter domination. In the low country, where geography,
economy, and language separated white and black, those few blacks
who spoke, dressed, acted, and looked like whites might be allowed
some white prerogatives. But, if low country planters could argue
that no white man could do the work required to grow rice commercially, no one in the Chesapeake could reasonably deny that

whites could grow tobacco. The fundamental unity of Chesapeake life and the long-term instability of African-creole differences pushed blacks together in the white mind and in fact.

During the middle years of the eighteenth century, changes in the Chesapeake economy and society further diminished differences within black society and created a unified Afro-American culture. The success of the tobacco economy enlarged the area of settlement and allowed planters to increase their holdings. The most successful planters, anxious to protect themselves from the rigors of the world marketplace, strove for plantation self-sufficiency. The great estates of the Chesapeake became self-contained enterprises with slaves taking positions as artisans, tradesmen, wagoners, and sometimes, managers; the plantation was "like a Town," as a tutor on Robert Carter's estate observed, "but most of the Inhabitants are black." The increased sophistication of the Chesapeake economy propelled many more blacks into artisanal positions and the larger units of production, tighter patterns of settlement, and the greater mobility allowed by the growing network of roads ended the deadening isolation of the upcountry quarter. Bondsmen increasingly lived in large groups, and those who did not could generally find black companionship within a few miles' walk. Finally, better food, clothing, and shelter and, perhaps, the development of immunities to New World diseases enabled blacks to live longer, healthier lives.

As part of their drive for self-sufficiency, Chesapeake slaveholders encouraged the development of an indigenous slave population. Spurred by the proven ability of Africans to survive and reproduce and pressed in the international slave market by the superior resources of West Indian sugar magnates and low land rice growers, Chesapeake planters strove to correct the sexual imbalance within the black population, perhaps by importing a large proportion of women or lessening the burden of female slaves. Blacks quickly took advantage of this new circumstance and placed their family life on a firmer footing. Husbands and wives petitioned their owners to allow them to reside together on the same quarter and saw to it that their families were fed, beyond their masters' rations. Planters, for their part, were usually receptive to slaves' demands for a secure family life, both because it reflected their own values and because they profited mightily from the addition of slave children. Thomas Jefferson frankly considered "a woman who brings a child every two years as more profitable than the best man on the farm [for] what she produces is an addition to capital, while his labor disappears in mere consumption." Under these circumstances, the black population increased rapidly. Planters relied less and less on African importation and, by the 1740s, most of the growth of the black population came from natural increase. Within a generation, African importation was, for all practical purposes, no longer a significant source of slave labor. In the early 1770s, the period of the greatest importation into the low country, only five hundred of the five thousand slaves added annually to the black population of Virginia derived directly from Africa.

The establishment of the black family marked the re-emergence of Afro-American culture in the Chesapeake. Although Africans continued to enter the region, albeit at a slower pace, the nature of the slave trade minimized their impact on the development of black society in the region. Unlike those in the low country, newly arrived Africans could rarely hope to remain together. Rather than funnel their cargo through a single port, Chesapeake slavers peddled it in small lots at the many tobacco landings that lined the bay's extensive perimeter. Planters rarely bought more than a few slaves at a time, and larger purchasers, usually the great planter-merchants, often acted as jobbers, quickly reselling these slaves to backcountry freeholders. The resulting fragmentation sent newly arrived Africans in all directions and prevented the maintenance of tribal or shipboard ties. Chesapeake slaveholders cared little about the origins of their slaves. In their eyes, newly arrived Africans were not Iboes, Coromantees, or Angolans, but "new Negroes." While the unicentered slave trade sustained and strengthened African culture in the lowcountry, the Chesapeake slave trade facilitated the absorption of Africans into the evolving creole society.

Differences between creoles and Africans did not disappear with the creation of a self-sustaining Afro-American population. The creoles' advantages—language skills, familiarity with the countryside, artisanal standing, and knowledge of the plantation routine—continued to propel them into positions of authority within the slave hierarchy. In some ways, the growing complexity of the Chesapeake economy widened the distance between Africans and creoles, at least at first. Most of the skilled and managerial positions within the region's expanding iron industry went to creole blacks as did the artisanal work in flour mills and weaving houses. On some plantations, moreover, artisan and house status became lodged in particular families with parents passing privileged positions on to their children. Increasingly, skilled slaves entered the market economy by selling their own time and earning money from "overwork," thereby gaining a large measure of freedom. For the most part, Africans remained on rude, backwoods plantations tending the broad-leaf weed. Since creole slaves sold at a premium price and most great planters had already established self-sustaining slave forces, small planters purchased nearly all of the newly arrived Africans after mid-century. These upward-striving men generally owned the least developed, most distant farms. Their labor requirements remained primitive compared to the sophisticated division of labor on the self-contained plantation-towns.

Over the long term, however, economic changes sped the integration of Africans into Afro-American society. Under the pressure of a world-wide food shortage, Chesapeake planters turned from the production of tobacco to that of foodstuff, especially wheat. The demands of wheat cultivation transformed the nature of labor in the region. Whereas tobacco farming required season-long labor, wheat farming employed workers steadily only during planting and harvesting. The remainder of the year, laborers had little to do with the crop. At the same time, however, wheat required a larger and more skilled labor force to transport the grain to market and to store it, mill it, and reship it as flour, bread, or bulk grain. Economic changes encouraged masters to teach their slaves skills and to hire them out during the slack season. At first, these opportunities went mostly to creoles, but as the wheat economy grew, spurring urbanization and manufacturing, the demands for artisans and hirelings outstripped the creole population. An increasing number of Africans were placed in positions previously reserved for creoles. The process of cultural transformation that earlier in the eighteenth century had taken a generation or more was considerably shorter at mid-century. Africans became Afro-Americans with increasing rapidity as the century wore on, eliminating the differences within black society that African importation had created.

Chesapeake blacks enjoyed considerably less autonomy than their low country counterparts. Resident planters, small units of production, and the presence of large numbers of whites meant that most blacks lived and worked in close proximity to whites. While low country planters fled to coastal cities for a large part of the year, the resident planter was a fixture of Chesapeake life. Small freeholders labored alongside slaves, and great planters prided themselves on regulating all aspects of their far-flung estates through a combination of direct personal supervision and plantation-based overseers. The latter were usually white, drawn from the region's white majority. Those few blacks who achieved managerial positions, moreover, enjoyed considerably less authority than lowland drivers. The presence of numerous nonslaveholding whites circumscribed black opportunities in other ways as well. While Chesapeake slaves commonly kept gardens and flocks of barnyard animals, white competitors limited their market and created a variety of social tensions. If low country masters sometimes encouraged their slaves to produce nonstaple garden crops, whites in the Chesapeake—slaveholders and nonslaveholders alike—complained that blacks stole more than they raised and worked to curb the practice. Thus, at every turn, economy and society conspired to constrain black autonomy.

The requirements of tobacco cultivation reinforced the planters' concern about daily work routine. Whereas the task system insulated low country blacks against white intervention and maximized black control over their work, the constant attention demanded by tobacco impelled Chesapeake planters to oversee the tedious process of cultivating, topping, worming, suckering, and curing tobacco. The desire of Chesapeake masters to control their slaves went beyond the supervision of labor. Believing that slaves depended on them "for every necessity of life," they intervened in the most intimate aspects of black life. "I hope you will take care that the Negroes both men and women I sent you up last always go by the names we gave them," Robert "King" Carter reminded his steward. "I am sure we repeated them so often . . . that everyone knew their names & would readily answer to them." Chesapeake planters sought to shape domestic relations, cure physical maladies, and form personalities. However miserably they failed to ensure black domestic tranquility and reform slave drunkards, paternalism at close quarters in the Chesapeake had a far more potent influence on black life than the distant paternalism that developed in the low country. Chesapeake blacks developed no distinct language and rarely utilized African day names for their children. Afro-American culture in the Chesapeake evolved parallel with Anglo-American culture and with a considerable measure of congruence.

The diverse development of Afro-American culture during the seventeenth and eighteenth centuries reveals the importance of time and place in the study of American slavery. Black people in colonial America shared many things: a common African lineage, a common racial oppressor, a common desire to create the richest life possible for themselves and their posterity in the most difficult of circumstances. But these commonalities took different shape and meaning within the diverse circumstances of the North American mainland. The nature of the slave trade, the various demographic configurations of whites and blacks, and the demands of particular staples—to name some of the factors influencing the development of slave society—created at least three distinctive patterns of Afro-American life. Perhaps a finer analysis will reveal still others.

This diversity did not end with the American Revolution. While African-creole differences slowly disappeared as the centerpole of black society with the closing of the slave trade and the steady growth of an Afro-American population, other sources of cohesion and division came to the fore. Differences between freemen and bondsmen, urban and rural folk, skilled and unskilled workers, and browns and blacks united and divided black people, and made black society every bit as variable and diverse during the nineteenth century as in the eighteenth. Indeed the diversity of black life increased substantially during the antebellum years as political changes abolished slavery in some places and strengthened it in others, as demographic changes set in motion by the Great Migration across the Lower South took effect, as the introduction of new crops enlarged the South's repertoire of staples, and as the kaleidoscopic movement of the world market sent the American economy in all directions.

If slave society during the colonial era can be comprehended only through a careful delineation of temporal and spatial differences among Northern, Chesapeake, and lowcountry colonies, a similar division will be necessary for a full understanding of black life in nineteenth-century America. The actions of black people during the American Revolution, the Civil War, and the long years of bondage between these two cataclysmic events cannot be understood merely as a function of the dynamics of slavery or the possibilities of liberty, but must be viewed within the specific social circumstances and cultural traditions of black people. These varied from time to time and from place to place. Thus no matter how complete recent studies of black life appear, they are limited to the extent that they provide a static and singular vision of a dynamic and complex society.

Edmund S. Morgan

SLAVERY AND FREEDOM: THE AMERICAN PARADOX

This selection by Edmund S. Morgan, Sterling Professor of History at Yale University, complements Berlin's essay on the origins of slavery. The institutionalization of African slavery in colonial Virginia provided a solution to antagonistic class relations among white landowners, large and small, by creating a readily identifiable black underclass that yeomen and gentry alike had a common racial interest in suppressing. Secure in their racial unity, white Virginians could develop a representative government in a plantation society and would, during the Revolutionary era, defend their rights against British imperialism, but at the cost of ignoring the rights of African-Americans. Morgan's argument is particularly insightful in demonstrating how the connection between race and class bound freedom to slavery.

The story properly begins in England with the burst of population growth there that sent the number of Englishmen from perhaps three million in 1500 to four-and-one-half million by 1650. The increase did not occur in response to any corresponding growth in the capacity of the island's economy to support its people. And the result was precisely that misery which Madison pointed out to Jefferson as the consequence of "a high degree of populousness." Sixteenth-century England knew the same kind of unemployment and poverty that Jefferson witnessed in eighteenth-century France and [Andrew] Fletcher in seventeenth-century Scotland. Alarming numbers of idle and hungry men drifted about the country looking for

Edmund S. Morgan, "Slavery and Freedom: The American Paradox," *Journal of American History*, 59, June 1972, pp. 14–29. Reprinted by permission.

work or plunder. The government did what it could to make men of means hire them, but it also adopted increasingly severe measures against their wandering, their thieving, their roistering, and indeed their very existence. Whom the workhouses and prisons could not swallow the gallows would have to, or perhaps the army. When England had military expeditions to conduct abroad, every parish packed off its most unwanted inhabitants to the almost certain death that awaited them from the diseases of the camp.

As the mass of idle rogues and beggars grew and increasingly threatened the peace of England, the efforts to cope with them increasingly threatened the liberties of Englishmen. Englishmen prided themselves on a "gentle government," a government that had been releasing its subjects from old forms of bondage and endowing them with new liberties, making the "rights of Englishmen" a phrase to conjure with. But there was nothing gentle about the government's treatment of the poor; and as more Englishmen became poor, other Englishmen had less to be proud of. Thoughtful men could see an obvious solution: get the surplus Englishmen out of England. Send them to the New World, where there were limitless opportunities for work. There they would redeem themselves, enrich the mother country, and spread English liberty abroad.

The great publicist for this program was Richard Hakluyt. His *Principall Navigations, Voiages and Discoveries of the English nation* was not merely the narrative of voyages by Englishmen around the globe, but a powerful suggestion that the world ought to be English or at least ought to be ruled by Englishmen. Hakluyt's was a dream of empire, but of benevolent empire, in which England would confer the blessings of her own free government on the less fortunate peoples of the world. It is doubtless true that Englishmen, along with other Europeans, were already imbued with prejudice against men of darker complexions than their own. And it is also true that the principal beneficiaries of Hakluyt's empire would be Englishmen. But Hakluyt's dream cannot be dismissed as mere hypocrisy any more than Jefferson's affirmation of human equality can be so dismissed. Hakluyt's compassion for the poor and oppressed was not confined to the English poor, and in Francis Drake's exploits in the Caribbean Hakluyt saw, not a thinly disguised form of piracy, but a model for English liberation of men of all colors who labored under the tyranny of the Spaniard.

Drake had gone ashore at Panama in 1572 and made friends with an extraordinary band of runaway Negro slaves. "Cimarrons" they were called, and they lived a free and hardy life in the wilderness, periodically raiding the Spanish settlements to carry off more of their people. They discovered in Drake a man who hated the Spanish as much as they did and who had the arms and men to mount a stronger attack than they could manage by themselves. Drake wanted Spanish gold, and the Cimarrons wanted Spanish iron for tools. They both wanted Spanish deaths. The alliance was a natural one and apparently untroubled by racial prejudice. Together the English and the Cimarrons robbed the mule train carrying the annual supply of Peruvian treasure across the isthmus. And before Drake sailed for England with his loot, he arranged for future meetings. When Hakluyt heard of this alliance, he concocted his first colonizing proposal, a scheme for seizing the Straits of Magellan and transporting Cimarrons there, along with surplus Englishmen. The straits would be a strategic strong point for England's world empire, since they controlled the route from Atlantic to Pacific. Despite the severe climate of the place, the Cimarrons and their English friends would all live warmly together, clad in English woolens, "well lodged and by our nation made free from the tyrannous Spanyard, and quietly and courteously governed by our nation."

The scheme for a colony in the Straits of Magellan never worked out, but Hakluyt's vision endured, of liberated natives and surplus Englishmen, courteously governed in English colonies around the world. Sir Walter Raleigh caught the vision. He dreamt of wresting the treasure of the Incas from the Spaniard by allying with the Indians of Guiana and sending Englishmen to live with them, lead them in rebellion against Spain, and govern them in the English manner. Raleigh also dreamt of a similar colony in the country he named Virginia. Hakluyt helped him plan it. And Drake stood ready to supply Negroes and Indians, liberated from Spanish tyranny in the Caribbean, to help the enterprise.

Virginia from the beginning was conceived not only as a haven for England's suffering poor, but as a spearhead of English liberty in an oppressed world. That was the dream; but when it began to materialize at Roanoke Island in 1585, something went wrong. Drake did his part by liberating Spanish Caribbean slaves, and carrying to Roanoke those who wished to join him. But the English settlers whom Raleigh sent there proved unworthy of the role assigned them. By the time Drake arrived they had shown themselves less than courteous to the Indians on whose assistance they depended. The first group of settlers murdered the chief who befriended them, and then gave up and ran for home aboard Drake's returning ships. The second group simply disappeared, presumably killed by the Indians.

What was lost in this famous lost colony was more than the band of colonists who have never been traced. What was also lost and never quite recovered in subsequent ventures was the dream of Englishman and Indian living side by side in peace and liberty. When the English finally planted a permanent colony at Jamestown they came as conquerors, and their government was far from gentle. The Indians willing to endure it were too few in numbers and too broken in spirit to play a significant part in the settlement.

Without their help, Virginia offered a bleak alternative to the workhouse or the gallows for the first English poor who were transported there. During the first two decades of the colony's existence, most of the arriving immigrants found precious little English liberty in Virginia. But by the 1630s the colony seemed to be working out, at least in part, as its first planners had hoped. Impoverished Englishmen were arriving every year in large numbers, engaged to serve the existing planters for a term of years, with the prospect of setting up their own households a few years later. The settlers were spreading up Virginia's great rivers, carving out plantations, living comfortably from their corn fields and from the cattle they ranged in the forests, and at the same time earning perhaps ten or twelve pounds a year per man from the tobacco they planted. A representative legislative assembly secured the traditional liberties of Englishmen and enabled a larger proportion of the population to participate in their own government than had ever been the case in England. The colony even began to look a little like the cosmopolitan haven of liberty that Hakluyt had first envisaged. Men of all countries appeared there: French, Spanish, Dutch, Turkish, Portuguese, and African. Virginia took them in and began to make Englishmen out of them.

It seems clear that most of the Africans, perhaps all of them, came as slaves, a status that had become obsolete in England, while it was becoming the expected condition of Africans outside Africa and of a good many inside. It is equally clear that a substantial number of Virginia's Negroes were free or became free. And all of them, whether servant, slave, or free, enjoyed most of the same rights and duties as other Virginians. There is no evidence during the period before 1660 that they were subjected to a more severe discipline than other servants. They could sue and be sued in court. They did penance in the parish church for having illegitimate children. They earned money of their own, bought and sold and raised cattle of their own. Sometimes they bought their own freedom. In other cases, masters bequeathed them not only freedom but land, cattle, and houses. Northampton, the only county for which full records exist, had at least ten free Negro households by 1668.

As Negroes took their place in the community, they learned English ways, including even the truculence toward authority that has always been associated with the rights of Englishmen. Tony Longo, a free Negro of Northampton, when served a warrant to appear as a witness in court, responded with a scatological opinion of warrants, called the man who served it an idle rascal, and told him to go about his business. The man offered to go with him at any time before a justice of the peace so that his evidence could be recorded. He would go with him at night, tomorrow, the next day, next week, any time. But Longo was busy getting in his corn. He dismissed all pleas with a "Well, well, Ile goe when my Corne is in," and refused to receive the warrant.

The judges understandably found this to be contempt of court; but it was the kind of contempt that free Englishmen often showed to authority, and it was combined with a devotion to work that English moralists were doing their best to inculcate more widely in England. As England had absorbed people of every nationality over the centuries and turned them into Englishmen, Virginia's Englishmen were absorbing their own share of foreigners, including Negroes, and seemed to be successfully moulding a New World community on the English model.

But a closer look will show that the situation was not quite so promising as at first it seems. It is well known that Virginia in its first fifteen or twenty years killed off most of the men who went there. It is less well known that it continued to do so. If my estimate of the volume of immigration is anywhere near correct, Virginia must have been a death trap for at least another fifteen years and probably for twenty or twenty-five. In 1625 the population stood at

1,300 or 1,400; in 1640 it was about 8,000. In the fifteen years between those dates at least 15,000 persons must have come to the colony. If so, 15,000 immigrants increased the population by less than 7,000. There is no evidence of a large return migration. It seems probable that the death rate throughout this period was comparable only to that found in Europe during the peak years of a plague. Virginia, in other words, was absorbing England's surplus laborers mainly by killing them. The success of those who survived and rose from servant to planter must be attributed partly to the fact that so few did survive.

After 1640, when the diseases responsible for the high death rate began to decline and the population began a quick rise, it became increasingly difficult for an indigent immigrant to pull himself up in the world. The population probably passed 25,000 by 1662, hardly what Madison would have called a high degree of populousness. Yet the rapid rise brought serious trouble for Virginia. It brought the engrossment of tidewater land in thousands and tens of thousands of acres by speculators, who recognized that the demand would rise. It brought a huge expansion of tobacco production, which helped to depress the price of tobacco and the earnings of the men who planted it. It brought efforts by planters to prolong the terms of servants, since they were now living longer and therefore had a longer expectancy of usefulness.

It would, in fact, be difficult to assess all the consequences of the increased longevity; but for our purposes one development was crucial, and that was the appearance in Virginia of a growing number of freemen who had served their terms but who were now unable to afford land of their own except on the frontiers or in the interior. In years when tobacco prices were especially low or crops especially poor, men who had been just scraping by were obliged to go back to work for their larger neighbors simply in order to stay alive. By 1676 it was estimated that one fourth of Virginia's freemen were without land of their own. And in the same year Francis Moryson, a member of the governor's council, explained the term "freedmen" as used in Virginia to mean "persons without house and land," implying that this was now the normal condition of servants who had attained freedom.

Some of them resigned themselves to working for wages; others preferred a meager living on dangerous frontier land or a hand-to-mouth existence, roaming from one county to another, renting a bit of land here, squatting on some there, dodging the tax collector, drinking, quarreling, stealing hogs, and enticing servants to run away with them.

The presence of this growing class of poverty-stricken Virginians was not a little frightening to the planters who had made it to the top or who had arrived in the colony already at the top, with ample supplies of servants and capital. They were caught in a dilemma. They wanted the immigrants who kept pouring in every year. Indeed they needed them and prized them the more as they lived longer. But as more and more turned free each year, Virginia seemed to have inherited the problem that she was helping England to solve. Virginia, complained Nicholas Spencer, secretary of the colony, was "a sinke to drayen England of her filth and scum."

The men who worried the uppercrust looked even more dangerous in Virginia than they had in England. They were, to begin with, young, because it was young persons that the planters wanted for work in the fields; and the young have always seemed impatient of control by their elders and superiors, if not downright rebellious. They were also predominantly single men. Because the planters did not think women, or at least English women, fit for work in the fields, men outnumbered women among immigrants by three or four to one throughout the century. Consequently most of the freedmen had no wife or family to tame their wilder impulses and serve as hostages to the respectable world.

Finally, what made these wild young men particularly dangerous was that they were armed and had to be armed. Life in Virginia required guns. The plantations were exposed to attack from Indians by land and from privateers and petty-thieving pirates by sea. Whenever England was at war with the French or the Dutch, the settlers had to be ready to defend themselves. In 1667 the Dutch in a single raid captured twenty merchant ships in the James River, together with the English warship that was supposed to be defending them; and in 1673 they captured eleven more. On these occasions Governor William Berkeley gathered the planters in arms and at least prevented the enemy from making a landing. But while he stood off the Dutch he worried about the ragged crew at his back. Of the ablebodied men in the colony he estimated that "at least one third are Single freedmen (whose Labour will hardly maintaine them) or men much in debt, both which wee may reasonably expect upon any Small advantage the Enemy may gaine upon us, wold revolt to them in hopes of bettering their Condicion by Shareing the Plunder of the Country with them."

Berkeley's fears were justified. Three years later, sparked not by a Dutch invasion but by an Indian attack, rebellion swept Virginia. It began almost as Berkeley had predicted, when a group of volunteer Indian fighters turned from a fruitless expedition against the Indians to attack their rulers. Bacon's Rebellion was the largest popular rising in the colonies before the American Revolution. Sooner or later nearly everyone in Virginia got in on it, but it began in the frontier counties of Henrico and New Kent, among men whom the governor and his friends consistently characterized as rabble. As it spread eastward, it turned out that there were rabble everywhere, and Berkeley understandably raised his estimate of their numbers. "How miserable that man is," he exclaimed, "that Governes a People wher six parts of seaven at least are Poore Endebted Discontented and Armed."

Virginia's poor had reason to be envious and angry against the men who owned the land and imported the servants and ran the government. But the rebellion produced no real program of reform, no ideology, not even any revolutionary slogans. It was a search for plunder, not for principles. And when the rebels had redistributed whatever wealth they could lay their hands on, the rebellion subsided almost as quickly as it had begun.

It had been a shattering experience, however, for Virginia's first families. They had seen each other fall in with the rebels in order to save their skins or their possessions or even to share in the plunder. When it was over, they eyed one another distrustfully, on the lookout for any new Bacons in their midst, who might be tempted to lead the still restive rabble on more plundering expeditions. When William Byrd and Laurence Smith proposed to solve the problems of defense against the Indians by establishing semi-independent buffer settlements on the upper reaches of the rivers, in each of which they would engage to keep fifty men in arms, the assembly at first reacted favorably. But it quickly occurred to the governor and council that this would in fact mean gathering a crowd of Virginia's wild bachelors and furnishing them with an abundant supply of arms and ammunition. Byrd had himself led such a crowd in at least one plundering foray during the rebellion. To put him or anyone else in charge of a large and permanent gang of armed men was to invite them to descend again on the people whom they were supposed to be protecting.

The nervousness of those who had property worth plundering continued throughout the century, spurred in 1682 by the tobacco-cutting riots in which men roved about destroying crops in the fields, in the desperate hope of producing a shortage that would raise the price of the leaf. And periodically in nearby Maryland and North Carolina, where the same conditions existed as in Virginia, there were tumults that threatened to spread to Virginia.

As Virginia thus acquired a social problem analogous to England's own, the colony began to deal with it as England had done, by restricting the liberties of those who did not have the proper badge of freedom, namely the property that government was supposed to protect. One way was to extend the terms of service for servants entering the colony without indentures. Formerly they had served until twenty-one; now the age was advanced to twenty-four. There had always been laws requiring them to serve extra time for running away; now the laws added corporal punishment and, in order to make habitual offenders more readily recognizable, specified that their hair be cropped. New laws restricted the movement of servants on the highways and also increased the amount of extra time to be served for running away. In addition to serving two days for every day's absence, the captured runaway was now frequently required to compensate by labor for the loss to the crop that he had failed to tend and for the cost of his apprehension, including rewards paid for his capture. A three week's holiday might result in a year's extra service. If a servant struck his master, he was to serve another year. For killing a hog he had to serve the owner a year and the informer another year. Since the owner of the hog, and the owner of the servant, and the informer were frequently the same man, and since a hog was worth at best less than one tenth the hire of a servant for a year, the law was very profitable to masters. One Lancaster master was awarded six years extra service from a servant who killed three of his hogs, worth about thirty shillings.

The effect of these measures was to keep servants for as long as possible from gaining their freedom, especially the kind of servants who were most likely to cause trouble. At the same time the engrossment of land was driving many back to servitude after a brief taste of freedom. Freedmen who engaged to work for wages by so doing became servants again, subject to most of the same restrictions as other servants.

Nevertheless, in spite of all the legal and economic pressures to keep men in service, the ranks of the freedmen grew, and so did poverty and discontent. To prevent the wild bachelors from gaining an influence in the government, the assembly in 1670 limited voting to landholders and householders. But to disfranchise the growing mass of single freemen was not to deprive them of the weapons they had wielded so effectively under Nathaniel Bacon. It is questionable how far Virginia could safely have continued along this course, meeting discontent with repression and manning her plantations with annual importations of servants who would later add to the unruly ranks of the free. To be sure, the men at the bottom might have had both land and liberty, as the settlers of some other colonies did, if Virginia's frontier had been safe from Indians, or if the men at the top had been willing to forego some of their profits and to give up some of the lands they had engrossed. The English government itself made efforts to break up the great holdings that had helped to create the problem. But it is unlikely that the policy makers in Whitehall would have contended long against the successful.

In any case they did not have to. There was another solution, which allowed Virginia's magnates to keep their lands, yet arrested the discontent and the repression of other Englishmen, a solution which strengthened the rights of Englishmen and nourished that attachment to liberty which came to fruition in the Revolutionary generation of Virginia statesmen. But the solution put an end to the process of turning Africans into Englishmen. The rights of Englishmen were preserved by destroying the rights of Africans.

I do not mean to argue that Virginians deliberately turned to African Negro slavery as a means of preserving and extending the rights of Englishmen. Winthrop Jordan has suggested that slavery came to Virginia as an unthinking decision. We might go further and say that it came without a decision. It came automatically as Virginians bought the cheapest labor they could get. Once Virginia's heavy mortality ceased, an investment in slave labor was much more profitable than an investment in free labor; and the planters bought slaves as rapidly as traders made them available. In the last years of the seventeenth century they bought them in such numbers that slaves probably already constituted a majority or nearly a majority of the labor force by 1700. The demand was so great that traders for a time found a better market in Virginia than in Jamaica or Barbados. But the social benefits of an enslaved labor force, even if not consciously sought or recognized at the time by the men who bought the slaves, were larger than the economic benefits. The increase in the importation of slaves was matched by a decrease in the importation of indentured servants and consequently a decrease in the dangerous number of new freedmen who annually emerged seeking a place in society that they would be unable to achieve.

If Africans had been unavailable, it would probably have proved impossible to devise a way to keep a continuing supply of English immigrants in their place. There was a limit beyond which the abridgment of English liberties would have resulted not merely in rebellion but in protests from England and in the cutting off of the supply of further servants. At the time of Bacon's Rebellion the English commission of investigation had shown more sympathy with the rebels than with the well-to-do planters who had engrossed Virginia's lands. To have attempted the enslavement of English-born laborers would have caused more disorder than it cured. But to keep as slaves black men who arrived in that condition *was* possible and apparently regarded as plain common sense.

The attitude of English officials was well expressed by the attorney who reviewed for the Privy Council the slave codes established in Barbados in 1679. He found the laws of Barbados to be well designed for the good of his majesty's subjects there, for, he said, "although Negros in that Island are punishable in a different and more severe manner than other Subjects are for Offences of the like nature; yet I humbly conceive that the Laws there concerning Negros are reasonable Laws, for by reason of their numbers they become dangerous, and being a brutish sort of People and reckoned as goods and chattels in that Island, it is of necessity or at least convenient to have Laws for the Government of them different from the Laws of England, to prevent the great mischief that otherwise may happen to the Planters and Inhabitants in that Island." In Virginia too it seemed convenient and reasonable to have different laws for black and white. As the number of slaves increased, the assembly passed laws that carried forward with much greater severity the trend already under way in the colony's labor laws. But the new severity was reserved for people without white skin. The laws specifically exonerated the master who accidentally beat his slave to death, but they placed new limitations on his punishment of "Christian white servants."

Virginians worried about the risk of having in their midst a body of men who had every reason to hate them. The fear of a slave insurrection hung over them for nearly two centuries. But the danger from slaves actually proved to be less than that which the colony had faced from its restive and armed freedmen. Slaves had none of the rising expectations that so often produce human discontent. No one had told them that they had rights. They had been nurtured in heathen societies where they had lost their freedom; their children would be nurtured in a Christian society and never know freedom.

Moreover, slaves were less troubled by the sexual imbalance that helped to make Virginia's free laborers so restless. In an enslaved labor force women could be required to make tobacco just as the men did; and they also made children, who in a few years would be an asset to their master. From the beginning, therefore, traders imported women in a much higher ratio to men than was the case among English servants, and the level of discontent was correspondingly reduced. Virginians did not doubt that discontent would remain, but it could be repressed by methods that would not have been considered reasonable, convenient, or even safe, if applied to Englishmen. Slaves could be deprived of opportunities for association and rebellion. They could be kept unarmed and unorganized. They could be subjected to savage punishments by their owners without fear of legal reprisals. And since their color disclosed their probable status, the rest of society could keep close watch on them. It is scarcely surprising that no slave insurrection in American history approached Bacon's Rebellion in its extent or in its success.

Nor is it surprising that Virginia's freedmen never again posed a threat to society. Though in later years slavery was condemned because it was thought to compete with free labor, in the beginning it reduced by so much the number of freedmen who would otherwise have competed with each other. When the annual increment of freedmen fell off, the number that remained could more easily find an independent place in society, especially as the danger of Indian attack diminished and made settlement safer at the heads of the rivers or on the Carolina frontier. There might still remain a number of irredeemable, idle, and unruly freedmen, particularly among the convicts whom England exported to the colonies. But the numbers were small enough, so that they could be dealt with by the old expedient of drafting them for military expeditions. The way was thus made easier for the remaining freedmen to acquire property, maybe acquire a slave or two of their own, and join with their superiors in the enjoyment of those English liberties that differentiated them from their black laborers.

A free society divided between large landholders and small was much less driven by antagonisms than one divided between landholders and landless, masterless men. With the freedman's expectations, sobriety, and status restored, he was no longer a man to be feared. That fact, together with the presence of a growing mass of alien slaves, tended to draw the white settlers closer together and to reduce the importance of the class difference between yeoman farmer and large plantation owner.

The seventeenth century has sometimes been thought of as the day of the yeoman farmer in Virginia; but in many ways a stronger case can be made for the eighteenth century as the time when the yeoman farmer came into his own, because slavery relieved the small man of the pressures that had been reducing him to continued servitude. Such an interpretation conforms to the political development of the colony. During the seventeenth century the royally appointed governor's council, composed of the largest property owners in the colony, had been the most powerful governing body. But as the tide of slavery rose between 1680 and 1720 Virginia moved toward a government in which the yeoman farmer had a larger share. In spite of the rise of Virginia's great families on the black tide, the power of the council declined; and the elective House of Burgesses became the dominant organ of government. Its members nurtured a closer relationship with their yeoman constituency than had earlier been the case. And in its chambers Virginians developed the ideas they so fervently asserted in the Revolution: ideas about taxation, representation, and the rights of Englishmen, and ideas about the prerogatives and powers and sacred calling of the independent, property-holding yeoman farmer—commonwealth ideas.

In the eighteenth century, because they were no longer threatened by a dangerous free laboring class, Virginians could afford these ideas, whereas in Berkeley's time they could not. Berkeley himself was obsessed with the experience of the English civil wars and the danger of rebellion. He despised and feared the New Englanders for their association with the Puritans who had made England, however briefly, a commonwealth. He was proud that Virginia, unlike New England, had no free schools and no printing press, because books and schools bred heresy and sedition. He must have taken satisfaction in the fact that when his people did rebel against him under Bacon, they generated no republican ideas, no philosophy of rebellion or of human rights. Yet a century later, without benefit of rebellions, Virginians had learned republican lessons, had introduced schools and printing presses, and were as ready as New Englanders to recite the aphorisms of the commonwealthmen.

It was slavery, I suggest, more than any other single factor, that had made the difference, slavery that enabled Virginia to nourish representative government in a plantation society, slavery that transformed the Virginia of Governor Berkeley to the Virginia of Jefferson, slavery that made the Virginians dare to speak a political language that magnified the rights of freemen, and slavery, therefore, that brought Virginians into the same commonwealth political tradition with New Englanders. The very institution that was to divide North and South after the Revolution may have made possible their union in a republican government.

Thus began the American paradox of slavery and freedom, intertwined and interdependent, the rights of Englishmen supported on the wrongs of Africans. The American Revolution only made the contradictions more glaring, as the slaveholding colonists proclaimed to a candid world the rights not simply of Englishmen but of all men. To explain the origin of the contradictions, if the explanation I have suggested is valid, does not eliminate them or make them less ugly. But it may enable us to understand a little better the strength of the ties that bound freedom to slavery, even in so noble a mind as Jefferson's. And it may perhaps make us wonder about the ties that bind more devious tyrannies to our own freedoms and give us still today our own American paradox.

David Brion Davis

THE UNCERTAIN ANTISLAVERY COMMITMENT OF THOMAS JEFFERSON

The United States' founders did not resolve the paradox of slavery and freedom that Morgan discussed in the previous selection. Thomas Jefferson is a case in point. His democratic ideals, eloquently expressed in the Declaration of Independence, inspired the later antislavery cause. He was one of the first statesmen anywhere to propose specific measures to restrict and eradicate black slavery. Yet, as David Brion Davis argues, Jefferson's personal commitment against slavery was ambiguous. Although he transcended his age in some ways, his social identification with Virginia's slaveholding gentry bounded his idealism with the prejudices of his class. He agonized about the legitimacy of slavery, but he ultimately defended the institution. In his last years he supported its expansion during the Missouri crisis of 1820 and demeaned abolitionism as a mere Federalist machination. David Brion Davis is Sterling Professor of History at Yale University and recipient of the Pulitzer prize for *The Problem of Slavery in the Age of Revolution* (1975), from which this selection is taken.

There can be no question that by the 1760s many sensitive Virginians, even among the planter elite, regarded Negro slavery with the deepest moral repugnance. Writing privately in 1761, Robert Beverley confided "'tis something so very contradictory to Humanity, that I am really ashamed of my Country whenever I consider of it; & if ever I bid adieu to Virginia, it will be from that cause alone." Governor Francis Fauquier, who was intimate with the Williamsburg intellectual circle that included George Wythe, Dr. William Small, and the young Thomas Jefferson, expressed the hope, in his will, that none of his slaves would condemn him on the Day of Judgment: "For with what face can I expect mercy from an offended God, if I have not myself shewn mercy to these dependent on me." George Washington spoke for the more enlightened sector of his class when he expressed the wish, in private correspondence, for legislative

Reprinted from *The Problem of Slavery in the Age of Revolution, 1770–1823,* pp. 169–184 by David Brion Davis. Copyright © 1975 by Cornell University. Used by permission of the publisher, Cornell University Press.

emancipation by "slow, sure, and imperceptible degrees." Can such sentiments be termed "antislavery" without diluting the concept of any meaning?

Instead of ennobling the antislavery cause with a touch of his enormous prestige, President Washington privately discountenanced even a cautiously worded Quaker memorial against the slave trade, terming it "very mal-apropos," and an "illjudged piece of business [that] occasioned a great waste of time." One may note that Benjamin Franklin, as president of the Pennsylvania Abolition Society, signed a somewhat bolder companion petition; and in a published response to Congressional speeches vilifying the Quakers, Franklin satirized the southern defenses of slavery by putting them in the mouth of an Algerian pirate. In 1789, Beverley Randolph, then governor of Virginia, sent copies of Virginia slave laws to the Pennsylvania Abolition Society, adding that "it will always give me pleasure to give any aid in my Power to forward the humane & benevolent Designs of the Philadelphia Society." James Wood, also while presiding as governor of Virginia, served as vice-president of the Virginia Abolition Society.

In contrast, Washington became indignant when the Pennsylvania Society sought to bring the slaves of government officials resident in Philadelphia under the protection of Pennsylvania law. Afraid that some of his own servants might find "the idea of freedom" "too great a temptation for them to resist," he instructed Tobias Lear to send back to Virginia any slaves who, being unregistered in accordance with Pennsylvania law, might seek liberation after six months' residence: "I wish to have it accomplished under pretext that may deceive both them and the Public; and none I think would so effectively do this, as Mrs. Washington coming to Virginia next month." Washington's sincerity is not the issue. He often wished he could free himself, as well as his state, from this "very troublesome species of property." When he drew up his last will, in 1799, he provided for the emancipation of his own slaves, after "the decease of my wife." But antislavery is a questionable classification for a master who threatened to have a misbehaving youth shipped off to the West Indies, and who feared, two years before his death, that he would have to break his resolution against buying more slaves because his cook had run away. . . .

Jefferson's position is considerably more ambiguous. One must emphasize that he gave occasional and extremely quiet encouragement to Negro education and to antislavery opinion among the planter class. By 1835 this would have been unthinkable for any major political leader in the South. Nor were there many planters in any country who could write that

> the whole commerce between master and slave is a perpetual exercise of the most boisterous passions, the most unremitting despotism on the one part, and degrading submissions on the other. Our children see this, and learn to imitate it.

Such rhetoric soon acquired a life of its own, transmuting the "Jefferson image" into an antislavery force. No one can deny that Jefferson's democratic ideals were of monumental importance for the later antislavery cause. But the question of Jefferson's relation to the antislavery of his time requires an examination of his various roles and specific audiences.

According to Professor [Winthrop] Jordan, it was "neither timidity nor concern for reputation" which restrained Jefferson from public criticism of slavery or from endorsement of the antislavery cause. Rather, the statesman's caution arose from an acute consciousness of the depth of American racial prejudice and from a fear "that premature endorsement by a figure of his prominence might easily damage the antislavery cause." This was essentially Jefferson's own explanation. But Benjamin Franklin, Alexander Hamilton, and John Jay were figures of prominence who either owned or had owned Negro slaves; they were by no means free from racial prejudice or unaware of the difficulties of emancipation. Yet none of these circumstances deterred them from joining and lending their prestige to the earliest abolition societies.

I am not concerned with assigning moral credit or with ranking political leaders according to their abolitionist "contributions." Neither Hamilton nor Jay boldly championed the cause; and it is likely that Jay's inaction, as governor of New York, delayed the enactment of New York's gradual emancipation law. The point to be stressed is that early antislavery organization posed no threat to the vital interests of the northeastern states. In the North, abolitionist

societies could win sanction and support from national political leaders as well as from the reigning mercantile elites. In the South, however, the abolitionist societies carried far more subversive implications. It was not accidental that they were virtually ignored by
Jefferson and the other major political leaders who professed an ab-
horrence of slavery.

From the time of Jefferson's election to the Virginia House of
Burgesses to his departure for France as American Minister, his political experience with slavery amounted to a series of rebuffs from
the class which first accorded him recognition and prestige. Late in
life he recalled that soon after his election to the House of Burgesses,
at the age of twenty-six, he succeeded in persuading Richard Bland
to move "for certain moderate extensions of the protection of the
laws" to slaves. Although Bland was "one of the oldest, ablest, and
most respected members," he was "denounced as an enemy of his
country, and was treated with the grossest indecorum." Jefferson,
because of his youth, "was more spared in the debate." He clearly
thought this story contained a lesson for twenty-seven-year-old Edward Coles, who had written the aged and respected former President, hopeful that "in the calm of this retirement you might, most
beneficially to society, and with much addition to your own fame,
avail yourself of that love and confidence to put into complete practice those hallowed principles contained in that renowned Declaration, of which you were the immortal author." Jefferson urged Coles
to work "softly but steadily" for emancipation, promising to give the
cause "all my prayers, & these are the only weapons of an old man."

As a young man, he had dared a good bit more. In his *Summary View* of 1774 he had attacked the British crown for refusing to
allow colonies to restrict or prohibit the further importation of
slaves. This was a safe stand in Virginia, but Jefferson also asserted
that "the abolition of domestic slavery is the great object of desire in
those colonies where it was unhappily introduced in their infant
state." He surely knew this was an exaggeration, in the light of his
experience with Richard Bland, but it strengthened the case against
England and no doubt expressed his own true desire as well as that
of mentors like Bland and George Wythe. In the Declaration of Independence, however, he made no mention of emancipation but
condemned King George for enslaving innocent Africans, for encouraging the "execrable commerce" in men, and for inciting Amer-

ican Negroes to rise in arms against their masters. Congress struck out the entire section. Thus in writing the document that gave him international fame, Jefferson learned that on the question of slavery one yielded to older and more cautious men, and especially to outspoken objections from any segment of the planter class. In 1776 he also met defeat when, in his drafts of a constitution for Virginia, he introduced an unacceptable clause prohibiting any future importation of slaves. At the end of the Revolution he was apparently emboldened by the national spirit of thanksgiving and the expectation of a new republican era. In his 1783 draft of a new constitution for Virginia he provided for the freedom of all children born of slaves after the year 1800. This is the only definite record of a formal proposal by Jefferson for gradual emancipation; along with the measure his committee submitted to Congress in 1784 for excluding slaves from the western territories, again after the year 1800, it represents the high-water mark of his reform zeal. But both propositions were defeated.

One cannot question the genuineness of Jefferson's liberal dreams. If he had died in 1784, at the age of forty-one, it could be said without further qualification that he was one of the first statesmen in any part of the world to advocate concrete measures for restricting and eradicating Negro slavery. One may add, parenthetically, that in 1780 Edmund Burke drafted a bill for ameliorating the treatment of West Indian slaves, in preparation for their ultimate emancipation; but since he feared splitting the Whig party, he kept the plan secret for twelve years, and termed the abolition of the slave trade a "very chimerical object." In Britain, however, there were far weaker forces limiting the assimilation of antislavery philosophy. It is significant that Jefferson's individual efforts had virtually ceased by the time the first abolition societies appeared.

Jefferson played a central role in revising the laws of Virginia. Since this prodigious undertaking aimed at bringing the entire structure of law into conformity with republican principles, it offered unprecedented opportunities for the reform of slave codes, for the amelioration of slavery, or even for experiments at gradual emancipation. Surprisingly enough, Jefferson's proposed bills retained most of the inhumane features of the colonial slave law, and his innovations were largely too conservative for the legislature to adopt. For example, he was particularly harsh in depriving free Negroes of legal protection and in insisting on their expulsion from the common-wealth. Jefferson later claimed that the revisers had planned on in-troducing on the floor of the legislature an amendment for gradual emancipation and colonization. No draft of the amendment has sur-vived, and it seems clear that its supporters were not prepared to defend the measure against legislative opponents and the angry pe-titioners already mentioned. As Merrill D. Peterson has recently written, Jefferson continued to favor the plan of gradual emancipa-tion proposed in the *Notes on Virginia* in 1785; yet "neither he nor any other prominent Virginian was ever willing to risk friends, po-sition, and influence to fight for it."

In 1786, when Jefferson was in France and was contributing detailed information for an article on the United States in the *Ency-clopédie méthodique,* he wrote a strained reply to the editor's question: Why had Virginia adopted a new slave law without some provision for emancipation? Jefferson told of his planned amendment, hasten-ing to add that his own presence in the Virginia legislature would not have reversed the decision to suppress the untimely clause. He seemed anxious to avoid raising any suspicion of political conflict over slavery. The disposition of the legislature was simply not "ripe" for emancipation. And here Jefferson began experimenting with the locutions which for the rest of his life would characterize his re-sponse to such questions. Since his replies became so standardized, it is not unfair to conflate a number of examples: there was "not a man on earth" who more "ardently desired" emancipation, or who was more prepared to make "any sacrifice" to "relieve us from this heavy reproach, in any practicable way"; but—and Jefferson's buts deserve underscoring—the public mind needed "ripening" and would not yet "bear the proposition." To a French audience condi-tioned by the Abbé Raynal's bombastic rhetoric he exclaimed over the inconsistency of a slaveholding nation that fought for natural rights: "What a stupendous, what an incomprehensible machine is man!" In the style of Raynal, Jefferson talked, with uncharacteristic awkwardness, of "exterminating thunder" and "cosmic justice": when the slaves' groans "shall have involved heaven itself in darkness, doubtless a god of justice will awaken to their distress."

It is curious that the author of the Declaration of Indepen-dence should now justify inaction on the ground that an unsuccess-ful struggle against injustice would "rivet still closer the chains of bondage, and retard the moment of delivery to this oppressed description of men." We do not ordinarily associate Jeffersonian democracy with a quietistic surrender to fate; yet he advised his French editor that we must "await with patience the workings of an overruling providence, and hope that that is preparing deliverance of these our suffering brethren." At the age of forty-three Jefferson placed all his hope in the younger generation. In Virginia, he said, the emancipation cause was winning the support of "nearly the whole of the young men as fast as they come into public life." But what would these young men think when they heard their intellectual mentor recommending faith in providence as a substitute for social action? Jefferson gave no public sanction or moral encouragement to this alleged army of young emancipators; there is no record of his approving or even acknowledging the existence of the Virginia Abolition Society. Instead, his icy caution provided a precedent and model for the younger generation of politicians from both North and South who would attack every effort to discuss the slavery question as a reckless tampering with the "seals" which Jefferson and the other Founders had "wisely placed" on the nation's most incendiary issue. If the great father of democracy had refrained from giving public voice to his convictions, how could lesser men presume superior wisdom?

It is true that Jefferson's celebrated *Notes on Virginia* combined the antislavery ideals of the Enlightenment with a clinical diagnosis of Negro inferiority. But one must not forget that this work originated in 1781 as a body of information on Virginia for a small audience of French statesmen and intellectuals; that Jefferson opposed publishing the enlarged manuscript, in part because of his strictures on slavery; and that he intended the small and anonymous edition published in France in 1785 for strictly private circulation. He seems to have had two purposes for digressing on the general subject of Negro slavery: he wished to show that American planters shared the prevailing spirit of *bienfaisance* and *éclaircissement;* he also sought to explain why the abolition of slavery would require the deportation and colonization of Negroes. When it appeared that the book might be published without his consent, Jefferson became alarmed at the thought of American planters' reading his antislavery rhetoric. In 1785 he wrote the Marquis de Chastellux that the passages on slavery, if made public, might "produce an irritation" that would damage the cause of emancipation. In the next year Chastellux would damage the cause of emancipation by making derogatory comments on American Quakers, Negroes, and abolitionists, in his *Voyages dans l'Amérique septentrionale,* a book which drew heavily on Jefferson's *Notes* and which provoked an angry rebuttal from the abolitionist Brissot de Warville. Jefferson did not indicate how he expected to encourage the cause of emancipation without producing irritation. He told Chastellux that if he received sufficient reassurance from American friends, he would present a copy of the *Notes* to each student at William and Mary College: "It is to them I look, to the rising generations, and not to the one now in power for these great reformations." And yet John Adams, who belonged to the generation in power, wrote Jefferson that the passages on slavery were "worth Diamonds." James Monroe thought the *Notes* could be safely circulated, but promised to keep the book private until Jefferson consented to general publication. Jefferson agreed to have copies distributed among members of Congress, but was adamant that his authorship remain unknown. He would not take the risk of placing his own prestige squarely behind his antislavery views. Some thirty years later he could still affirm his willingness to make any sacrifice for the cause of emancipation and then add, with tragic opacity, "But I have not perceived the growth of this disposition in the rising generation, of which I once had sanguine hopes."

The truth was that Jefferson had only a theoretical interest in promoting the cause of abolition. When still in France, and incidentally while helping one J. D. Derieux buy land and slaves in America, he received inquiries from both the French and British abolition societies. Brissot reported the formation of the *Amis des noirs,* whose immediate object, like that of the parent London society, was limited to combating the slave trade. Brissot and Etienne Clavière requested that Jefferson attend a general meeting. No doubt it would have been imprudent if not improper for the American Minister to have joined a French reform society (John Jay, for example, resigned from the New York Manumission Society when he was appointed Chief Justice of the Supreme Court). Jefferson knew that he represented South Carolina as well as Virginia; his efforts to find new markets for American produce, including rice, had increased his awareness of the importance of slave labor in the national economy. He might informally have provided the *Amis* with valuable information, but he clearly wanted nothing to do with antislavery organizations. One fears, in any event, there was something disingenuous about his insistence to Brissot that while he was "willing to encounter every sacrifice" for the abolition of slavery as well as of the slave trade, any association with the *Amis* might render him less able to serve the cause in America. The purity he preserved in France did not equip him to speak out later against the spread of slavery into Kentucky, Tennessee, Mississippi Territory, or Louisiana.

The communication from London was less demanding. Edward Bancroft, an American inventor and double agent in the Revolution, had been talking with some friends who were members of the London Abolition Society. He had retold a story he had heard Jefferson tell at a dinner in France, concerning a benevolent Virginia planter who had tried to free his Negroes and pay them wages for labor. The point of the story, as Bancroft recalled, was that the Negroes had proved incapable of self-government, the "most sensible" desiring to return to slavery. Since the British abolitionists wanted more than hearsay evidence, Bancroft appealed to Jefferson for exact particulars. After a four-month delay, Jefferson replied that he could not remember telling such a story. He refused to go on record with any conclusions about the effects of emancipation. But so far as he knew from the experiments in Virginia, to free Negroes was "like abandoning children." Slavery had rendered them utterly incapable of self-control. Even the Quakers had been obliged to give daily supervision and even to whip the Negroes they had emancipated. This was essentially the message British abolitionists would continue to receive from West Indian planters. But Jefferson was unwilling to abandon his role as scientist and philanthropist. He abruptly announced to Bancroft that he personally intended to import German workers equal in number to the adult slaves he owned, intermingling them on farms of fifty acres. Presumably the Germans, with their "habits of property and foresight," would set an example for the slaves. But since Jefferson was at this time in critical financial straits and was faced with the need of selling land or slaves to pay his debts, he could not have taken the plan very seriously.

After his return to America the most remarkable thing about Jefferson's stand on slavery is his immense silence. The revolution in

St. Domingue, followed by the Gabriel plot* in Virginia, prompted him to occasional apocalyptic warnings about being "the murderers of our own children," or being forced, "after dreadful scenes and sufferings to release them in their own way, which, without such suffering we might now model after our own convenience." But such insights into the nature of power were balanced by Jefferson's self-comforting assurance that "interest is really going over to the side of morality. The value of the slave is every day lessening." If this seemed true in 1805 (and it was not true), how would Jefferson define morality when the value of slaves was every day increasing?

Political responsibilities help to justify Jefferson's policy of having "carefully avoided every public act or manifestation" on the subject of slavery. As President he felt he could not even reply to a warm appeal for his subscription to an antislavery poem, although he subscribed to other literary works and apparently had no hesitation over the public act of signing a law which opened Louisiana to settlement by slaveholders. He wrote to his friend Dr. George Logan, who was the only Quaker in the United States Senate, asking him to explain to the antislavery poet why the President could not openly support the "holy" cause: "Should an occasion ever occur in which I can interpose with decisive effect, I shall certainly know & do my duty with promptitude & zeal. But in the meantime it would only be disarming myself of influence to be taking small means." Again we find Jefferson conserving his influence and power for some decisive and well-timed blow against Negro bondage. But during his long retirement, when he was unencumbered by the responsibilities of office and was being deified as the apostle of liberty and the sage of Monticello, he kept his peace.

He was challenged, then, "in the calm of this retirement" by Edward Coles, one of the members of the rising generation in whom he had invested such hope. Coles had attended William and Mary and was thus part of the select audience Jefferson had hoped would read *Notes on Virginia*. By 1814, Coles had determined to emancipate the slaves he had inherited from his father, even if this required moving to a free state or territory. After apologizing for seeming so pres-

*Gabriel Prosser, a black artisan, planned an insurrection of African-Americans that would attack Richmond, Virginia, on August 30, 1800. Whites, however, learned of the plot before it could be executed. Prosser and other conspirators were arrested and hanged.

umptuous, Coles confronted Jefferson with the truths he had tried so hard to evade. Obviously it would be easier for "the revered fathers of all our political and social blessings" to begin the work of gradual emancipation than it would be for any succeeding statesmen. "And it is a duty," Coles went on, "as I conceive, that devolves particularly on you, from your known philosophical and enlarged view of subjects, and from the principles you have professed and practiced through a long and useful life." Coles, who had been President Madison's private secretary, was familiar with Jefferson's rationalizations: "I hope the fear of failing, at this time, will have no influence in preventing you from employing your pen to eradicate this degrading feature of British Colonial policy, which is still permitted to exist, notwithstanding its repugnance as well to the principles of our revolution as to our free institutions." Coles tried to persuade Jefferson that temporary failure could not damage his future reputation. After the former President had been "taken from us by the course of nature," his memory would be "consecrated"; his opinions and writings would have an "irresistible influence . . . in all questions connected with the rights of man."

Since Coles put Jefferson's antislavery commitment to the test, it is well to examine the statesman's reply with some care. Although he had postponed speaking out against slavery until the time was ripe, he now insisted that his views had "long since been in possession of the public." Nevertheless, the younger generation had not been aroused to action: "Your solitary but welcome voice is the first which has brought this sound to my ear; and I have considered the general silence which prevails on this subject as indicating an apathy unfavorable to every hope." To this excuse Coles made the obvious reply: it required men of influence and reputation "to arouse and enlighten the public sentiment, which in matters of this kind ought not to be expected to lead, but to be led; nor ought it to be wondered at that there should prevail a degree of apathy with the general mass of mankind, where a mere passive principle of right has to contend against the weighty influence of habit and interest."

Jefferson tried to reassure Coles that moral progress was inevitable: "It is an encouraging observation that no good measure was ever proposed, which, if duly pursued, failed to prevail in the end. We have proof of this in the history of the endeavors in the English parliament to suppress that very trade which brought this evil on us." But surely Jefferson knew that both Pitt and Fox had given their immense prestige to the British abolition cause; nor had British reformers talked about awaiting with patience the workings of an overruling providence. In response to Jefferson's familiar plea that "this enterprise is for the young," Coles reiterated the importance of experience, influence, and reputation, and pointed out that Jefferson was not as old as Franklin had been when leading the antislavery movement in Pennsylvania. But what must have disheartened Coles the most was Jefferson's strong advice that he should remain in Virginia and take good care of his slaves: "I hope then, my dear sir, you will reconcile yourself to your country and its unfortunate condition." Although Coles would remain a loyal disciple of Jefferson, he realized there was no hope of working for gradual emancipation in Virginia. The only alternative to reconciling himself to slavery was emigration to Illinois.

The exchange with Edward Coles dramatized Jefferson's fundamental commitment to his "country" as well as his extraordinary capacity to sound like an enlightened reformer while upholding the interests of the planter class. By "class" I mean something far more complex than a group united or governed by purely economic interest. Jefferson lived and moved within a cultural milieu dominated by the master-slave relationship, a relationship that included considerably more than "the most unremitting despotism on the one part, and degrading submissions on the other." The first childhood memory of the author of the Declaration of Independence was of being carried on a pillow by a mounted Negro slave. Jefferson was attuned to the values, loyalties, sanctions, taboos, and expectations of Virginia's wealthiest families, most of whom owned more than one hundred slaves. To a large extent he shared their collective sense of propriety, their moral imperatives, their definitions of available options. When Jefferson feared that he might harm the cause of liberty by overstepping prudent bounds, he gave expression to the genuine conviction that his power to do good depended on maintaining his reputation, or in other words, his social identity.

In some respects, of course, Jefferson transcended both his society and his age; in other respects he shared the more generalized opinions and prejudices of his time. For example, he felt that the only "practicable plan" of emancipation would be to liberate and eventually deport some future generation of Negroes; the children would be put to "industrious occupations," as wards of the state, as soon as their labor equalled the cost of their maintenance. This would mean permanently separating the children from their mothers, but the program would reduce both the public expense of emancipation and the compensation due to the mothers' owners. It must be stressed that there was nothing peculiarly "southern" about such reasoning. Neither racism nor a calculated concern for the rights of property was a monopoly of the slaveholding class.

On the other hand, if Jefferson could blame England for the "trade which brought this evil on us," he could also blame northeastern Federalists for trying to divide the nation by excluding slaves from Missouri. Ironically, in defending the extension of slavery into Missouri, Jefferson used precisely the same arguments which British slave traders had used long before. It was not a moral question, he insisted, since the removal of slaves from one state or country to another did not make new slaves; their status remained unchanged. Moreover, if slaves were spread over a larger surface, "their happiness would be increased."

Jefferson's record on slavery can only be judged by the values of his contemporaries and by the consistency between his own professed beliefs and actions. One needs to remember that he was a man burdened by many conflicting fears, roles, and responsibilities. One can understand and sympathize with his occasional feelings of despair, as when he wrote in 1820 that "we have a wolf by the ears, and we can neither hold him, nor safely let him go. Justice is in one scale, and self-preservation in the other." But for Jefferson the scale tipped heavily toward self-preservation, which meant the preservation of a social order based on slavery. Despite his glimpses of a more humane and just world, he could not doubt the basic legitimacy of his social universe. He knew that any serious threat to slavery was also a threat to this universe, however he might wish to dissociate the two. He was, to be sure, equivocal and indecisive; because of his immense prestige, he thereby sanctioned equivocation and indecision. But when the chips were down, as in the Missouri crisis, he threw his weight behind slavery's expansion, and bequeathed to the South the image of antislavery as a Federalist mask for political and economic exploitation. If early antislavery became identified with political partisanship and with conservatives like Hamilton, Jay, and Rufus King, it was partly by default.

III

Slave Life and Culture

Lawrence Levine

SLAVE SPIRITUALS

Religion lay at the heart of slave culture. It was far less the opiate of the masses, as Karl Marx thought, than a belief system by which slaves interpreted and shaped their own world, often in ways that challenged the legitimacy of white supremacy. Lawrence Levine, professor of history at the University of California, Berkeley, argues that the spirituals—the sacred songs of slaves—incorporated the divine into almost all aspects of their world. The emotional power of the spirituals, with their promise of redemption and salvation, was a testament to the way that slaves used Christianity to transcend their bondage. Drawing on the importance of music to their African ancestors, African-American slaves created a distinct cultural form that provided a sense of community as well as an alternative to the world of the slaveholder.

It is significant that the most common form of slave music we know of is sacred song. I use the term "sacred" not in its present usage as something antithetical to the secular world; neither the slaves nor their African forebears ever drew modernity's clear line between the sacred and the secular. The uses to which spirituals were put are an unmistakable indication of this. They were not sung solely or even primarily in churches or praise houses but were used as rowing songs, field songs, work songs, and social songs. Seated in a long cypress bark canoe on the Altamaha River in Georgia in 1845, Sir Charles Lyell listened to the six slave rowers improvise songs complimenting their master's family and celebrating a black woman of the neighborhood by comparing her beauty to that of the red bird. "Occasionally they struck up a hymn, taught them by the Methodists, in which the most sacred subjects were handled with strange familiarity, and which, though nothing irreverent was meant, sounded oddly to our ears, and, when following a love ditty, almost profane." Mary Dickson Arrowood recalled slave boatmen in the late

1850s singing the following spirituals which, characteristically, were as congenial to the work situation as to the praise house:

> Breddren, don' git weary,
> Breddren, don' git weary,
> Breddren, don' git weary,
> Fo' de work is most done.
>
> De ship is in de harbor, harbor, harbor,
> De ship is in de harbor,
> To wait upon de Lord. . . .
>
> 'E got 'e ca'go raidy, raidy, raidy,
> 'E got 'e ca'go raidy,
> Fo' to wait upon de Lord.

On the Sea Islands during the Civil War, Lucy McKim heard the spiritual *Poor Rosy* sung in a wide variety of contexts and tempos:

> On the water, the oars dip "Poor Rosy" to an even andante; a stout boy and girl at the hominy-mill will make the same "Poor Rosy" fly, to keep up with the whirling stone; and in the evening, after the day's work is done, "Heab'n shall-a be my home" [the final line of each stanza] peals up slowly and mournfully from the distant quarters.

For the slaves, then, songs of God and the mythic heroes of their religion were not confined to a specific time or place, but were appropriate to almost every situation. It is in this sense that I use the concept sacred—not to signify a rejection of the present world but to describe the process of incorporating within this world all the elements of the divine. The religious historian Mircea Eliade, whose definition of sacred has shaped my own, maintains that for people in traditional societies religion is a means of extending the world spatially upward so that communication with the other world becomes ritually possible, and extending it temporally backward so that the paradigmatic acts of the gods and mythical ancestors can be continually re-enacted and indefinitely recoverable. By creating sacred time and space, Man can perpetually live in the presence of his gods, can hold on to the certainty that within one's own lifetime "rebirth" is continually possible, and can impose order on the chaos of the universe. "Life," as Eliade puts it, "is lived on a twofold plane; it takes its course as human existence and, at the same time, shares in a trans-human life, that of the cosmos or the gods."

Claude Lévi-Strauss, who found these same cosmological outlooks in South America and Asia, has eloquently expressed the difficulties modern Westerners have in relating to them. As a boy he lived with his grandfather, the rabbi of Versailles, in a house which was linked to the synagogue by a long inner corridor. To the young Lévi-Strauss that long passage was appropriately symbolic: "Even to set foot in that corridor was an awesome experience; it formed an impassable frontier between the profane world and that other world from which was lacking precisely that human warmth which was the indispensable condition to my recognizing it as sacred." For men and women of traditional societies, such as those the slaves had originally come from, such corridors were absent. This is not to deny that the slaves were capable of making distinctions between this world and the next. Of course they were, and some of their songs do reflect a desire to release their hold upon the temporal present. "Why don't you give up de world?" they sang at times. "We must leave de world behind." Or, again:

This world is not my home.
This world is not my home.
This world's a howling wilderness,
This world is not my home.

But for the most part when they looked upon the cosmos they saw Man, Nature, and God as a unity, distinct but inseparable aspects of a sacred whole.

This notion of sacredness gets at the essence of the spirituals, and through them at the essence of the slave's world view. Denied the possibility of achieving an adjustment to the external world of the antebellum South which involved meaningful forms of personal integration, attainment of status, and feelings of individual worth that all human beings crave and need, the slaves created a new world by transcending the narrow confines of the one in which they were forced to live. They extended the boundaries of their restrictive universe backward until it fused with the world of the Old Testament, and upward until it became one with the world beyond. The spirituals are the record of a people who found the status, the harmony, the values, the order they needed to survive by internally creating an expanded universe, by literally willing themselves reborn. In this respect I agree with the anthropologist Paul Radin that

> the ante-bellum Negro was not converted to God. He converted God to himself. In the Christian God he found a fixed point and he needed a fixed point, for both within and outside of himself, he could see only vacillation and endless shifting. . . . There was no other safety for people faced on all sides by doubt and the threat of personal disintegration, by the thwarting of instincts and the annihilation of values.

The spirituals are a testament not only to the perpetuation of significant elements of an older world view among the slaves but also to the continuation of a strong sense of community. Just as the process by which the spirituals were created allowed for simultaneous individual and communal creativity, so their very structure provided simultaneous outlets for individual and communal expression. The overriding antiphonal structure of the spirituals—the call and response pattern which Negroes brought with them from Africa and which was reinforced in America by the practice of lining out hymns—placed the individual in continual dialogue with his community, allowing him at one and the same time to preserve his voice as a distinct entity and to blend it with those of his fellows. Here again slave music confronts us with evidence which indicates that, however seriously the slave system may have diminished the central communality that had bound African societies together, it was never able to destroy it totally or to leave the individual atomized and psychically defenseless before his white masters. In fact, the form and structure of slave music presented the slave with a potential outlet for his individual feelings even while it continually drew him back into the communal presence and permitted him the comfort of basking in the warmth of the shared assumptions of those around him. Those shared assumptions can be further examined by an analysis of the content of slave songs.

The most persistent single image the slave songs contain is that of the chosen people. The vast majority of the spirituals identify the singers as "de people dat is born of God," "We are the people of God," "we are de people of de Lord," "I really do believe I'm a child of God," "I'm a child ob God, wid my soul sot free," "I'm born of

God, I know I am." Nor is there ever any doubt that "To the promised land I'm bound to go," "I walk de heavenly road," "Heav'n shall-a be my home," "I gwine to meet my Saviour," "I seek my Lord and I find Him," "I'll hear the trumpet sound / In that morning."

The force of this image cannot be diminished by the observation that similar images were present in the religious singing of white evangelical churches during the first half of the nineteenth century. White Americans could be expected to sing of triumph and salvation, given their long-standing heritage of the idea of a chosen people which was reinforced in this era by the belief in inevitable progress and manifest destiny, the spread-eagle oratory, the bombastic folklore, and, paradoxically, the deep insecurities concomitant with the tasks of taming a continent and developing an identity. But for this same message to be expressed by Negro slaves who were told endlessly that they were members of the lowliest of races *is* significant. It offers an insight into the kinds of barriers the slaves had available to them against the internalization of the stereotyped images their masters held and attempted consciously and unconsciously to foist upon them.

Not only did slaves believe that they would be chosen by the Lord, there is evidence that many of them felt their owners would be denied salvation. On a trip through the South, Harriet Martineau recorded the instance of a mistress being told by one of her slaves, "You no holy. We be holy. You in no state of salvation." "Slaves knew enough of the orthodox theology of the time to consign all bad slaveholders to hell," Frederick Douglass wrote in his autobiography. Some went even further than this. "No white people went to Heaven," a correspondent in the *Southern Workman* noted in 1897, summing up the attitude of his fellow slaves before the Civil War and added, "Many believe the same until this day." The fugitive slave Charles Ball insisted that his fellow slaves refused to picture Heaven as a place where whites and blacks lived in perfect equality and boundless affection. "The idea of a revolution in the conditions of the whites and the blacks, is the corner-stone of the religion of the latter," he maintained. "Heaven will be no heaven to him [the slave], if he is not to be avenged of his enemies." One hundred years later a former slave bore witness to Ball's assertion: "This is one reason why I believe in a hell. I don't believe a just God is going to take no such man as that [her master] into His Kingdom." Martha Harrison recounted how her master, "Old Bufford," who beat her mother savagely for refusing to sleep with him, offered on his death bed to spend seven thousand dollars to pay his way out of hell, "but he couldn'ta got out of hell, the way he beat my mammy." Another former slave recalled that when her mistress died the slaves filed into the house "just a hollering and crying and holding their hands over their eyes, just hollering for all they could. Soon as they got outside of the house they would say, 'Old God damn son-of-a-bitch, she gone on down to hell.'" Mary Reynolds described the brutality of Solomon the white overseer on the Louisiana plantation where she had been a slave and concluded simply, "I know that Solomon is burning in hell today, and it pleasures me to know it."

Whether or not these reactions were typical, it is clear that a great many slaves agreed with H. B. Holloway that "It's going to be an awful thing up yonder when they hold a judgment over the way that things was done down here." The prospect pleased slaves enough to become part of their repertoire of jokes. The fugitive slave Lewis Clarke recounted two anecdotes with which the slaves on his Kentucky plantation used to delight each other. The first described the final conversation between a dying master and his slave: "Goodby, Jack; I have a long journey to go; farewell." "Farewell, massa! pleasant journey: you soon be dere, massa—*all de way down hill.*" The second told of a slave's reaction to the news that he would be rewarded by being buried in the same vault with his master: "Well, massa, one way I am satisfied, and one way I am not. I like to have good coffin when I die [but] I fraid, massa, when the debbil come take you body, he make mistake, and get mine."

The confinement of much of the slave's new world to dreams and fantasies does not free us from the historical obligation of examining its contours, weighing its implications for the development of the slave's psychic and emotional structure, and eschewing the kind of reasoning that has led one historian to imply that, since the slaves had no alternatives open to them, their fantasy life was "limited to catfish and watermelons." Their spirituals indicate clearly that there *were* alternatives open to them—alternatives which they themselves fashioned out of the fusion of their African heritage and their new religion—and that their fantasy life was so rich and so important to them that it demands understanding if we are even to begin to comprehend their inner world.

The God the slaves sang of was neither remote nor abstract, but as intimate, personal, and immediate as the gods of Africa had been. "O when I talk I talk wid God," "Mass Jesus is my bosom friend," "I'm goin' to walk with [talk with, live with, see] King Jesus by myself, by myself," were refrains that echoed through the spirituals.

> In de mornin' when I rise,
>   Tell my Jesus huddy [howdy] oh,
> I wash my hands in de mornin' glory,
>   Tell my Jesus huddy oh.
>
> Gwine to argue wid de Father and chatter wid de son,
> The last trumpet shall sound, I'll be there.
> Gwine talk 'bout de bright world dey des' come from.
> The last trumpet shall sound, I'll be there.
>
> Gwine to write to Massa Jesus,
> To send some Valiant soldier
> To turn back Pharaoh's army, Hallelu!

"Good news, member, good news member," the slaves sang jubilantly, "And I heard-e from Heav'n today."

The images of these songs were carried over into slave religious experiences. In a small South Carolina town in the 1850s, a white visitor questioned a young slave about his recent conversion experience:

> "An den I went to hebben."
> "What!" said I.
> "An' den I went to hebben."
> "Stop, Julius. You mean you had a dream, and thought you went to heaven."
> "No, Sah: an' den I went to hebben, and dere I see de Lord Jesus, *a sittin' behind de door an' a reading his Bible.*"

There was no question, the white interrogator concluded, of the slave's "unmistakable sincerity" or of the fact that his fellow slave parishioners believed him implicitly. "We must see, feel and hear something," an ex-slave exclaimed, "for our God talks to his children." During a slave service in New Orleans in January of 1851,

Fredrika Bremer witnessed the conversion of a black woman who, transported by religious enthusiasm, lept up and down with outstretched arms crying out "Hallelujah! Hallelujah!" and then, falling prostrate on the floor, lapsed into rigid quiescence. Gradually she recovered consciousness: "she talked to herself in a low voice, and such a beautiful, blissful expression was portrayed in her countenance that I would willingly experience that which she then experienced, saw, or perceived. It was no ordinary, no earthly scene. Her countenance was, as it were, transfigured."

In these states of transfiguration slave converts commonly saw and conversed with God or Christ: "I looked to the east and there was . . . God. He looked neither to the right nor to the left. I was afraid and fell on my face. . . . I heard a voice from God saying, 'My little one, be not afraid for lo! I am with you always.'" "I looked away to the east and saw Jesus. . . . I saw God sitting in a big armchair." "I first came to know of God when I was a little child. He started talking to me when I was no more than nine years old." "I seen Christ when His hair parted in the center." "I saw Him when he freed my soul from hell." "I saw in a vision a snow-white train once and it moved like lightning. Jesus was on board and He told me that He was the Conductor." "I saw the Lord in the east part of the world. . . . His hair was parted in the middle and he looked like he had been dipped in snow and he was talking to me." For the slave, Heaven and Hell were not concepts but places which could well be experienced during one's lifetime; God and Christ and Satan were not symbols but personages with whom meetings or confrontations were quite possible.

The heroes of the Scriptures—"Sister Mary," "Brudder Jonah," "Brudder Moses," "Brudder Daniel"—were greeted with similar intimacy and immediacy. In the world of the spirituals, it was not the masters and mistresses but God and Jesus and the entire pantheon of Old Testament figures who set the standards, established the precedents, and defined the values; who, in short, constituted the "significant others." The world described by the slave songs was a black world in which no reference was ever made to any white contemporaries. The slave's positive reference group was composed entirely of his own peers: his mother, father, sister, brother, uncles, aunts, preacher, fellow "sinners" and "mourners" of whom he sang endlessly, to whom he sent messages via the dying, and with whom he was reunited joyfully in the next world.

The same sense of sacred time and space which shaped the slave's portraits of his gods and heroes also made his visions of the past and future immediate and compelling. Descriptions of the Crucifixion communicate a sense of the actual presence of the singers: "Dey pierced Him in the side . . . Dey nail Him to de cross . . . Dey rivet His feet . . . Dey hanged him high . . . Dey stretch Him wide. . . ."

> Oh sometimes it causes me to tremble,—tremble,—tremble.
> Were you there when they crucified my Lord?

In 1818 a group of white Quaker students observed a Negro camp meeting. They watched in fascination and bewilderment as the black worshippers moved slowly around and around in a circle chanting:

> We're traveling to Immanuel's land,
>   Glory! Halle-lu-jah.

Occasionally the dancers paused to blow a tin horn. The meaning of the ceremony gradually dawned upon one of the white youths: he was watching "Joshua's chosen men marching around the walls of Jericho, blowing the rams' horns and shouting, until the walls fell." The students were witnessing the slaves' "ring shout"—that counterclockwise, shuffling dance which frequently lasted long into the night. The shout often became a medium through which the ecstatic dancers were transformed into actual participants in historic actions: Joshua's army marching around the walls of Jericho, the children of Israel following Moses out of Egypt. The shout, as Sir Charles Lyell perceived in 1845, frequently served as a substitute for the secular dance. It was allowed even where dancing was proscribed—"Hit ain't railly dancin' 'less de feets is crossed," "dancin' ain't sinful iffen de foots ain't crossed," two participants explained—and constituted still one more compelling feature of black religion. "Those who have witnessed these shouts can never forget them," Abigail Christensen has written. "The fascination of the music and the swaying motion of the dance is so great that one can hardly refrain from joining the magic circle in response to the invitation of the enthusiastic clappers, 'Now, brudder!' 'Shout, sister!' 'Come, belieber!' 'Mauma Rosa kin shout!' 'Uncle Danyel!' 'Join, shouters!'"

The thin line between time dimensions is nowhere better illustrated than in the slave's visions of the future, which were, of course, a direct negation of his present. Among the most striking spirituals are those which pile detail upon detail in describing the Day of Judgment: "You'll see de world on fire . . . see de element a meltin', . . . see the stars a fallin' . . . see the moon a bleedin' . . . see the forked lightning, . . . Hear the rumblin' thunder . . . see the righteous marching, . . . see my Jesus coming . . . ," and the world to come where "Dere's no sun to burn you . . . no hard trials . . . no whips a crackin' . . . no stormy weather . . . no tribulation . . . no evil-doers . . . All is gladness in de Kingdom." This vividness was matched by the slave's certainty that he would partake of the triumph of judgment and the joys of the new world:

> Dere's room enough, room enough, room enough in de heaven, my Lord
> Room enough, room enough, I can't stay behind.

Continually, the slaves sang of reaching out beyond the world that confined them, of seeing Jesus "in de wilderness," of praying "in de lonesome valley," of breathing in the freedom of the mountain peaks:

> Did yo' ever
> Stan' on mountun
> Wash yo' han's
> In a cloud?

Continually, they held out the possibility of imminent rebirth: "I look at de worl' an' de worl' look new, . . . I look at my hands an' they look so too . . . I looked at my feet, my feet was too."

These possibilities, these certainties were not surprising. The religious revivals which swept large numbers of slaves into the Christian fold in the late eighteenth and early nineteenth centuries were increasingly based upon notions of individual, volitional conversion and, in the words of one southern minister, "a free salvation to all men thro' the blood of the Lamb." They were based on a practical and implied, if not invariably theological or overt, Arminianism: God would save all who believed in Him; Salvation was there for all to take hold of if they would. This doctrine more and more came to characterize the revivals of the Presbyterians and Baptists as well as those of the more openly Arminian Methodists. The effects of this message upon the slaves who were exposed to and converted by it are illustrated graphically in the spirituals which were the products of these revivals and which continued to spread the evangelical word long after the revivals had passed into history. "What kind o' shoes is dem-a you wear? . . . Dat you can walk upon de air?" slaves asked in one of their spirituals, and answered by emphasizing the element of choice: "Dem shoes I wear am de gospel shoes; . . . An' you can wear dem ef-a you choose." "You got a right, I got a right," they sang, "We all got a right to de tree ob life."

The religious music of the slaves is almost devoid of feelings of depravity or unworthiness, but is rather, as I have tried to show, pervaded by a sense of change, transcendence, ultimate justice, and personal worth. The spirituals have been referred to as "sorrow songs," and in some respects they were. The slaves sang of "rollin' thro' an unfriendly world," of being "a-trouble in de mind," of living in a world which was a "howling wilderness," "a hell to me," of feeling like a "motherless child," "a po' little orphan chile in de worl'," a "home-e-less child," of fearing that "Trouble will bury me down."

But these feelings were rarely pervasive or permanent; almost always they were overshadowed by a triumphant note of affirmation. Even so despairing a wail as *Nobody Knows the Trouble I've Had* could suddenly have its mood transformed by lines like: "One morning I was a-walking down, . . . Saw some berries a-hanging down, . . . I pick de berry and I suck de juice, . . . Just as sweet as de honey in de comb." Similarly, amid the deep sorrow of *Sometimes I Feel Like a Motherless Chile,* sudden release could come with the lines: "Sometimes I feel like / A eagle in de air. . . . Spread my wings an' / Fly, fly, fly." Slaves spent little time singing of the horrors of hell or damnation. Their songs of the Devil pictured a harsh but almost semicomic figure (often, one suspects, a surrogate for the white man), over whom they triumphed with reassuring regularity:

> The Devil's mad and I'm glad,
> He lost the soul he thought he had.
>
> Ole Satan toss a ball at me.
> O me no weary yet . . .
>
> Him tink de ball would hit my soul.
> O me no weary yet . . .
>
> De ball for hell and I for heaven.
> O me no weary yet . . .
>
> Ole Satan thought he had a mighty aim;
> He missed my soul and caught my sins.
> Cry Amen, cry Amen, cry Amen to God!
>
> He took my sins upon his back;
> Went muttering and grumbling down to hell.
> Cry Amen, cry Amen, cry Amen to God!
>
> Ole Satan's church is here below.
> Up to God's free church I hope to go.
> Cry Amen, cry Amen, cry Amen to God!

For all their inevitable sadness, slave songs were characterized more by a feeling of confidence than of despair. There was confidence that contemporary power relationships were not immutable: "Did not old Pharaoh get lost, get lost, get lost, . . . get lost in the Red Sea?"; confidence in the possibilities of instantaneous change: "Jesus make de dumb to speak. . . . Jesus make de cripple walk. . . . Jesus give de blind his sight. . . . Jesus do most anything"; confidence in the rewards of persistence: "Keep a' inching along like a poor inchworm, / Jesus will come by'nd bye"; confidence that nothing could stand in the way of the justice they would receive: "You kin hender me here, but you can't do it dah," "O no man, no man, no man can hinder me"; confidence in the prospects of the future: "We'll walk de golden streets / Of de New Jerusalem." Religion, the slaves sang, "is good for anything, . . . Religion make you happy, . . . Religion gib me patience . . . O member, get Religion . . . Religion is so sweet."

The slaves often pursued the "sweetness" of their religion in the face of many obstacles. Becky Ilsey, who was sixteen when she was emancipated, recalled many years later:

> 'Fo' de war when we'd have a meetin' at night, wuz mos' always 'way in de woods or de bushes some whar so de white folks couldn't hear, an' when dey'd sing a spiritual an' de spirit 'gin to shout some de elders would go 'mongst de folks an' put dey han' over dey mouf an' some times put a clof in dey mouf an' say: "Spirit don talk so loud or de patterol break us up." You know dey had white patterols what went 'roun' at night to see de niggers didn't cut up no devilment, an' den de meetin' would break up an' some would go to one house an' some to er nudder an' dey would groan er w'ile, den go home.

Elizabeth Ross Hite testified that although she and her fellow slaves on a Louisiana plantation were Catholics, "lots didn't like that 'ligion."

> We used to hide behind some bricks and hold church ourselves. You see, the Catholic preachers from France wouldn't let us shout, and the Lawd done said you gotta shout if you want to be saved. That's in the Bible.
>
> Sometimes we held church all night long, 'til way in the mornin'. We burned some grease in a can for the preacher to see the Bible by. . . .
>
> See, our master didn't like us to have much 'ligion, said it made us lag in our work. He jest wanted us to be Catholicses on Sundays and go to mass and not study 'bout nothin' like that on week days. He didn't want us shoutin' and moanin' all day 'long, but you gotta shout and you gotta moan if you wants to be saved.

Slaves broke the proscription against unsupervised or unauthorized meetings by holding their services in secret, well-hidden areas, usually referred to as "hush-harbors." Amanda McCray testified that on her Florida plantation there was a praying ground where "the grass never had a chance ter grow fer the troubled knees that kept it crushed down," and Andrew Moss remembered that on the Georgia plantation where he grew up all the slaves had their private prayer grounds: "My Mammy's was a ole twisted thick-rooted muscadine bush. She'd go in dar and pray for deliverance of de slaves."

Even here the slaves were often discovered by the white patrols. "Den dey would rush in an' start whippin' an' beatin' de slaves unmerciful," West Turner of Virginia reported. ". . . an' do you know some o' dem devils was mean an' sinful 'nough to say, 'If I ketch you here servin' God, I'll beat you. You ain't got no time to serve God. We bought you to serve us.'" Slaves found many ways to continue to speak with their gods. Patsy Larkin recalled that on her plantation the slaves would steal away into the cane thickets and pray in a prostrate position with their faces close to the ground so that no sound would escape. Kalvin Woods, a slave preacher, described how slave women would take old quilts and rags and soak them before hanging them up in the shape of a small room, "and the slaves who were interested about it would huddle up behind these quilts to do their praying, preaching and singing. These wet rags were used to keep the sound of their voices from penetrating the air." On a Louisiana plantation the slaves would gather in the woods at night, form a circle on their knees, and pray over a vessel of water to drown the sound. The most commonly used method, in which the slaves had great confidence, was simply to turn a large pot upside down. "All the noise would go into that kettle," an ex-slave explained. "They could shout and sing all they wanted to and the noise wouldn't go outside."

Religious services were not confined to formal meetings, open or secret, but were often informal and spontaneous. One former slave remembered how religious enthusiasm could begin simply with a group of slaves sitting in front of their cabins after supper on a summer evening. Someone might start humming an old hymn; the humming would spread from house to house and would be transformed into song. "It wouldn't be long before some of them got happy and started to shouting. Many of them got converted at just such meetings." Wherever the slaves practiced their religion—in formal church settings, in their own praise houses, in camp meetings, in their secret hush-harbors—it was characterized by physical and spiritual enthusiasm and involvement. A white visitor observing a slave religious gathering on a Georgia plantation noted that they sang "with all their souls and with all their bodies in unison; for their bodies rocked, their heads nodded, their feet stamped, their knees shook, their elbows and their hands beat time to the tune and the words which they sang with evident delight. One must see these people singing if one is rightly to understand their life." Attempting to explain why the slaves shouted, an old slave preacher testified, "There is a joy on the inside and it wells up so strong that we can't keep still. It is fire in the bones. Any time that fire touches a man, he will jump."

The slaves were no more passive receptors of sermons than they were of hymns and spirituals; they became participants in both forms of worship. Attending a slave service in New Orleans in the 1850s, Frederick Olmsted carefully recorded a single passage of the black preacher's sermon which was punctuated every few sentences with cries from the parishioners of "yes, glory!" "that's it, hit him again! hit him again! oh, glory! hi! hi! glory!" "glory, glory, glory,!" "Glory!—oh, yes! yes!—sweet Lord! sweet Lord!" "yes, sir! oh, Lord, yes!" "yes! yes!" "oh! Lord! help us!" "Ha! ha! HA!" "Glory to the Lord!" The responses were not confined to ejaculations of this kind, "but shouts, and groans, terrific shrieks, and indescribable expressions of ecstacy—of pleasure or agony—and even stamping, jumping, and clapping of hands, were added. The tumult often resembled that of an excited political meeting." For many slaves shouting was both a compelling personal need and a religious requirement. A well-known joke told of a master who was so embarrassed by the uproar his slave made every Sunday at church that he promised him a new pair of boots if he would stop making so much noise. The slave agreed to try, and at the next meeting he did his best to keep quiet so that he might win his prize, but the "spirit" proved too great a force to contain. "Glory to God!" he finally cried out. "Boots or no boots, glory to God!"

The slaves clearly craved the affirmation and promise of their religion. It would be a mistake, however, to see this urge as exclusively other-worldly. When Thomas Wentworth Higginson observed that the spirituals exhibited "nothing but patience for this life,—nothing but triumph in the next," he, and later observers who elaborated upon this judgment, were indulging in hyperbole. Although Jesus was ubiquitous in the spirituals, it was not invariably the Jesus of the New Testament of whom the slaves sang, but frequently a Jesus transformed into an Old Testament warrior whose victories were temporal as well as spiritual: "Mass Jesus" who engaged in personal combat with the Devil; "King Jesus" seated on a milk-white horse with sword and shield in hand. "Ride on, King

Jesus," "Ride on, conquering King," "The God I serve is a man of war," the slaves sang. This transformation of Jesus is symptomatic of the slaves' selectivity in choosing those parts of the Bible which were to serve as the basis of their religious consciousness. Howard Thurman, a Negro minister who as a boy had the duty of reading the Bible to his grandmother, was perplexed by her refusal to allow him to read from the Epistles of Paul.

> When at length I asked the reason, she told me that during the days of slavery, the minister (white) on the plantation was always preaching from the Pauline letters—"Slaves, be obedient to your masters," etc. "I vowed to myself," she said, "that if freedom ever came and I learned to read, I would never read that part of the Bible!"

This experience and reaction were typical. Slaves simply refused to be uncritical recipients of a religion defined and controlled by white intermediaries and interpreters. No matter how respectfully and attentively they might listen to the white preachers, no matter how well they might sing the traditional hymns, it was their own preachers and their own songs that stirred them the most. Observing his black soldiers at religious services, Colonel Higginson wrote: "they sang reluctantly, even on Sunday, the long and short metres of the hymn-books, always gladly yielding to the more potent excitement of their own 'spirituals.'" In Alabama, Ella Storrs Christian noted in her diary: "When Baptist Negroes attended the church of their masters, or when their mistress sang with them, they used hymn books, but in their own meetings they often made up their own words and tunes. They said their songs had 'more religion than those in the books.'" "Dat ole white preachin' wasn't nothin,'" Nancy Williams observed. "Ole white preachers used to talk wid dey tongues widdout sayin' nothin' but Jesus told us slaves to talk wid our hearts." "White folks can't pray right to de black man's God," Henrietta Perry agreed. "Cain't nobody do it for you. You got to call on God yourself when de spirit tell you." . . .

Slave songs present us with abundant evidence that in the structure of their music and dance, in the uses to which music was put, in the survival of the oral tradition, in the retention of such practices as spirit possession which often accompanied the creation of spirituals, and in the ways in which the slaves expressed their new religion, important elements of their shared African heritage remained alive not just as quaint cultural vestiges but as vitally creative elements of slave culture. This could never have happened if slavery had so completely closed in around the slave, so totally penetrated his personality structure as to reduce him to a kind of *tabula rasa* upon which the white man could write what he chose.

Slave songs provide us with the beginnings of a very different kind of hypothesis: that the preliterate, premodern Africans, with their sacred world view, were so imperfectly acculturated into the secular American society into which they were thrust, were so completely denied access to the ideology and dreams which formed the core of the consciousness of other Americans, that they were forced to fall back upon the only cultural frames of reference that made any sense to them and gave them any feeling of security. I use the word "forced" advisedly. Even if the slaves had had the opportunity to enter fully into the life of the larger society, they might still have chosen to retain and perpetuate certain elements of their African heritage. But the point is that they really had no choice. True acculturation was denied to most slaves. The alternatives were either to remain in a state of cultural limbo, divested of the old cultural patterns but not allowed to adopt those of their new homeland—which in the long run is no alternative at all—or to cling to as many as possible of the old ways of thinking and acting. The slaves' oral tradition, their music, and their religious outlook served this latter function and constituted a cultural refuge at least potentially capable of protecting their personalities from some of the worst ravages of the slave system.

IMAGES OF SLAVERY:
A PHOTOGRAPHIC ESSAY

The United States outlawed the foreign slave trade after 1808, but, as this 1860 depiction shows, the practice continued well into the nineteenth-century. The crowded conditions reflected the captain's desire to maximize profit from the human cargo. (From a daguerreotype published in *Harper's Weekly*, June 2, 1860.)

Defined legally as chattel, an article of movable property, slaves were advertised as commodities, available for purchase in the antebellum South. (Library of Congress)

On the auction block, slaves were displayed, examined, and sold to the highest bidder. The bidders in this illustration are shown as men of high social standing in their formal dress and top hats. (Chicago Historical Society)

Slave owners commonly whipped their slaves. Another form of coercion was the iron collar with attached bells that afflicted pain and restricted movement [top]. The young woman depicted with a similar pronged collar on a nineteenth-century New Orleans street was punished for attempting to run away [bottom]. (Courtesy The Historic New Orleans Collection, Museum/Research Center)

The slave quarters on this Georgia plantation were grouped together, organized around individual family units and set apart from the master's dwelling. These nineteenth-century quarters were more substantial than the crude huts in which most slaves lived. (Historic Mobile Preservation Society Archives, Mobile, Alabama)

This folk painting from the late 1700s shows the distinctive African-American culture that developed in the slave quarters. African traditions are reflected in the headwraps, the dance, and types of musical instruments. Significantly, no whites are present; the master's house is seen in the background. (Abby Aldrich Rockefeller Folk Art Center)

The law did not recognize slave marriages. The slave family was subjected to other flagrant abuses, including having individual members sold apart. Nevertheless slaves highly valued their personal relationships, as this 1862 photograph of several generations of a South Carolina family documents. (Library of Congress)

The cultivation of cotton forced long hours of toil on the slave. Led by a black slave driver, a large work gang, including women, returns from the fields carrying sacks of cotton on their heads, African-style. (New York Historical Society, New York City)

The bill of sale [top] bonds the "Slave Louisa" to the child she attends as well as "his heirs and assigns forever." The intimate relationship between white child and black nurse provided the emotional source of the planter's nostalgia for "dear old mammy," the surrogate slave mother. (Both figures courtesy Missouri Historical Society)

Beginning in 1862, the first African-American regiments were formed during the Civil War, adding nearly 180,000 troops whose courage and commitment significantly enhanced the Union cause. These well-dressed soldiers were typically led by white officers who volunteered for the assignment. (Chicago Historical Society)

Albert J. Raboteau

CONJURE

In addition to the spiritual, conjure—a traditional form of West African magic—was another important component of slave culture. At the center of the supernatural world of the slave was a well-established folk belief in conjure, herbalism, ghost lore, witchcraft, and fortune-telling. In this excerpt Albert J. Raboteau, who teaches in the Department of Religion at Princeton University, discusses the role of conjure. The conjurer, a highly regarded figure in the slave community, provided a means of redress for deeply felt social needs often caused or aggravated by slavery. Raboteau argues that the world of magic complemented African-American Christianity and provided a means of cultural self-definition.

A rich tradition of folk belief and practice, including conjure, herbalism, ghost lore, witchcraft, and fortune-telling, flourished in the slave quarters. The power of the supernatural impinged on the daily lives of slaves and affected their relationships with one another and with the world around them. Like Christianity, conjure was a system of belief, a way of perceiving the world which placed people in the context of another world no less "real" than the ordinary one. Many slaves, and whites as well, knew the world of conjure to be real because they had experienced its power. In part, conjure was a theory which made sense of the mysterious and inexplicable occurrences of life. Duncan Gaines, former Virginia slave, described this explanatory function of conjure when he recalled that during slave times "there was much talk of 'hoodooism' and anyone ill for a long time without getting relief from herb medicine was thought to be 'fixed' or suffering from some sin that his father had committed." The concept of suffering for the guilt of the father is biblical; the concept of being victimized by a "fix" is conjure. Both attempt to locate the cause of irrational suffering. Among Africans and their descendants in America illness which did not respond to natural medicines and the sudden, unpredictable occurrence of misfortune were the result of another's animosity. Slaves believed adversity was due not to blind fate or mere happenstance but to the ill will of someone working through a conjurer.

Not only was conjure a theory for explaining the mystery of evil, but it was also a practice for doing something about it. Because the conjure doctor had the power to "fix" and to remove "fixes," to harm and to cure, it was possible to locate the source of misfortune and control it. Therefore the conjurer, as a man of power—and supernatural power at that—enjoyed a measure of authority in the slave community directly proportional to belief in his power. Variously known as root doctor, hoodoo doctor, two-facer, and wangateur (from *oanga*-charm), he was respected and feared by those blacks and whites who had implicit faith in his power. Conjurers cultivated an aura of mystery which lent credibility to their reputations as men familiar with supernatural lore. Distinctive features, such as "red eyes" and "blue gums," unusual dress, and the accoutrements of his trade—a crooked cane, charms, and conjure bag—all were outward manifestations of the root worker's special expertise. The ultimate source of the conjurer's power was either God or the devil. Being born the seventh son of a seventh son or being born with a caul also were seen as sources of power. In addition, it was believed that the lore of conjure could be passed on from teacher to pupil.

Conjurers were said to be two-faced or two-handed because they could do "left-handed work"—"charm" a person—or "right-handed" work—counteract a charm. Conjurers employed to do left-handed work used both direct and indirect methods. A substance, perhaps a root or a toad's head, could be ground into powder and then mixed or dissolved in the food or drink of the intended victim. The substance used sometimes was poisonous. It would be interesting to know how many cases of slaves' poisoning their masters involved conjure. The indirect approach was to place the charm near the victim where contact or at least proximity would transmit the harm intended. A charm, also known as hand, trick, toby, mojo, and gris-gris, might lurk anywhere—under the doorstep, inside a mattress, out in the yard, or alongside a path the victim was sure to take. Tricks placed by the roadside could even distinguish their targets from other passersby if hair from the victim or dirt from his footprint was wrapped up in the charm.

A virtual job summary of conjure was detailed by Rosanha Frazier, ex-slave born in Mississippi, who blamed her loss of sight upon a "hoodoo-nigger."

Dey powder up de rattle offen de snake and tie it up in de little old rag bag and dey do devilment with it. Dey git old scorpion and make bad medicine. Dey git dirt out de graveyard and dat dirt, after dey speak on it, would make you go crazy.

When dey wants conjure you, dey sneak round and git de hair combin' or de finger or toenail, or anything natural 'bout your body and works de hoodoo on it.

Dey make de straw man or de clay man and dey puts de pin in he leg and you leg gwineter git hurt or sore jus' where dey puts de pin. Iffen dey puts de pin through de heart you gwineter die . . .

Dey make de charm to wear round de neck or de ankle and dey make de love powder too out de love vine, what grow in de wood. Dey bites de leaves and powders 'em. Dey sho' works, I done try 'em.

Among the materials used by the conjure doctor, gopher dust (graveyard dirt) was believed to be particularly potent. Red flannel, useful for wrapping charms, bottles, pins, bones, reptiles, scorpions, horse hair, roots, and herbs of various sorts made up the root doctor's stock-in-trade. However, it was the spell and the ritual invoked by the conjurer which gave the various items power. It was believed that each charm had a spirit. Consequently charms were moistened with liquor to strengthen their power by strengthening their spirits.

Even ordinary possessions—a knife, a hat, a shoe—could be fixed by the conjurer's spell, so that the unsuspecting owner would be conjured upon contact. One had to be extra careful in disposing of worn clothing, nail clippings, cut hair, and washrags lest they fall into the hands of an enemy. Their close contact with the body made them dangerous instruments for conjure, as one old root doctor from Georgia explained: "Duh haiah is one uh duh mos powful tings yuh enemy kin git hold ub cuz it grow neah duh brain an a han made outuh haiah kin sho affec duh brain."

The variety of illnesses, injuries, and misfortunes blamed on conjure was endless. One especially gruesome and frequently mentioned fix reportedly culminated with snakes or spiders roaming up and down inside the victim's body. The conjurer supposedly accomplished this trick by putting the blood of a spider or snake within the person and from this blood the spider or snake would be spawned. Mental as well as physical illness was explained by conjure. "Wennebuh a pusson go crazy, wut is dat but conjuh?" asked Fred Jones, an elderly informant for the Georgia Writers' Project. The point of his rhetorical question was supported by two early analysts of conjure: "insanity on the plantation was often laid to 'conjuration' and consequently took in the patient the form that the belief in conjuration would naturally give it."

A central tenet of conjure was that any spell worked by a conjurer could be removed only by a conjurer; a medical doctor was useless. Even the conjure doctor could be effective only if he was called before the "hand" had done irreversible harm. If called in time, the root doctor took several steps to effect a cure. First he determined whether the illness was due to conjure or not. A small piece of silver was commonly used in diagnosis: if it turned black when placed in the patient's mouth or hand, he had been conjured. Once established that the patient had been conjured, the next step was to discover where the trick had been hidden and to identify the party who had ordered the conjuring done. Then the conjurer cured the patient by destroying or nullifying the power of the charm. Since most conjurers were also herbalists, medicinal potions, salves, and leaf effusions were usually part of the magical ritual. The final step in the cure, if the patient wished it, was to get revenge by turning the charm against the one who sent it. It was said that if you discovered a trick and burned it, the sender would burn, and that if you threw it into water, he would drown. At any rate, the sender could be repaid in kind, and any client of a conjurer had to take that risk into account and live with the fear of retribution.

The reasons for which slaves sought the conjurer's assistance were not all so deadly serious. Affairs of the heart, for example, supplied the conjurer with a great deal of business. Henry Bibb was one of many slaves who turned to conjure to aid romance:

> One of these conjurers, for a small sum agreed to teach me to make any girl love me that I wished. After I had paid him, he told me to get a bull frog, and take a certain bone out of the frog, dry it, and when I got a chance I must step up to any girl whom I wished to

make love me, and scratch her somewhere on her naked skin with this bone, and she would be certain to love me, and would follow me in spite of herself; no matter who she might be engaged to, nor who she might be walking with.

Bibb, not surprisingly, failed in his first attempt but decided to try again. Seeking out another conjurer, he was advised to get a lock of hair from any girl and wear it in his shoes and the girl would then love him above anybody else. Unfortunately, the girl Bibb asked for a lock of hair refused to cooperate. "Believing that my success depended greatly upon this bunch of hair," Bibb explained, "I grasped hold of a lock . . . which caused her to screech, but I never let go until I had pulled it out. This of course made the girl mad with me, and I accomplished nothing but gained her displeasure."

Marital peace was preserved, according to Aunt Irene, a former slave from Alabama, by conjurers who sold "hush water in a jug. Hush water was jes' plain water what dey fixed so if you drink it you would be quiet an' patient. De mens would git it to give to dey wives to make 'em hush up." Conjurers also sold talismans—good-luck charms to ward off sickness, misfortune, or another's animosity.

The ability to tell fortunes was another supernatural skill possessed by some slave conjurers (though not all conjurers were fortune-tellers or vice versa). William Wells Brown, although skeptical (at least in hindsight), went to an old soothsayer in St. Louis named Frank, who predicted the escape from slavery which Brown was contemplating: "Whether the old man was a prophet, or the son of a prophet, I cannot say; but there is one thing certain, many of his predictions were verified. I am no believer in soothsaying; yet I am . . . at a loss to know how Uncle Frank could tell so accurately what would occur in the future. Among the many things he told was one which was enough to pay me for all the trouble of looking him up. It was that I *should be free*! He further said, that in trying to get my liberty I would meet with many severe trials. I thought to myself any fool could tell me that!" One can't help wondering what influence Uncle Frank's prediction had upon Brown's determination to brave those "severe trials" in his eventual escape from slavery.

More than a few slaves were skeptical about the power of conjurers, especially after a charm failed to work. But even then a quick-witted conjurer might save face by blaming the dissatisfied customer for failing to follow instructions. In the story of a trick doctor related by Puckett, a slave received a hand which would enable him to "cuss out" his master without being harmed. The slave tried it and received a terrible beating for his insolence. When he went back to the conjurer to complain, he was informed, "I gi' you a runin' han'! (a charm which would give the possessor swiftness . . .) Why didn't yer run?"

A failed charm might lead a slave to lose faith in that particular charm, or in the conjurer who supplied it, without destroying his belief in conjure as such. Doubts were tempered by the prevalence of belief. Jacob Stroyer, for example, confessed: "I held the idea that there were such things, for I thought the majority of the people believed it, and that they ought to know more than could one man."

Trouble might inspire in an unbeliever a willing suspension of disbelief. This seems to have been the case with Frederick Douglass, who prided himself on being above conjure. "I had a positive aversion to all pretenders to 'divination.' It was beneath one of my intelligence to countenance such dealings with the devil as the power implied." But when Douglass was bedeviled by Covey, the slave breaker, he accepted a root which Sandy the local conjurer told him would prevent Covey or any other white man from whipping him. In some individuals, such as Douglass, conjure stirred ambivalence— what the intellect denied, the emotions and the imagination affirmed, or, as one folklorist astutely observed, "Practices are more enduring than theories."

The simple fact is that slave conjurers kept their credibility and their authority because their power worked. Whatever explanation the modern observer offers—outright poisoning, probable coincidence, psychosomatic suggestion, or psychic phenomenon—some became sick and some were cured by conjure. Undoubtedly the conjurer's knowledge of both medicinal and poisonous herbs, his astuteness in judging human nature, and the sound practical advice he gave accounted for a good deal of his success. Still, the magical words he spoke and the esoteric rites he performed, the imaginative world of power which he represented and the folk traditions he bore, were important to slave culture and should not be lightly dismissed.

Despite skeptics and charlatans, the conjurer's reputation, on some plantations at least, reached legendary proportions. The tale of one remarkable conjurer named Dinkie was told by William Wells

Brown. Dinkie held everyone on the plantation, white or black, in his power. Able to come and go at his pleasure, he never worked. "No one interfered with him . . . Dinkie hunted, slept, was at the table at meal time, roamed through the woods, went to the city, and returned when he pleased. Everybody treated him with respect," even the white ladies who sought him out for love potions and forecasts of romance. When a new overseer, unfamiliar with Dinkie's status, tried to force him to work in the fields, Dinkie, by some secret means, set him straight. His power, it was rumored, came from his being in league with Satan. Whatever the source of his power, it was clear to all that Dinkie was his own master.

The conjurer's exploits, like those ascribed to Dinkie, were discussed with awe and, one suspects, a good deal of embellishment and enjoyment in the quarters. According to one former slave, the children on his plantation liked to play conjure man in a game called hoodoo doctor. A figure to be feared, the conjurer became also a folk character, and stories which told of his resourcefulness, independence, and power were a source of vicarious pleasure to slaves whose own independence and power were so severely restricted.

Nothing challenged the credibility of the conjurer as much as his claim that he could conjure white folks. Whether whites were susceptible to conjure was problematic, as the testimony of ex-slaves reveals. Some ex-slaves argued that only blacks could be conjured. One claimed, for instance: "They had in those days a Hoodoo nigger, who could hoodoo niggers, but couldn't make ole master stop whipping him, with the hoodooism." A clear-cut explanation for the immunity of whites was that whites did not believe in conjure and you had to believe in it for conjure to work. On the other hand, many slaves believed that conjure would work against whites; at least, they tried to prove it. Hoodoo doctors frequently were asked "to save the slave from punishment, to enable him to escape the 'patrolers,' or, in the case of a runaway, to enable him to return home without suffering from his master's anger." In order to "soften the master's heart and sooth his anger," slaves were given roots to chew. Using a jack, fortune-tellers predicted whether a slave would receive a whipping or not. Powders and charms were placed in or near the big house to improve the white folks' disposition. Eugene Genovese has noted several cases of conjured whites in the antebellum South.

That whites did succumb to conjure is not surprising given the similarity of their own folk beliefs and also the probable influence of slave folklore upon white children.

One of the arguments advanced by C. C. Jones for the conversion of the slaves to Christianity was the danger that "superstitions brought from Africa" might be used to turn the slaves dangerously against their masters. "On certain occasions they [slaves] have been made to believe that while they carried about their persons some charm with which they had been furnished, they were *invulnerable*. . . . They have been known to be so perfectly and fearfully under the influence of some leader or conjurer or minister, that they have not dared to disobey him in the least particular; nor to disclose their own intended or perpetrated crimes, in view of inevitable death itself . . ." The historical precedent Jones had in mind was no doubt the Denmark Vesey Conspiracy of 1822, in which the conjurer Gullah (or Cooter) Jack had great influence over the conspirators, who called him the "little man who can't be shot, killed or taken." According to a witness at his trial, Jack gave his recruits "some dry food, consisting of parched corn and ground nuts, and said eat that and nothing else on the morning [the rebellion] breaks out, and when you join us as we pass put into your mouth this crab-claw and you can't then be wounded . . ."

The countercultural nature of conjure was implied by the belief that conjure was African. To be sure, hoodoo combined African and European magical lore. It is significant, however, that both slaves and whites repeatedly connected conjure with Africa. Over and over again hoodoo doctors were described as "African-born" or as "pure Africans." Sandy the conjurer was described by Frederick Douglass as a "genuine African" whose magical powers were inherited from the East. William Wells Brown reported that Dinkie was "a full blooded African and reportedly descended from a king in his native Africa." A former Georgia slave, named Thomas Smith, cited the ability of Aaron to turn his rod into a serpent before Pharaoh as an example of the magical expertise of Africa. "Dat happen in Africa de Bible say. Ain' dat show dat Africa wuz a lan uh magic powah since de begginnin uh history? Well duh descendants ub Africans hab duh same gif tuh do unnatchal ting." Black folk in coastal Georgia and the Sea Islands preserved numerous stories about the miraculous ability of their African-born ancestors to fly back to Africa when they were mistreated on the plantations of America. William Adams, ex-slave from Texas and himself a conjurer, felt that "De old folks in dem days knows more about de signs dat de Lawd uses to reveal His laws dan de folks of today. It am also true of de cullud folks in Africa; dey native land." The prevalence of the idea that conjure was African in origin and that Africans were especially powerful conjurers indicates that slaves thought of hoodoo as their own separate tradition. Whites might be susceptible to conjure, but almost never were they conjurers.

Revenge against overseers and masters was a clear theme in the folktales and ghostlore told by slaves to one another and to their children. In these tales ghosts, witches, and conjurers redressed the wrongs which the slaves could not. The following stories from Edisto Island, South Carolina, surely must have appealed to the slaves' frustrated sense of justice:

> [A slave] wen' to a witch man. When his master 'mence to whip him, eve'y cut he give de man, his [master's] wife way off at home feel de cut. Sen' wor' please stop cut lick de man. When he [master] got home, his wife was wash down wid blood.

> His master beat him so sevare, so de man went to a witch. De witch said, "Never min'! you go home. Tomorrow you will see me." When de man got up in de mornin', de white man was jus' as happy as happy can be; but de more de sun goes down, he commence ter sleep. At de same time he call to his Negro, "Tomorrow you go an' do such an' such a tas'." Given' out his orders kyan hardly hol' up his head. As soon as de sun was down, he down too, he down yet. De witch done dat. He [witch] come but he stay in his home an' done dat.

In yet another example, recorded shortly after the Civil War, a conjurer and his son take revenge upon an overseer:

> Dey goes to de overseer's house, an' give de sign an' slip t'rough de keyhole. Den dey unbar de door on de inside an' take out de overseer an' his son, widout deir knowin' it; an de conjeror tetch de overseer wid his switch an' he turns to a bull, an' tetch de overseer's son an' he turns to a bull-yerlin.' Den de conjeror mounts de bull an' de boy he mounts de bull-yerlin, an' sets off a long way over de creek to blight a man's wheat what de conjeror had a spite agin.

In these stories—as in the tales of Jack, Brer Rabbit, or High John—the slaves could identify with the protagonist and vicariously enjoy their exercise of power over whites. With their emphasis on revenge, the stories also served as muted protests for the slaves who did not dare to complain overtly about the injustice of their situation.

Then, too, the world of conjure answered deeply felt needs within the slaves' own community, where white control inhibited the free outward expression of social conflict. For example, masters limited fighting among slaves in order to protect their human property from serious damage and to preserve order on the plantation. In addition, the common burden of slavery itself tended to create group solidarity, as did Christian fellowship, which prohibited fighting, backbiting, and animosity between "brothers and sisters in Christ." The very closeness of the quarters necessitated a degree of tolerance while at the same time exacerbating personal tensions. Given these constrictions, conjure served as a perfect vehicle for expressing and alleviating anger, jealousy, and sheer ill will among slaves. When unable to settle disputes openly, the slaves turned to the secret system of conjure. Primarily, conjure was a method of control: first, the control which comes from knowledge—being able to explain crucial phenomena, such as illness, misfortune and evil; second, the control which comes from the capacity to act effectively—it was "a force . . . by which mankind can (or thinks he can) achieve almost every desired end . . ."; third, a means of control over the future through reading the "signs"; fourth, an aid to social control because it supplied a system whereby conflict, otherwise stifled, could be aired.

The pervasiveness of conjure in the quarters suggests a problem: What was the relationship of conjure to Christianity, of the conjurer to the slave preacher? The practice of conjure was, at least in theory, in conflict with Christian beliefs about the providence of God, and indeed one way of relating conjure to Christianity was to make the former the realm of the devil, in effect creating a balance of good and evil. Willis Easter recited a song his mother had taught him "to keep from bein' conjure" which illustrates this point:

> Keep 'way from me, hoodoo and witch, Lead my path from de porehouse gate; I pines for golden harps and sich, Lawd, I'll jes' set down

and wait. Old Satan am a liar and conjurer, too—If you don't watch out, he'll conjure you.

Another former slave put it this way: "I'm a believer, an' dis here voodoo an' hoodoo an' sper'ts ain't nothin' but a lot of folks outten Christ."

And yet conjure was not always employed for evil. Puckett noted that conjurers in the twentieth century were all very religious. Closer to the slavery period, Herron and Bacon observed that the source of the conjurers' power was not well defined. One informant stated, "I have always heard that those doctors sold themselves to the Devil before they were given the power." Another reported that all the conjure doctors she had heard of claimed "a special revelation from God." Some conjurers saw nothing strange in calling upon God to assist their cures. (While it is an intriguing possibility, I have found no evidence of conjurers who were also ministers.) The conflict between Christianity and conjure was more theoretical than actual. Even those slaves who condemned conjure as evil did not deny its reality. Moreover, among black folk there was a refusal to dichotomize power into good and evil—a refusal which Herskovits and others see as African. In the slave community the power to heal and the power to harm resided in one person, the conjurer; in Africa these powers resided in any one of the gods who had to be propitiated in order to avoid misfortune and illness. There is an amoral quality to conjure which makes it stray outside norms of good and evil. Whether it was good or bad, one had to respect power that worked. In a world of practical power, good was power which worked *for* you, bad was power which turned *against* you. The primary categories were not good and evil but security and danger. Therefore an unequivocal rejection of conjure was not only unnecessary but foolhardy. To be safe, one kept on the right side of all spiritual power.

Moreover, Christian tradition itself has always been attuned to special gifts (charisms) of the Spirit as they are manifested in prophecy, healing, and miracles. As a result, Christianity, especially on the popular level, has a certain tendency to appropriate and baptize magical lore from other traditions. In an important sense, conjure and Christianity were not so much antithetical as complementary. Discussing the differences between magic and religion, M. J. Field gives a succinct statement of this complementary relationship in her book on witchcraft in West Africa, *Search for Security*:

> Classical anthropology distinguishes between religion and magic by saying that religion involves a deity whom man implores, magic involves forces which man commands. . . . It may be added, first that religion usually postulates a deity who is good and who demands goodness, whereas magic is of two kinds, good and bad. Furthermore, a deity generally has at his disposal a diversity of blessings and punishments, whereas each special magic is directed to one narrowly circumscribed end [;] . . . magics, unlike deities, make no moral demands and, above all, will operate automatically and inexorably. . . . Magic, or, as it is more often called in West Africa, "medicine," always involves concrete apparatus . . . and a ritual in which the apparatus is handled. There is no activity in life which cannot be assisted by medicine.

Conjure could, without contradiction, exist side by side with Christianity in the same individual and in the same community because, for the slaves, conjure answered purposes which Christianity did not and Christianity answered purposes which conjure did not.

Kenneth F. Kiple and Virginia H. King

NUTRITION AND NUTRIMENTS

West Africans, like all other indigenous peoples, were well adapted to their homeland. They had, for example, developed a greater resistance to malaria and yellow fever than had Europeans, who were seldom exposed to tropical diseases prior to the African slave trade and the colonization of the New World. The disease differential between Africans and Europeans reinforced the white belief that slavery racially suited blacks because disproportionately fewer slaves than masters died of ma-

From *Another Dimension to the Black Diaspora: Diet, Disease, and Racism*, by Kenneth F. Kiple and Virginia H. King, 1981, pp. 79–94. Reprinted with the permission of Cambridge University Press.

laria and yellow fever. The forced migration of West Africans to North America placed them at risk for new diseases and dietary deficiencies. In this selection Kenneth F. Kiple and Virginia H. King, historians at Bowling Green State University, Ohio, pose the question not only of "whether the slave diet was adequate, but rather, was it adequate for persons of West African descent?" They are concerned with the complex relationship of nutrition, genetics, and physical environment, subjects of recent investigation by historians.

One of the many controversies touched off by Robert Fogel and Stanley Engerman's "cliometric" examination of the peculiar institution concerns slave nutrition. [In 1974, these two economic historians published *Time on the Cross,* a quantitative or "cliometric" study of slavery. Although indicting slavery as evil, they ignited a major controversy by arguing that the objective conditions—including diet—under which slaves lived were better than those of northern white laborers.] The cliometricians portrayed the slave diet as not only substantial calorically but as actually exceeding "modern (1964) recommended daily levels of the chief nutrients." . . .

We have accepted these findings, modified them with assumptions suggested by antebellum literature and black genetic circumstances and then used the amounts of foods in question as the basis for a chemical analysis of the slave diet with an eye to ascertaining its quality. It is only here with the matter of quality that we find ourselves most sharply in disagreement with the cliometricians; not because of any specific errors they have made, but rather because the question we pose is not whether the slave diet was qualitatively adequate, but whether it was qualitatively adequate for persons of West African descent.

The question, of course, is novel, while the relationships between nutrition, genetics, and physical environment are complex. Moreover, the medical and nutritional literature upon which our analysis rests is in itself occasionally novel, complex and (in some cases) controversial. With this word of caution, let us begin with the quantitative aspects of slave comestibles. . . .

Planters, large and small, across much of the South and particularly in the cotton belt consistently claimed that they issued an average of about three pounds of pork "clear of bone" per week per working slave. In fact, this allotment has been confirmed by students of slavery so often as to become a truism. Fogel and Engerman, on the other hand, could only feed a slave 88 pounds of pork annually on the basis of their "systematic data" drawn from the 1860 manuscript censuses. There are problems with these "systematic" data where pork is concerned, however, that suggest that their estimations may considerably understate slave pork consumption. First, the manuscript census schedules Fogel and Engerman consulted for the number of hogs per plantation do not reveal that swine were permitted to run "wild" on most cotton belt plantations.

Thus owners had only a vague notion of how many they "owned." Although plantation records of the region usually distinguish between "tame" and "wild" pork in the storehouse awaiting consumption, it seems highly probable that many planters when counting live swine for census purposes thought only of those which were penned up for fattening. Second, slaves themselves were often permitted to raise hogs, which they frequently sold to their masters, and it is doubtful that the number of slave-owned swine on a plantation are reflected in the manuscript census. Third, and most important, cotton belt plantations were scarcely self-sufficient manors, and outside purchases of pork were considerable for many, if not most, planters. For these reasons, there seems little cause to doubt planter claims that working slaves received on the average the 3 pounds of pork weekly.

By contrast, there were sufficient cattle on the plantations of the South to permit the Fogel and Engerman assumption that slaves enjoyed a fairly high level of beef consumption. Yet much literary evidence contradicts this assumption. A Yankee agronomist, Solon Robinson, put it clearly enough while visiting cotton belt plantations. He discovered that on many of them pork production was insufficient to feed the slaves without outside purchasing yet observed that the plantations also possessed many cattle. "Well, if you can't raise pork, why not feed your negroes on beef?" was the query, and the reply: "Simply because it would raise a revolt, sooner than all the whiplashes ever braided in Massachusetts. Fat pork and corn bread is the natural aliment of a negro. Deprive him of these and he is miserable. Give him his regular allowance and the negro enjoys . . . 'heaven on earth.'"

Perhaps slave preference for pork might have been overcome were it not for the inferior preserving qualities of beef. Unlike pork, it neither pickled nor smoked well; dried it was extremely unpalatable. Therefore, when beef was served on the plantation it was served fresh. This occurred, however, on special occasions only and usually in the winter months, because the cold retarded spoilage. Thus, for some slaves, at least, beef consumption was limited to the holiday season around Christmas time.

Another problem with beef was that planters on the whole were very skeptical of fresh meat, believing that it caused sickness among the blacks (which it undoubtedly did when it was not all that fresh). In fact, in much of the South, whites also feared fresh meat and continued to do so even after it was readily available, and they had facilities for refrigeration.

But in addition to slave preference for pork, there was also the planters' conviction that hog was the only proper meat for laborers. A physician, writing in 1859, clearly articulated the planters' belief that "fatty articles of diet are peculiarly appropriate on account of their heat producing properties" and "fat bacon and pork are the most nourishing of all foods for the Negro."

Earlier in the century, the conviction had been the same. Bacon was the proper "nourishment" for slaves, and "a pound goes as far as three pounds of beefsteak." During the intervening decades, planters and physicians lost few opportunities to remind one another in agricultural and medical journals of the efficacy of pork. Fresh beef might be served on occasion, but pork was the fuel upon which the efficiency of labor depended.

So why all the plantation cattle? The answer, it seems, is that cattle (as opposed to hogs) "were maintained primarily for manure and only incidently for meat and milk." The notion of cattle raising as a profitable enterprise *per se* was dismissed by planters, who made little effort to improve their breeds and permitted cattle, like hogs, a semiwild existence foraging in fallow fields for themselves. When the cattle became too numerous, their superior traveling powers (over swine) made it relatively easy for them to be driven to towns and cities. There fresh beef could be marketed quickly thus avoiding the problems of beef's inferior preserving qualities and the absence of a packing industry in the South.

To summarize then, slave meat preferences and planters' notions regarding black health combined to suggest strongly that cattle were employed mostly as fertilizer producers. They may eventually have wound up in the market place but, except for the occasional barbecue or holiday feast, not in slave stomachs.

A shift from one product of cattle to another brings up the problem of plantation milk consumption. As with beef consumption, one might conclude on a priori grounds that the presence of many cattle on the plantation meant an abundance of milk for the slaves. This is incorrect, however, for reasons that fall alternately under the headings of milk production and black biology.

To begin with, the antebellum South was notorious for low milk production. Travelers crossing the Mason-Dixon line on a southward trek reported that milk was fairly plentiful in border states such as Kentucky yet "a great rarity" in the Deep South. Part of the reason was that cattle, like hogs, were not usually penned up but rather permitted to run wild and forage for themselves. The result was that they were frequently too wild to be milked.

Another reason was the poor quality of the animals themselves. For example, a traveler reported that southern cows did not calve more than once in two years and that even when they did give milk, the yield was "far less in quantity" than that produced by northern cows. Hence the classic plight of the South Carolina planter whose cattle were such bad "milkers" that he and his family were forced to rely on goat milk for coffee. Still one more difficulty was the poor quality of southern milk described by one unenthusiastic visitor as "blue and watery." The butter churned from it was routinely denounced as "sickly looking," while that inveterate observer of things southern, Frederick Law Olmsted, complained more than once of "what to both eye and tongue seemed lard," but what was termed butter. Apparently then only the more progressive plantations saw much in the way of milk, and this usually was of poor quality. Still, even on these units it was only available on a seasonal basis, limited to the warmest months of spring and summer which of course presented many spoilage problems. In part then, because of scarcity, milk, when produced, went mostly to the white population and it became "customary" to not "feed dairy products to slaves." Where a small milk surplus was produced, it usually went to the slave children.

Yet what appears to have been a slovenly southern attitude toward milk production may well have had an important rationale behind it, for a good portion of the South's population—the blacks—

could not drink much of it in the first place and planters knew it. Today it is estimated that somewhere between 70 and 80 percent of the adult Afro-American population is lactose intolerant as opposed to 5 to 19 percent of their white counterparts.

This phenomenon of lactose intolerance is not fully understood. All infants are obviously lactose tolerant, else they could not live. But sometime after weaning, a majority of the world's population loses the ability to digest milk, meaning the level of the lactase enzyme that metabolizes milk's lactose into absorbable sugars decreases. When this occurs and the individual persists in drinking milk he is rudely rewarded with abdominal cramps, bloating, and diarrhea. Sooner or later he connects milk with the problem and eliminates it from his diet. A study has found that 72 percent of lactose intolerant Americans stop drinking milk completely because of the complications that result.

Most persons of northern European descent as well as some other peoples scattered around the world, however, do not lose the lactase enzyme. This means that milk remains a regular part of their dietary regimen throughout a lifetime. A sensible hypothesis advanced to account for the development of lactose tolerance, at least its development among northern Europeans, is that the lactase enzyme was genetically encouraged among ancient residents because of the prevalence of rickets and osteomalacia caused by a lack of sunshine. The result would have been many pelvic deformities among females and consequently a reduction in their reproductivity. The lactase enzyme was therefore encouraged because milk provides its consumer with both a rickets preventative (calcium) and a substitute for vitamin D (lactose) to facilitate the absorption of that calcium.

By contrast in West Africa there was no lack of abundant sunshine. Moreover, the presence of the tsetse fly made the raising of cattle virtually impossible, effectively discouraging the development of a milk-drinking culture. These twin factors were instrumental in creating a historical situation of low milk consumption with no need for humans to develop high levels of the lactase enzyme.

Yesterday on the plantation the rate of lactose intolerance was probably even higher than that of today, perhaps even approaching 100 percent by the time adulthood was reached. With blacks, the problem begins soon after infancy, and the level of intolerance increases with age, whereas with whites the difficulty remains constant with age. Thus, studies have revealed that by age eleven at least 40 to 45 percent of black youngsters exhibit symptoms of lactose intolerance, about 60 percent of black teenagers manifest symptoms, with the rate reaching the 70 to 80 percent range for adults.

No wonder that when milk consumption is mentioned in connection with the plantations it is invariably the children who are doing the consuming. Yet it seems that even many children were noticeably lactose intolerant, for planters warned one another that they "should have no sweet milk"; "none but sour, or buttermilk," advised one perceptive master. Planters could not know that the souring process converted the lactose to lactic acid, which made the milk more digestible. But in a very real way they may have pioneered in the treatment of lactose intolerance.

In summary then, slaves consumed very little milk, first because the South produced little of it, and second because they could not drink it. Ingestion of as little as one eight-ounce glass of milk will trigger symptoms in the lactose intolerant. So even where milk was available consumption was probably limited to a daily dollop in their coffee. For children, milk was sometimes available, but on a seasonal basis only. Thus, in the words of one student of southern foods, "although the food habits of whites and slaves were similar in many respects, one of the greatest differences was in the relative amount of dairy products consumed."

Cowpeas and sweet potatoes are considered together because questions of the quantities consumed hinge on amounts fed to livestock and problems of storage. Unquestionably both were grown in large quantities on southern plantations, and superficially a glance at the manuscript census schedules would convince one that at least these two items appeared on slave tables in profusion.

Yet in the case of the cowpea (the black-eyed pea, field pea, crowder pea, etc.), one should not make the assumption that slaves desired or even ate them if offered. Today cowpeas are viewed as the quintessence of southern dining (particularly by Yankees) and the "soul" of soul food. As late as the eve of the War Between the States, however, most Southerners, black and white, regarded these legumes as "fodder" which was by far their major use. The herbage was used as forage, while the seed of the plant was a "major source of food for cattle, horses, mules, and hogs in all cotton and corn growing areas." It is true that some planters who found blacks to be "fond" of the "common field pea," delightedly advised one another of this cheap source of slave food and even suggested drying them and putting some aside for later consumption. Still, the very fact that a few planters were exhorting others to dry and store cowpeas suggests that the vast majority of the slaves did not enjoy them on a year-round basis. Rather most of the slaves who were fond of cowpeas and whose masters made them available consumed them for a few weeks only while they were in season.

A similar problem exists in the case of sweet potatoes, which manuscript census data on southern production indicate were piled on slave tables to the extent of 318 pounds annually per male aged 18 to 35. But to have apportioned sweet potatoes in this manner meant that livestock went hungry. For sweet potatoes were "frequently employed to supplement corn in the fattening of stock" and often left right in the fields for the animals. In fact, sweet potatoes were regarded as the best and quickest means (when boiled) of fattening hogs for the winter killing season and were often employed lavishly for this purpose. This does not mean of course that slaves did not eat sweet potatoes. Indeed some planters stored them for year-round consumption; however others, perhaps most, regarded them as a seasonal food and encouraged the slaves to feast on them while they lasted.

Moreover, those planters who did store sweet potatoes expected some loss from rot no matter how well the pile was ventilated. And the standard method of cooking sweet potatoes—tossing them into a fire or popping them into the coals of a cookstove—meant a good deal of waste. When done, the sweet meat of the center was extracted and the charred husk thrown aside. Thus, after the sweet potatoes were shared with livestock and storage and cooking losses are subtracted, it would seem likely that only a portion of the sweet potatoes produced on the plantation actually found their way into slave stomachs.

Planters claimed, and their records bear them out, that it was practically a tradition to allot one peck of cornmeal weekly per slave which translates into something over one pound daily. Yet, probably most did not consume all of this large ration. On plantations that permitted slave enterprise, bondsmen frequently fed a portion of their rations to the family hogs and chickens, which were raised to procure tobacco, liquor, and Sunday clothes. On other plantations, it was customary that slaves exchange surplus cornmeal for these luxury items. Cornmeal also served as food for the family dog(s) that few slave cabins were without.

Finally, as was the case with sweet potatoes, often a great deal of cornmeal was lost in cooking methods. So long as cornbread was prepared in the plantation kitchen in pans, no particular loss occurred. A favorite method of preparing "pone" or hoecakes or cornash cakes, however, was "to mix the meal with a little water, then lay the mixture in the fire to bake," perhaps on a hoe. "When it is 'done brown,' the ashes are scraped off," and a good deal less meal was consumed than went into the fire.

Undoubtedly because of biscuits, another perennial frontrunner in southern cuisine, the assumption is sometimes made that wheat flour was plentiful in the South. Most of the South, however, lies outside of the wheat region. Thus, in the Deep South states of Georgia, Alabama, Mississippi, and Louisiana the 1860 wheat production would have yielded only 57 pounds of wheat flour per man, woman, and child—slave and white combined—so of course whites, not blacks, were the big consumers of wheat bread.

Actually, even in a state such as Arkansas where the yield of wheat per person was twice that of the Deep South, it is still "unlikely that slaves ate wheat bread to any great extent. The high prices of wheat flour as compared to corn meal prevented the widespread use of wheat bread for slaves, as well as for many of the white people of the period." Rather, the only way that wheat flour found its way into the slave diet on most cotton belt plantations was in the form of those cherished biscuits served occasionally on Sundays and/or holidays. As with cattle, the bulk of the little wheat raised on plantations seems to have been intended for the market and not for local consumption.

There remains the question of the extent to which the basic hog-and-hominy core of the slave diet was "commuted and/or supplemented" with comestibles other than those already mentioned, a question that defies any ready answer. The evidence suggests that a majority of slaves was permitted to raise produce, poultry, and pigs, but a sizable minority was not.

Moreover, many ex-slaves testified that they did not care for green vegetables of any kind. Rather they only became a standard part of black fare following the Civil War. Thus, pin money, rather than a variety in viands, was frequently the chief motive in slave enterprises such as gardening as well as hog and chicken raising. Fish and game, including the oft-mentioned possum, undoubtedly graced some slave tables. But on how many tables, and how frequently did these supplements appear?

A few planters seem to have made heroic efforts to grow and stockpile sufficient vegetables for year-round slave consumption, but others apparently begrudged their slaves even basic meat and meal provisions and attempted to stint on them. There were those who believed (correctly) that molasses was healthy for slaves and issued it liberally, yet there were others who feared that molasses, at least in the diet of children, would lead to dirt-eating. Still others issued molasses in lieu of meat, and there were those who presumably found molasses too expensive to serve or too bothersome or both. Many planters appointed individuals to cook for the slaves in an attempt to ensure that they received variety in their victuals. Many more, however, expected the slaves to cook for themselves, and all too frequently after the blacks had spent a long and wearisome day in the fields that cooking was badly done.

Although evidence was presented to suggest that in many cases slaves did not consume foods in the quantities the Fogel and Engerman estimates might indicate, we certainly do not mean to imply that slaves in the American South were on the verge of starvation. Rather, it seems a safe assumption that some slaves enjoyed a wide variety of foods; others suffered from a seldom if ever supplemented hog-and-corn routine, while most existed on a basic meat-and-meal core with some supplementation, including the fish and game they provided for themselves. Unquestionably, the core itself supplied enough in the way of calories. Calculations by the United Nations Food and Agriculture Organization suggest that the caloric requirement for a medium-sized male in his mid-twenties performing moderately heavy agricultural labor for ten hours is between 3,200 and 4,000 calories daily. If something approaching a pound of the cornmeal ration were converted into cornpone and consumed along with the half pound or so of pork allotted daily and a sweet potato or two, this caloric requirement would have been met. Whether the diet was nutritionally adequate for the slaves, however, is another question entirely. . . .

A high quality protein is one that contains all eight essential amino acids in sufficient amounts to support and sustain life. Thus, the value of any protein depends on the various amino acids it contains. Methods have been devised to give protein a chemical score ranging from high (animal protein) to low (vegetable protein), although two foods of relatively poor values when combined may constitute—depending on their amino acid pattern—a good protein. For example, cowpeas do not offer a complete protein. On the other hand, they are high in tryptophan and lysine, precisely those amino acids in which corn is deficient. Thus, those slaves whose masters did dry and store this legume for serving on a year-round basis would (if they consumed them with corn) have received a good amount of fairly complete protein. Yet earlier we asserted that this was hardly common practice, and therefore corn alone, the slaves' biggest source of protein, would have left them with an apparent protein deficiency.

Now had the slaves eaten a half pound of pork daily consisting of a composite of trimmed, lean cuts (ham, loin, shoulder) which averaged 78 percent lean and 22 percent fat they would have derived much of what today would be their recommended daily allowance (RDA) of protein (36 of a RDA of 56 grams).

Slaveholders, antebellum physicians, ex-slaves, visitors to the South, and students of slavery alike, however, made no mention of slaves' dining on hams or loins, except, of course, those stolen on occasion from the master's storehouse. Rather, they unanimously set slave tables with fat pork and fat bacon, in part because it was inexpensive, and in part because of a planter conviction that "fatty articles of diet are peculiarly appropriate on account of their heat-producing properties," and for hard-working slaves "fat bacon and pork are the most nourishing of all foods." Therefore, a medium-fat class of pork, with cuts consisting of bacon or belly and backfat, probably more closely approximated the quality of pork consumed by the slaves, and this would have yielded about a third (18 grams) of their daily protein requirements.

A pound of cornmeal contains about 41 grams of protein, the meat ration about 18 and a couple of good-sized sweet potatoes another half dozen or so which put the slave close to his RDA for protein (and doubtless other comestibles consumed actually put him over). Nonetheless about three-quarters of the protein (sweet potatoes also yield an incomplete protein) was of low quality.

Superficially it would seem that slaves derived a fair amount of vitamin A from corn. This is not true, however, for it was white corn, not yellow, that was normally raised for human consumption in the South, and white corn contains absolutely no vitamin A.

Some sweet potatoes, on the other hand, yield a great deal of this vitamin, as evidenced by the orange hue of the flesh. Yet there are sweet potatoes, and then there are sweet potatoes, with the nutritive values of vitamin A varying depending on the kind from less than 0.1 per 100 grams to 4.1. Put another way some kinds of sweet potatoes contain forty times more vitamin A than others. Of the varieties grown in the antebellum South, Richard Sutch has unearthed evidence to indicate that the colors of their flesh ranged from a "yellowish tint" to "very white," the light colors suggesting that the varieties of antebellum sweet potatoes to which slaves had access were not high in vitamin A.

Fresh cowpeas contained some vitamin A (a cup would have provided about one-tenth of the daily RDA), and because the vitamin can be stored by the body (even though fresh peas were only consumed seasonally) they would also have made a contribution toward an adequate year-round supply.

Vitamin C cannot be stored; therefore, the ascorbic acid yielded by fresh cowpeas and sweet potatoes, constituting the only vitamin C in the core diet, would have been of temporary benefit only. Those who ate garden greens or fruit also would have benefited from a seasonal dose of this vitamin. Yet the testimony of ex-slaves indicates that many did not care for vegetables or fruit; planters frequently considered fruit a source of slave disease, and one visitor to the South summed up the general attitude toward vegetables in Mississippi by suggesting tongue-in-cheek that they were "forbidden by law."

Thus, for many slaves their vitamin C intake seems to have been a matter of a haphazard seasonal injection only, and many were without the vitamin for a good portion of the year. Moreover, greens and fresh cowpeas were normally subjected to thorough cooking (a lamentable southern practice that persists today), and as is well known heat destroys ascorbic acid; consequently something between 15 and 40 percent of the potential seasonal offering of vitamin C was probably lost.

Much vitamin C as well is lost in sweet potatoes when stored;

conversely the vitamin A content increases slightly during storage but not enough to have made any appreciable difference. There is, however, a good reason for suspecting a substantial loss of vitamin A. Much mention is made of rancid fat pork and cooking fat on the plantation. Vitamin A is a fat-soluble vitamin, meaning that it is rendered usable by fatty acids. But if that fat is rancid, the solvents it contains destroy, rather than dissolve, the vitamin. Additionally, research suggests that the body must have sunlight to release the bulk of its vitamin A that is stored in the liver. Hence those slaves whose masters either did not keep sweet potatoes for the winter months, or ran out early in the winter, would not have enjoyed the full benefits of the vitamin A their body had stored. Finally, the low serum level of vitamin A (despite a normal level in the liver) in black subjects has led at least one group of researchers to hypothesize that their ability to mobilize this vitamin may be impaired.

Given all of these factors, then, it would seem that most slaves were somewhat vitamin C deficient for much of the year. By contrast vitamin A may have been sufficiently supplied to the majority of the slaves. Yet variables such as the kinds of potatoes consumed and the complexity of vitamin A's utilization caution that others may have actually been vitamin A deficient as well.

Raw dried peas furnish almost twice as much thiamine (B_1), riboflavin (B_2) and niacin (B_3) as fresh cowpeas, so once more those slaves with progressive masters would have fared far better nutritionally than those forced to consume only what the season had to offer. But even for these individuals the remainder of their core diet was dismally deficient in the B complex, save thiamine. Corn is notoriously lacking in B_2 and B_3, and with even a full pound of cornmeal supplying only one-quarter to one-half of the daily RDA, slaves would have been hard pressed to make up the remainder. Consuming between ten and twelve good-sized sweet potatoes, for example, would have done it, but in this case plantations would have produced more pudgy thralls than cotton.

The ration of fat pork would have been little help because it was largely fat, producing only 16 percent of the niacin and 15 percent of the riboflavin requirements. Thus, slaves were receiving little of vitamins B_2 and B_3. Moreover, the apparent satisfaction of the B_1 requirement is deceptive because the more carbohydrates in the diet, the higher the requirement of thiamine. Similarly, the deficiency of vitamin B_2 is more serious than one might suppose because its requirement is linked to the fat content of the diet: the more fats, the more riboflavin required. Again the requirement for niacin is based on calories (with which the slave diet abounded): the more calories, the greater the demand for niacin.

Additionally, cooking losses must be considered in the original supply of the B complex, particularly given the great amount of boiling and frying that took place in the slave quarters. Fully 25 to 50 percent of vitamin B_1 in pork is lost in cooking along with significant amounts of vitamins B_2 and B_3. Finally, in the case of niacin, the whole of the slave diet concealed another adverse effect. For although the amount of niacin in the slave diet was very low, the body might have produced niacin by converting what little tryptophan the diet did yield. Yet because that diet (because of cornmeal in particular) also contained an excess of leucine, the body's niacin production was inhibited. Similarly, vitamin B_2 is crucial in the conversion of tryptophan to niacin, but the slave comestibles were deficient in riboflavin. The absence of sufficient niacin in turn suggests that the slaves were unable to properly metabolize the carbohydrates, fats, and proteins in the diet, which means they could not possibly have received the full benefit of those nutrients.

Vitamin D exists in several forms, but, because it is naturally present in few foods, most of it comes from cholecalciferol (D_3) which is obtained by irradiation on the skin from a chemical precursor present in living skin cells called 7-dehydrocholesterol. Season changes and different geographical regions affect vitamin D levels in individuals. The darker pigmentation of the black protected against sun damage in Africa. His black skin, however, transmits ultraviolet radiation only one-third as well as white skin. Thus, it is believed that pigment reduces the synthesis of vitamin D by the skin. And therefore the black transplanted to more northerly latitudes found himself low in vitamin D, especially during the winter and spring months of pale sunlight, shorter days, and overcast skies. Whites, in other words, because of a lack of pigment, have access to sufficient vitamin D in North America; blacks frequently do not.

Vitamin D is crucial in the intestinal absorption of calcium, but it is also important for normal growth and skeletal development and the bone mineral mobilization process, a process that could have replenished the dangerously low serum calcium levels, which for the following reasons were undoubtedly characteristic of the slaves.

First, the core of the slave diet was composed of fat pork and cornmeal. The yield of phosphorus from this core, while not extraordinarily high by itself, is overwhelmingly high in relation to the low calcium offering of the diet. Lactose-intolerant slaves would have derived little calcium from milk, while the greens, sweet potatoes, etc., which supplemented the core, although a source of some calcium, could not have provided enough to overcome a year-round imbalance because of their seasonal appearance on tables. This excessive amount of phosphorous in relation to calcium in turn would have hindered the absorption of the little calcium the slaves did receive, and therefore increased their requirements. Similarly, the fatty acids flowing from fat pork also interfered with the bodily absorption of calcium, as do the oxalic acids contained in greens that form insoluble salts to impair absorption of the pair of minerals in question.

Second, if calcium did not already have a difficult time playing a proper nutritional role in the slave regimen, it was further frustrated by the peculiar nature of the proteins inherent in that regimen. High-quality protein promotes efficient absorption of calcium. Yet high-quality protein content was not an outstanding feature of the slave regimen. Clearly, then, many circumstances combined to deny calcium a full nutritional participation in the slave diet, yet even at this point these circumstances might have been at least partially overcome had it not been for two more factors that were also hostile to calcium absorption.

An adequate source of vitamin C also would have increased the absorption of what calcium was available; conversely, vitamin C is so crucial to calcium accumulation that its deficiency can cause calcium deficiency. Yet ascorbic acid cannot be stored by the body, and no one seriously argues that slaves received a year-round supply of this vitamin. Finally, the two remaining factors that could have enhanced the absorption of calcium are lactose and vitamin D (the reason milk is fortified with this vitamin today), but as already noted pigment that was kindly to blacks in their West African homeland militated against an adequate year-round supply of this vitamin in temperate North America. Thus, even if one's calcium intake is adequate (the slaves' clearly was not), it will be very poorly absorbed if one's vitamin D levels are inadequate (which the slaves' doubtless were for at least a portion of the year). . . .

To summarize then, West Africans were marvelously adapted for survival in their homeland. These mechanisms contained the potential for provoking severe nutritional difficulties, however, once their possessor was removed from West Africa's specialized environment. This potential should have been realized after the blacks' forced migration to North America. To repeat ourselves, therefore, the important question concerning slave nutrition that we are posing is not whether the slave diet was adequate, but rather, was it adequate for persons of West African descent? Nutritional analysis thus far suggests not.

IV

Family and Gender

Allan Kulikoff

THE LIFE CYCLE OF SLAVES

Allan Kulikoff, professor of history at Northern Illinois University, spe-
cializes in the history of the development of Chesapeake slavery. In the
essay reprinted here, he concludes that slave families in the mid-eighteenth century were often unstable, a revision of Herbert G. Gutman's
thesis in the selection that follows. Nevertheless, Kulikoff argues that a
flexible kinship network helped slaves adjust to the disruption of forced
separation and provided them with an alternative cultural system to the
authority of the master. At the same time, critical stages in the life of the
slave—infancy, work in the tobacco fields, leaving home, courtship and
marriage, child rearing, and old age—shaped their individual and collective existence. Professor Kulikoff's study is marked by the extensive use
of local records.

By the 1750s, a peculiarly Afro-American life cycle had developed.
Afro-Americans lived in a succession of different kinds of households. Children under ten years almost always lived with their mothers, and more than half on large plantations lived with both parents.
Between ten and fourteen years of age, large numbers of children left
their parents' homes. Some stayed with siblings and their families,
others were sold, and the rest lived with other kin or unrelated people. Women married in their late teens, had children, and established
households with their own children. More than two-fifths of the
women on large plantations and a fifth on small farms lived with
husbands as well as children. The same proportion of men as women
lived in nuclear households, but because children of separated
spouses usually lived with their mothers, large numbers of men, even
on big plantations, lived only with other men.

These life-cycle changes can perhaps best be approached
through a study of the critical events in the lives of Afro-Americans.
Those events probably included the following: infancy, leaving the

From *Tobacco and Slaves: The Development of Southern Cultures in the Chesapeake,
1680–1800,* by Allan Kulikoff, pp. 371–375, 377–380. Published for the Institute
of Early American History and Culture, Williamsburg, Virginia. © 1986 The University of North Carolina Press. Reprinted by permission of the author and publisher.

matricentral cell, beginning to work in the tobacco fields, leaving home, courtship and marriage, child rearing, and old age.

For the first few months of life, a newborn infant stayed in the matricentral cell, that is, received his identity and subsistence from his mother. A mother would take her new infant to the fields with her "and lay it uncovered on the ground . . . while she hoed her corn-row down and up. She would then suckle it a few minutes, and return to her labor, leaving the child in the same exposure." Even-tually, the child left its mother's lap and explored the world of the hut and quarter. In the evenings, he ate with his family and learned to love his parents, siblings, and other kinfolk. During the day the young child lived in an age-segregated world. While parents, other adults, and older siblings worked, children were "left, during a great portion of the day, on the ground at the doors of their huts, to their own struggles and efforts." They played with age-mates or were left at home with other children and perhaps an aged grandparent. Sib-lings and age-mates commonly lived together or in nearby houses. In Prince George's County [Maryland] in 1776, 86 percent of those from zero to four years of age and 82 percent of those from five to nine years of age lived on plantations with at least one other child near their own age. Many children lived in little communities of five or more children their own age. Children five to nine years old, too young to work full time, may have cared for younger siblings; in Prince George's in 1776, 83 percent of all children under five years of age lived on a plantation with at least one child five to nine years of age.

Black children began to work in the tobacco fields between seven and ten years of age. For the first time they joined fully in the daytime activities of adults. Those still living at home labored beside parents, brothers and sisters, cousins, uncles, aunts, and other kin-folk. (Even on smaller plantations, they worked with their mothers.) Most were trained to be field hands by white masters or overseers and by their parents. Though these young hands were forced to work for the master, they quickly learned from their kinfolk to work at the pace that black adults set and to practice the skills necessary to "put massa on."

At about the same age, some privileged boys began to learn a craft from whites or (on the larger plantations) from their skilled kinfolk. Charles Carroll's plantations provide an example of how skills were passed from one generation of Afro-Americans to the next. Six of the eighteen artisans on his plantations under twenty-five years of age in 1773 probably learned their trade from fathers and another four from other kinfolk skilled in that occupation. For example, Joe, twenty-one, and Jack, nineteen, were both coopers and both sons of Cooper Joe, sixty-three. Joe also learned to be a wheelwright and, in turn, probably helped train his brothers-in-law, Elisha, eleven, and Dennis, nine, as wheelwrights.

Beginning to work coincided with the departure of many children from their parents, siblings, and friends. The fact that about 54 percent of all slaves in single-slave households in Prince George's in 1776 were between seven and fifteen years of age suggests that children of those ages were typically forced to leave home. Young blacks were most frequently forced from large plantations to smaller farms. The parents' authority was eliminated, and the child left the only community he had known. Tension and unhappiness often resulted. For example, Hagar, age fourteen, ran away from her master in Baltimore in 1766. "She is supposed to be harbor'd in some Negro Quarter," he claimed, "as her Father and Mother Encourages her in Elopements, under a Pretense she is ill used at home."

Courtship and marriage (defined here as a stable sexual union) led to substantial but differential changes for slave women and men. The process began earlier for women: men probably married in their middle to late twenties, women in their late teens. Men, who initiated the courtship, typically searched for wives by visiting a number of neighboring plantations and often found a wife near home, though not on the same quarter. Some evidence for this custom, suggestive but hardly conclusive, can be seen in the sex and age of runaway slaves. Only 9 percent of all southern Maryland runaways, 1745–1779, and 12 percent of all Virginia runaways, 1730–1787, were women. Few men (relative to the total population) ran away in their late teens, but numbers rose in the early twenties when the search for wives began and crested between twenty-five and thirty-four, when most men married and began families. Courtship on occasion ended in a marriage ceremony, sometimes performed by a clergyman, sometimes celebrated by the slaves themselves.

Slave men had to search their neighborhood to find a compatible spouse because even the largest quarter contained few eligible women. Some of the potential mates were sisters or cousins, groups blacks refused to marry. When they were excluded, few choices remained on the quarter, and youths looked elsewhere. Charles Carroll united slave couples once they married, but that usually required either bride or groom to move. Only a fifth of the forty-seven identifiable couples on his plantations in 1773 had lived on the same quarter before they married. Either husband or wife, and sometimes both of them, moved in three-fifths of the cases. The other fifth of the couples remained on different quarters in 1773. Yet most planters owned too few slaves, on too few quarters, to permit a wide choice of spouses within their plantations; furthermore, they could not afford to purchase the husband or wife. Inevitably, a majority of slave couples remained separated for much of their married life.

Marriage was far less important for slave women than for white women; slave women, unlike their white counterparts, neither shared property with their husbands nor received subsistence from them. After the relationship was consummated, the woman probably stayed with her family (parents and siblings) until a child was born, unless she could form a household with her new husband. Childbearing, and the child rearing that followed, however, were highly important rites of passage for most slave women. Once she had a child, she moved from her mother's or parents' home to her own hut. The bonding between the slave mother and her child may have been far more important than her relationship with her husband, especially if he lived on another plantation. Motherhood, moreover, gave women a few valued privileges. Masters sometimes treated pregnant women and their newborn children with greater than usual solicitude. For example, Richard Corbin, a Virginia planter, insisted in 1759 that his steward be "Kind and Indulgent to pregnant women and not force them when with Child upon any service or hardship that will be injurious to them." Children were "to be well looked after."

Marriage and parenthood brought less change in the lives of most men. Many continued to live with other men. Able to visit his family only at night or on holidays, the nonresident husband could play only a small role in child rearing. If husband and wife lived together, however, they established a household. The resident father helped raise his children, taught them skills, and tried to protect them from the master. Landon Carter reacted violently when Manuel tried to help his daughter. "Manuel's Sarah, who pretended to be sick a week ago, and because I found nothing ailed her and would not let her lie up she run away above a week and was catched the night before last and locked up; but somebody broke open the door for her. It could be none but her father Manuel, and he I had whipped."

On large plantations, mothers could call upon a wide variety of kin to help them raise their children: husbands, siblings, cousins, uncles, or aunts might be living in nearby huts. Peter Harbard learned from his grandmother, father, and paternal uncles how his grandmother's indentures were burned by Henry Darnall, a large planter in Prince George's County, and how she was forced into bondage. He "frequently heard his grandmother Ann Joice say that if she had her *just right that she ought to be free and all her children. He hath also heard his Uncles David Jones, John Wood, Thomas Crane,* and also his father Francis Harbard declare as much." Peter's desire for freedom, learned from his kinfolk, never left him. In 1748, he ran away twice toward Philadelphia and freedom. He was recaptured but later purchased his freedom.

As Afro-Americans grew older, illness and lack of stamina cut into their productivity, and their kinfolk or masters had to provide for them. On rare occasions, masters granted special privileges to favored slaves. Landon Carter permitted Jack Lubbar and his wife "to live quite retired only under my constant kindness" during the last three years of his life, and after over half a century of service. When Thomas Clark died in 1766, he gave his son Charles "my faithful Negro man Jack whom I desire may be used tenderly in his old age." Charles Ball's grandfather lived as an old man by himself away from the other slaves he disliked. Similarly, John Wood, Peter Harbard's uncle, was given his own cabin in his old age.

Many old slaves progressed through several stages of downward mobility. Artisans and other skilled workers became common field hands. Although 10 percent of the men between forty and fifty-nine years of age were craftsmen in Prince George's, only 3 percent of men above sixty years of age held similar positions. Mulatto Ned, owned by Gabriel Parker of Calvert County, was a carpenter and cooper most of his life, but he had lost that job by 1750 when he was sixty-five. Abraham's status at Snowden's ironworks in Anne Arundel County changed from master founder to laborer when he could not work full time. As slaves became feeble, some masters refused to maintain them adequately or sold them to unwary buyers. An act passed by the Maryland assembly in 1752 complained that "sundry Persons in this Province have set disabled and superannuated Slaves free who have either perished through want or otherwise become a Burthen to others." The legislators uncovered a problem: in 1755, 20 percent of all the free Negroes in Maryland were "past labour or cripples," while only 2 percent of white men were in this category. To remedy the abuse, the assembly forbade manumission of slaves by will and insisted that masters feed and clothe their old and ill slaves. If slaveholders failed to comply, they could be fined four pounds for each offense.

As Afro-American slaves moved from plantation to plantation through the life cycle, they left behind many friends and kinfolk and established relations with slaves on other plantations. And when young blacks married off their quarter, they gained kinfolk on other plantations. Both of these patterns can be illustrated from the Carroll plantations. Sam and Sue, who lived on Sam's quarter at Doohoregan Manor, had seven children between 1729 and 1751. In 1774, six of them were spread over four different quarters at Doohoregan: one son lived with his father (his mother had died); a daughter lived with her family in a hut near her father's; a son and daughter lived at Frost's; one son headed Moses' quarter; and a son lived at Riggs. Marriages increased the size and geographic spread of Fanny's relations. A third of the slaves who lived away from Riggs Quarter (the main plantation) were kin to Fanny or her descendants. Two of Kate's children married into Fanny's family; Kate and one son lived at Frost's, and another son lived at Jacob's. Cecilia, the daughter of Carpenter Harry and Sophia, married one of Fanny's grandchildren. Harry and Sophia lived with three of their children at Frost's, and two of their sons lived at Riggs, where they were learning to be wheelwrights with kinsperson Joe, son of Cooper Joe.

Since husbands and wives, fathers and children, and friends and kinfolk were often physically separated, they had to devise ways of maintaining their close ties. At night and on Sundays and holidays, fathers and other kinfolk visited those family members who lived on other plantations. Fathers on occasion had regular visiting rights. Landon Carter's Guy, for instance, visited his wife (who lived on another quarter) every Monday evening. These visits symbolized the solidarity of slave families and permitted kinfolk to renew their friendships but did not allow nonresident fathers to participate in the daily rearing of their children.

Even though this forced separation of husbands from wives and children from parents tore slave families apart, slaves managed to create kinship networks from this destruction. Slave society was characterized by hundreds of connected and interlocking kinship networks that stretched across many plantations. A slave who wanted to run away would find kinfolk, friends of kinfolk, or kinfolk of friends along his route willing to harbor him for a while. As kinship networks among Afro-American slaves grew ever larger, the proportion of runaways who were harbored for significant periods of time on slave quarters seems to have increased in both Maryland and Virginia.

There were three different reasons for slaves to use this underground. Some blacks, like Harry—who left his master in 1779, stayed in the neighborhood for a few weeks, and then took off for Philadelphia—used their friends' and kinfolk's hospitality to reach freedom. Others wanted to visit. About 27 percent of all runaways from southern Maryland mentioned in newspaper advertisements from 1745 to 1779 (and 54 percent of all those whose destinations were described by masters) ran away to visit. For example, Page traveled back and forth between Piscataway and South River in 1749, a distance of about forty miles, and was not caught. He must have received help from many quarters along his route. And in 1756, Kate, thirty years old, ran away from her master, who lived near Georgetown on the Potomac. She went to South River (about thirty miles distant), where she had formerly lived. Friends concealed her there. Her master feared that since "she had been a great Rambler, and is well known in *Calvert* and *Anne-Arundel* Counties, besides other Parts of the Country," Kate would "indulge herself a little in visiting her old Acquaintance," but spend most of [her] time with her husband at West River.

Indeed, 9 percent of the southern Maryland runaways left masters to join their spouses. Sue and her child Jem, eighteen months old, went from Allen's Freshes to Port Tobacco, Charles County, a distance of about ten miles, "to go and see her Husband." Sam, age thirty, lived about thirty miles from his wife in Bryantown, Charles

County, when he visited her in 1755. Will had to go more than a hundred miles, from Charles to Frederick County, to visit his wife, because her master had taken her from Will's neighborhood to a distant quarter.

Slave families in the eighteenth-century Chesapeake were often unstable, but Afro-Americans learned to cope with displacement and separation from kindred with some success. Slaves created flexible kinship networks that permitted slaves to adjust to separation. Most slaves were either members of a kin-based household or could call upon kindred on their own or nearby quarters for aid and encouragement. A girl who grew up in a two-parent household on a large plantation, for instance, might be sold in her teens to a small planter, marry a slave from a neighboring farm, and raise her children with minimal help from her husband. She would have learned about alternative child-rearing methods from playmates whose fathers lived elsewhere and would have been familiar with the nocturnal movement of men to visit their families. Her husband's kindred could provide some help and friendship if they lived nearby. If she longed for her old home, she could run away and visit, knowing that kindred and friends would hide her from the whites.

In sum, slave kinship networks provided Afro-Americans with an alternative system of status and authority and thereby set outside limits to exploitation by the master. A slave had not only a place in the plantation work hierarchy, mostly determined by the master, but a position within his kin group. Slave culture and religion developed within this system: blacks participated as kindred at work and in song, dance, celebrations, prayer, and revivals at home.

Herbert G. Gutman

FAMILY LIFE

Until recently, the common wisdom among historians and in social welfare circles was that slavery had debilitated the African-American family,
leaving in its wake among the contemporary black underclass the phenomena of paternal abandonment, matriarchal households, and high
rates of illegitimacy. But Herbert G. Gutman, a pioneer in the history of
working-class culture, has argued in effect that slavery was not the direct
antecedent of modern conditions, which have more to do with racism
and unemployment in urban and industrial settings than with antebellum slavery. Slave families were subject to masters' decisions and behavior, which might result in the sale and geographic separation of family members, the sexual exploitation of black women, and the
humiliation of black men. Nevertheless, Gutman held, the slave family
was a stable unit with long-standing marital unions and strong kinship
ties. Among the South Carolina slaves whom he studied by analyzing a
lengthy birth register, he emphasized the possibilities of resilience and
independence for slaves, who often made choices about family life that
were unrelated to the beliefs and practices of the owning class. The late
Professor Gutman taught at the Graduate Center of the City University
of New York.

A single South Carolina slave birth register, which makes clear the
extent of familial and kin networks among Afro-American slaves and
shows that their development depended primarily upon the adaptive
capacities of several closely related slave generations, is reason to put
aside mimetic theories of Afro-American slave culture and to describe instead how common slave sexual, marital, familial, and social
choices were shaped by a neglected cumulative slave experience. In
this small South Carolina slave community, most children lived with
two parents, and most adults lived in long-lasting marriages. Children were frequently given the names of blood kin from outside the
immediate family, and the rules that shaped slave marriage were very
different from the rules that existed among the largest resident South
Carolina plantation owners. . . .

From *The Black Family in Slavery and Freedom, 1750–1925* by Herbert G. Gutman,
pp. 45–52. Copyright © 1976 by Herbert G. Gutman. Reprinted by permission
of Pantheon Books, a division of Random House, Inc.

The social and cultural practices of the slaves living on the South Carolina Good Hope plantation do not require that much be known about their owner. Slaves on other large plantations with very different owners and very different experiences . . . behaved similarly to the Good Hope slaves. These Santee River cotton-plantation slaves, furthermore, were not supervised by a resident owner. Their owner, Joseph Heatly Dulles, the son of an immigrant British hardware merchant who had sided with the British during the War of Independence, was born in 1795, grew up in Charleston, graduated from Yale, and spent nearly his entire adult life in Philadelphia. The owner of a plantation about sixty miles northeast of Charleston, Dulles died in Philadelphia, aged eighty-one. He was a direct forebear of John Foster and Allen Dulles, corporate lawyers and appointed public servants who figured prominently in reshaping mid-twentieth-century American society.

How a cumulative slave experience affected the beliefs and behavior of the Good Hope slaves is learned from a plantation birth register, which regularly recorded four demographic items about each newborn slave child: its date of birth, its given name, and the given names, when known, of both parents. Most plantation whites who recorded slave births rarely listed a father's name, a social and business convention that rested upon the belief that because a slave child's status followed that of its mother, the father's name did not have to be recorded. Because it listed most fathers' names, and also because of its relative completeness and the length of time it covered, the Good Hope birth register is an unusual historical document. The first recorded birth occurred in Africa in 1760 and the last ninety-seven years later, three years before Abraham Lincoln's election to the presidency. Listing the names of at least six blacks born in eighteenth-century Africa and twelve others not yet ten years old when the Civil War started, the birth register included more than two hundred slave men, women, and children and covered nearly the entire formative Afro-American experience: birth in Africa, enslavement, South Carolina plantation slavery, the development of an adaptive slave culture, emancipation, and finally life as legally free men and women.

In 1857, when the last recorded slave birth occurred, 175 men, women, and children made up the Good Hope slave community and nearly all were linked together by blood and marital ties that reached back into the eighteenth century. Children up to the age of ten were about one-third of the community, and about 10 percent of the slaves were men and women at least fifty years old. One hundred fifty-four children had been born between 1820 and 1857. About one in five died, mostly before their first birthday. None of the rest lived alone. Eleven had matured and married; the others lived either with one parent or, more commonly, with both parents. Twenty-eight immediate families made up this slave community. A widowed parent headed two families; three others contained childless couples; the rest each had in them a mother, a father, and their children. All but a few husbands and wives were close to each other in age. Eleven slaves, ten of them at least fifty years old, lived alone.

Kin networks linked slaves born in different generations, slaves listed as members of separate immediate families, and slaves living alone. A few examples illustrate the intensity of these ties:

In 1857, Patty, Captain, and Flora lived alone. Patty, born a mainland North American slave before her future owner's father Joseph Dulles left Ireland to become a Charleston merchant and an American slaveowner, was the oldest Good Hope slave and died in that year. Three generations of blood descendants survived her. An African by birth, the widower Captain was surrounded by married children and grandchildren. In 1857, his oldest grandson, Charles, was twenty-one and his youngest, Zekiel, a year old. The widowed Flora lived in the same community as her married sons Dick and Mike, their wives, four grandchildren, six married half brothers and half sisters, and twenty nephews and nieces.

By 1857, Prince and Elsy, husband and wife for thirty years, had three married daughters (a fourth daughter had died in infancy), seven grandchildren, and twenty-nine nieces and nephews. Prince was Patty's son, and his younger married sister Clarinda and brother Primus lived in the community with their spouses and children.

Phoebe and Cuffee headed single-parent households. It had not always been so. Cuffee and Gadsey had been husband and wife for at least twenty-three years. She had apparently died. Cuffee did not remarry. In 1857, he lived with two grown sons; his other children had married, and at least ten grandchildren and a great-grandchild lived in the community. Probably widowed, Phoebe was still living with five of her nine children. Jack had been the father of the first four; Tom the father of the rest. Phoebe's oldest daughter was married and had the same given name as Phoebe's mother. . . .

Two young and as yet unmarried mothers lived with their families of origin. The twenty-one-year-old Betty and her two-year-old daughter Leah lived with Betty's father, Burge, and his second wife, Rose. Betty had been named for her paternal grandmother. The seventeen-year-old Gadsey and her two-year-old daughter, Betsey, lived with Gadsey's mother, Duck, and her husband, Jake. Gadsey was not Jake's daughter; she had been born when Duck was living with Wilson.

Similar familial and kin connections existed among plantation slaves over the entire South in the 1840s and the 1850s. And the slaves living in the Good Hope community were typical in other ways of plantation blacks. The age at which a woman had a first child, the size of completed families, and the length of marriages in the Good Hope slave community hardly differed in other plantation communities.

Good Hope slave women bore a first child at an early age. The ages of twenty-three women whose first children were born between 1824 and 1856 are known: they had a first child at a median age of 19.6 years. The average age differed insignificantly. Three were not yet sixteen, and fourteen were between seventeen and twenty. Two each were aged twenty-one, twenty-two, and twenty-four. Adequate data on the age of southern white women at the birth of a first child are as yet unavailable; hence the similarities between slave and free white women remain unknown. But these South Carolina slave mothers were far younger at the birth of a first child than European women at that time. Peter Laslett finds that the average age at which seventeenth- and eighteenth-century Englishwomen married was twenty-four, and Pierre Goubert fixes the average age of eighteenth-century Frenchwomen at the birth of a first child at between twenty-six and twenty-seven. The only estimate available to us relating free American women to slaves—that of Moncure D. Conway, a Virginia slaveholder who became an antislavery critic—compared southern slave and free white women in the early 1860s and concluded that "the period of maternity is hastened, the average youth of negro mothers being nearly three years earlier than that of the free race."

Good Hope children grew up in large families. Among those born between 1800 and 1849, only one in seven had fewer than three siblings, and slightly more than half had seven or more siblings. Family size increased over time. Twenty-three women had a first child between 1820 and 1849, and not all had completed their families by 1857. About four in five had at least four children; ten women had at least seven children.

Good Hope children also knew their parents well because most married couples lived in long-lasting unions. The ages of twenty-three of the twenty-six fathers living with their wives or their wives and children in 1857 are known. Among those aged twenty-five to thirty-four, the typical marriage in 1857 had lasted at least seven years, and for men aged thirty-five to forty-four at least thirteen years. July, for example, was thirty-eight years old in 1857, and he and Nancy had been married for at least sixteen years. Six of the nine men forty-five and older had lived with the same wife for at least twenty years. Sambo was not typical of these older men; born in 1811, he was not listed in the birth register as a father until his forty-fourth year, when he and Lena had a child. Lena's first husband, William, had died of fever in 1851 and left her with their infant son, William. The boy's paternal great-grandfather had been a slave named William. Sambo and Lena named their first-born daughter for Sambo's older sister Nancy. Unlike Sambo, other elderly men had nearly all lived in long marriages, lasting on the average at least twenty-four years. Gabriel and Abram each had lived with their wives at least thirty-four years.

The community that the Good Hope slaves lived in by 1857 casts fresh light on slave, not owner, belief and behavior. The Good Hope absentee owners did not break up slave marriages, but in itself that does not explain Good Hope slave belief and behavior, because other slaves in less fortunate plantation settings behaved similarly. Examination of the full birth register indicates why the slaves themselves—denied the security of legal marriages and subjected to the severe external pressures associated with ownership—sustained lasting marriages and the slave social beliefs and practices associated with them. The North Carolina Supreme Court Justice who wrote in 1853 that "our law requires no solemnity or form in regard to the marriage of slaves, and whether they 'take up' with each other by express permission of their owners, or from a mere impulse of nature, in obedience to the command 'multiply and replenish the earth,' cannot, in the contemplation of the law, make any sort of difference" spoke a legal truth. But the judge, like most nineteenth-century Americans, confused law and culture and therefore had no understanding of why slaves who married outside the law often lived together for many years.

Elizabeth Fox-Genovese

SLAVE WOMEN

The new wave of slavery studies that began during the early 1970s largely explained the slave experience in masculine terms. More recently, historians such as Elizabeth Fox-Genovese, the Eleonore Raoul Professor of Humanities at Emory University, have sought to correct this bias. The lives of slave women, Fox-Genovese argues, were shaped by two competing sets of gender conventions: one of the masters and the other of the slave community. African-American womanhood thus was a compromise between African traditions and the values of slaveholders. Slave women created their own identity in relation to slave men but always in the context of the political and economic authority of the master. They resisted their enslavement in different ways, depending on their individual disposition and the means available to them. The resistance of slave to master encompassed a complex of social relations, including those of gender, race, and class.

White notions of the appropriate relations between women and men circumscribed many aspects of black lives, but although slave women suffered the restrictions of white gender conventions, they enjoyed few of the attendant protections. Slave women did not embrace white conventions as the model of their own womanhood, but those conventions did figure among the conditions within which they shaped their own ideals. The slaves' gender conventions resulted from a combination of West African traditions, white influences, and their own experiences within the Afro-American slave

From *Within the Plantation Household: Black and White Women of the Old South*, pp. 290–299, 308–309, 315–317, 319–320, 322–333 by Elizabeth Fox-Genovese. © 1988 The University of North Carolina Press. Reprinted by permission of the author and publisher.

community. Transplantation to the New World, however violent and disorienting, never eradicated African conventions but did divorce them from the material and institutional conditions in which they had flourished; and it exposed the slaves to the power of masters with views and attitudes different from their own.

The masters' conventions, as they developed, established the dominant pattern for gender relations in the South. That dominance hardly determined the ways in which slave women viewed themselves or even the gender relations of the slave community, but it did delineate the prevailing patterns of southern society confirmed by law and religion. Dominance, however, provided no guarantee that the slaveholders would observe their own conventions in their relations with their slaves. Minimally, slaveholders viewed their slaves as women and men and even tried to promote orderly gender relations, notably marriage, among them, but they did not consider themselves bound by gender conventions in their treatment of slaves.

The slaveholders' refusal to view their slaves as ladies and gentlemen entailed more than a refusal to grant them genteel social status. It withheld minimal respect for those attributes of masculinity and femininity that the slaveholders prized most highly for themselves. The popular images of "Buck" and "Sambo" and "Jezebel" and "Mammy" captured dominant white views of gender roles among slaves and, not least, white anxieties about their relations with servants whom they had tried to deprive of autonomy in gender roles as in all else. These conventions did not reflect the slaves' views, although there is painful irony in their having sometimes represented caricatures of slave values—the strength of men and the motherhood of women.

The notion of Buck—a white gender convention—represented a caricature or reversal of the notion of cavalier. It encoded white male fears of black sexuality in particular and of virility in general. The convention of the Buck emphasized white views of the single, sexually active black male as divorced from other social roles. As a shadow image of the cavalier, it reflected whites' bad faith about the master-slave relation. Since slave law denied the legality of black marriage and ownership of property, it is hardly surprising that the white image of the black man should have divorced sexuality from reproduction and social responsibility, including the protection of women. The Buck evoked a sexually active, perpetual adolescent.

Implicitly, it also evoked the threat of black sexuality to white women—a fascinating reversal since the main interracial sexual threat was that of white predators against black women. The presumed threat of black male sexuality never provoked the wild hysteria and violence in the Old South that it did in the New, but self-proclaimed slaveholding paternalists harbored their own anxieties.

The image of Sambo inverted that of Buck and embodied a reversal of white attitudes toward masculinity. For Sambo captured an image of docility in direct opposition to the white ideals of male honor. Divorced from the image of Buck, it offered an image of the black man as naturally subservient to the will of the white, as too lazy and supine to care about self-defense, much less the honorable attributes of freedom. The image reassured whites of their own ability to control their slaves—and of their safety within households in which slaves outnumbered them.

Similarly, the convention of the Mammy reflected recognizable white values. If implicitly the idea of the Mammy referred to motherhood and reproduction, it also claimed those privileges for the masters rather than for the slaves themselves. Just as Buck signaled the threat of master-slave relations, Mammy signaled the wish for organic harmony and projected a woman who suckled and reared white masters. The image displaced sexuality into nurture and transformed potential hostility into sustenance and love. It claimed for the white family the ultimate devotion of black women, who reared the children of others as if they were their own. Although the image of the Mammy echoed the importance that black slaves attached to women's roles as mothers, it derived more from the concerns of the master than from those of the slave. Presumably, it bore some relation to the masters' complex feelings about motherhood and, like the image of the Buck, testified to an abiding childishness that informed the appearance of command. Yet neither Buck nor Mammy faithfully captured the most common and direct influences of the gender conventions of the masters on the lives of the slaves.

The image of Jezebel explicitly contradicted the image of Mammy and that of the lady as well, although, like that of Mammy and unlike that of the lady, it presented a woman isolated from the men of her own community. Jezebel lived free of the social constraints that surrounded the sexuality of white women. She thus legitimated the wanton behavior of white men by proclaiming black women to be lusty wenches in whom sexual impulse overwhelmed all restraint. The image eased the consciences of white men by suggesting that black women asked for the treatment they received.

These four images betrayed the whites' discomfort with their own attitudes toward their slaves' relations to gender conventions. Each image represented a caricature of attributes that whites celebrated in themselves. Each emphasized physical attributes over social, as if whites had difficulty depicting their slaves in adult gender roles. In many instances, slaveholders did recognize their dependents as women and men with distinct personalities, but they had difficulty in recognizing them as social beings. This conflicted attitude on the part of the whites permeated the slaves' experience of the gender conventions by which they were constrained but by no means defined.

Sojourner Truth, in her famous speech to the women's rights advocates of the North, directly addressed the relation between the experience of slave women and the white conventions of womanhood. Those conventions, she angrily insisted, had not applied to slave women, who nonetheless remained women. White men had denied, and slave men had been unable to provide, slave women with the protection conventionally accorded white women. Sojourner Truth was addressing a northern audience for whom the status of woman essentially subsumed that of lady in an ideological commitment to equality among women and the recognition of womanhood itself as the social role of all women, whereas in the South, even a white woman required the status of lady in order to enjoy the full social protection of gender conventions. And Truth might also have pointed out that southern slave women were doubly removed from that protection. As slaves they had no claim to the status of lady, and as blacks they had trouble establishing even their claim to the status of woman. Much more readily at risk than their white sisters in the turbulent public sphere of the antebellum South, they were at risk in the domestic sphere as well. The conditions of slavery stripped slave women of most of the attributes of the conventional female role.

For the slaveholders, gender conventions included a strong component of social stratification as well as a foundation for personal identity. For the slaves, many of whom also responded to the appeal of social "quality," gender conventions derived their primary importance from their role in organizing and perpetuating the slave community. Both groups recognized the importance of gender conventions in the life of black people, but the slaveholders saw them primarily as a means of control, whereas the slaves saw them primarily as an anchor for individual and collective identity. Gender conventions, as manifested in the everyday lives of slaves, penetrated the continual struggle in which they defended their own views as forcefully as their condition between white household and slave community would permit.

If, in assigning tasks, masters normally assigned most slaves to separate women's and men's gangs, they also assigned slave women to work that they would not have considered appropriate for white women. They were less likely to assign slave men to tasks that would not have been considered appropriate for white men. Bennet Barrow perversely confirmed a master's awareness of the importance of gender conventions to slaves' sense of themselves, for he violated those conventions as a means of humiliation. On one occasion he set three rugged field hands to washing clothes; on another he forced certain "Bucks" to wear women's clothing. Lizzie Barker's mother's mistress punished her for a theft of which she had been wrongfully accused by making her wear trousers for a year. Once, when her mistress was away, Victoria Adams put on a pair of pants "an scrub de floor wid them on." Another slave reported her, and "Missums told me it was a sin for me to put on a man's pants, and she whip me pretty bad." The mistress claimed that the Bible said that "A man shall not put on a woman's clothes, nor a woman put on a man's clothes." Victoria Adams never saw that in the Bible, "but from then 'til now, I ain't put on no more pants." Most slaveholders probably did not indulge in malicious perversity or invoke the Bible to enforce observance of dress codes, but neither did they underestimate the importance of gender identity to their servants.

For self-interested or disinterested reasons masters encouraged their slaves to observe facsimiles of white gender conventions. They encouraged "marriage" among their slaves, and motherhood even more. They valued piety among their slaves, much as among their own women—provided that it did not lead to independent thought. They provided women with skirts and men with pants. At worst, they reduced gender to mere sexuality in their relations with their slaves, ignoring the attributes of manhood and womanhood that might encourage an independent identity for individuals or for the slave community. Unable to reduce their slaves to mere chattel, they could still dominate them in innumerable ways, notably through their own sexual exploitation of slave women. Despite occasional examples of tenderness and loyalty between masters and slave concubines, the masters' unchecked power over their slave women brought into the center of the household that public violence against which white women were protected. And while it demeaned slave women, it also threatened to unman slave men. Violation of the conventions emerged as the attack of one people and one class upon another.

Gender conventions never provided slave women with a seamless casing for their own identities. One facet of those identities derived from their membership in the plantation household, in which they functioned primarily as individuals in relation to the other members of "the family, white and black." Their gender carried significance for the ways in which others related to them, but little significance for their identities as members of a larger social system. Another facet of their identities derived from membership in the community of slaves, which overlapped with but also frequently transcended the plantation household, and within which gender did constitute an important form of social organization. Slave women drew from that community their most important sense of themselves as women in relation to men, children, and other women, for it provided the context for their independent lives as sisters, wives, daughters, mothers, and friends. The household nonetheless cast a long shadow over the slave community, which remained bound by the white society that encircled it and which it permeated.

In most of North American slave society, the overwhelming majority of slaves lived closer to the whites, who outnumbered them, than did slaves in the Caribbean or even in the Carolina-Georgia low-country. In 1860, 75 percent of all American slaves lived on plantations of fewer than fifty slaves, and more than half lived on farms of twenty or fewer. Yet the slave community remained rooted in the households of twenty or more slaves, which had clusters of slaves large enough to support a solid community life. From these clusters, ties among slaves extended throughout the county or district and beyond them throughout the state and region. Kinship ties established interlocking networks of slaves, as did the churches, whether established by whites or blacks. Since well over 90 percent of the slaves were illiterate, the threads that bound them together were primarily oral. Yet word-of-mouth transmissions traveled like the echoes of African drums, with successive recipients' picking up the relay and passing it on. Letters written for slaves by members of their white families helped to sustain the links, but they could not possibly reveal all the slaves were thinking. Afro-American religion and folklore testify to the slaves' determination to preserve and transform their discrete African heritage, but they were never able to do so in complete isolation from white influence.

In the Caribbean—where blacks vastly outnumbered whites, slaves customarily grew their own food on individual plots, and continual importation ensured a high proportion of native Africans among the slave community—slave women enjoyed much greater opportunity to preserve or recreate African patterns intact. In North America, such opportunities were rare. The dominant white conventions did not, as many West African societies did, ascribe to women a special association with agricultural labor and marketing. Slave women's participation in the heaviest forms of agricultural labor violated white conventions and thereby emphasized the status of slave over that of woman. Many Caribbean slave women at least partially retained a positive association with agriculture and marketing, but largely because of their greater separation from white cultural influences. In the South, most slave women could not do the same. To the extent that they participated in incidental gardening and marketing, they did so to contribute an "extra" rather than basic subsistence. They clearly had a strong sense of themselves as women in relation to slave men, but if that sense owed something to their African past, it derived from remembered tradition rather than from the daily reenactment of fundamental social relations of production.

During the nineteenth century, middle-class domesticity emerged as the dominant model of gender relations for American society. White southerners, especially slaveholders, embraced important features of it, even though the social relations of slavery contradicted some of its fundamental premises. Features of that model, especially the emphasis on bonds between parents and children, appealed to slaves as well as to slaveholders; yet in the case of slaves, in contrast to slaveholders, the model did not derive directly from their own traditions. The slaves came, not from European societies that had long been developing an interrelated system of ideas about conjugal relations, motherhood, and absolute property, but from African societies with very different ideas about personal and property relations.

Relations of property and marriage constitute fundamental systems whereby all societies establish links between their deepest beliefs about gender relations (relations between men and women) and relations of power (who rules whom and in the name of what). Since the relations between men and women lie at the core of any viable society and individual identity, the most extreme consequence of ruthless domination may well consist in the destruction of those relations. Conversely, the successful domination of one people by another almost invariably includes concessions to those relations and attempts to bind them to the acceptance of that domination as a legitimate order. All societies attach importance to the differences between women and men and draw upon them in their elaboration of social and political institutions, but they vary widely in their interpretation of the differences.

The southern model of womanhood did not protect slave women from hard physical labor or undermine their emotional self-reliance, any more than it protected them from the abuse of white— or black—men. For slave women did not institutionally suffer the domination or enjoy the protection of their own men. As husbands and fathers, slave men lacked the backing of the law. Among the slaves conjugal domesticity figured more as an act of faith, and the domination of women figured more as personal violence, than either did as established practice in the larger society. Enslavement prevented them from simply adopting white models of gender relations. Slave women and men could hardly ground their personal and community identities in "normal" middle-class models of the proper relations between women and men, for they could not establish legally binding marriages or assert legal authority over their own children.

Slaveholders, with varying degrees of enthusiasm and good faith, encouraged slaves to observe the patterns of conjugal domesticity that they valued for themselves, and the slaves, for their own reasons, frequently did. But slaveholders and slaves both knew that the forms remained fragile in the absence of solid institutional foundations. Slavery, as abolitionists were quick to point out, made a mockery of marriage and family life. Afro-American slave women transmitted their condition to their offspring even if the fathers were free. Their "marriages" to black men, slave or free, had no status at law. They could be separated from spouse or children without any recourse except personal pleas. Slave men could not protect their "wives" from the sexual assaults of white men. The slave "family" depended entirely on personal ties, which historically have required the support of legal, economic, and social sanctions. "Husbands" did not support their wives, who worked at the will of the master. They did not provide for their children or even fully determine their preparation for adult life. Under favorable conditions, a slave couple might lead a life comparable to that of rural or urban workers, but the similarities are more deceptive than instructive. The slaves' legal status weighed heavily on them. A recently emancipated slave made the point in the words with which Louisa McCord would so heartily have concurred: "*I praise God for this day!* I have long been praying for it. The Marriage Covenant is at the foundation of all our rights. In slavery we could not have *legalised* marriage: *now* we have it. Let us conduct ourselves worthy of such a blessing—and all the people will respect us—God will bless us, and we shall be established as a people."

With time, Afro-American slaves absorbed a heavy dose of the larger society's attitudes. Evidence reveals that a concern for family held consuming importance for Afro-Americans both in slavery times and after emancipation. Hence, historians have stressed the semblance of conjugal domesticity that many slaves sought to sustain, and they have implicitly reasoned from it to a picture of the slave cabin as a bravely defended if precarious home. Doubtless some commitment to an idea of home did inform slaves' attitudes toward their cabins, but the slaves knew better than any that the cabin home did not benefit from any of the supports, in absolute property or even legal marriage, that buttressed its free equivalent. After slavery, Afro-American men and women struggled mightily to implement their own free homes, complete with primarily domestic wives, and they resisted to the best of their abilities the need for a married woman to work outside the home. Under slavery they did not have such opportunities to protect family life, however much they nurtured an ideal of parents and children as a primary care unit. It remains difficult to determine whether they found the white version of middle-class domesticity a compelling ideal, although it is clear that antebellum free blacks, like late-nineteenth-century, middle-class blacks, valued it highly as a sign of respectability.

Both in their acceptance of and resistance to white norms, the slaves established distinct limits to the power of the slaveholders, which always fell short of the total power that the latter desired. Had such limitations not applied, there would be scant justification for talking about the slaves' gender relations and roles, for total power strips away the wrappings of gender, race, and class in which the sense of self normally comes swathed. Conversely, had the slaveholders not exercised considerable power over the daily lives of their slaves, those slave might, like many Caribbean slaves, have more readily built upon their African cultural inheritance. Behind Sojourner Truth's angry question—"and ar'n't I a woman?"—lay the implicit corollary: And whereby am I a woman? For slave women the answer lay astride the household and the slave community, astride two competing sets of gender conventions.

The lives of slave women, which unfolded between the plantation household and the slave community, constituted a compromise between an African past and a slaveholder-dominated American present, but the compromise was grounded in the slaves' own Afro-American present, which owed something to both and replicated neither. The American model of gender relations was predicated upon the ideal of the freedom of the individual man. But because, in the South, that ideal was predicated upon slavery as a social system, a fundamental contradiction informed the slaves' relation to it. However attractive, the essence of the ideal remained beyond the slaves' grasp. Yet the contradiction itself rendered the ideal compelling. African models of gender relations also remained influential, and kin networks persisted that granted, for example, special roles to the mother's brother. But in the absence of material foundations in African kin and productive relations, they could not fully ground the slaves' sense of themselves as members of the larger society.

Nor could slave women develop an "African" model of womanhood that emphasized their independence and self-reliance as women in contrast to white women's dependence on and subordination to white men. However attractive the view that they did, it does not take adequate account of slave women's relations with the men of their own community or with those of white society. The strongest case for the autonomy of slave women lies in their freedom from the domestic domination of their men—in their independent roles as working members of the household. Yet to emphasize their independence vis-à-vis slave men means to underscore their dependence upon—or subjection to—their owners. Slave women did not live free of male domination; they lived free of the legally enforceable domination of "their own" men. White slaveholding men did exercise legal power over slave women. White male heads of slaveholding households provided slave women with food, lodging, clothing, and medical care, assigned them tasks, supervised their work, disciplined them, determined the destiny of their children, and could impose nonnegotiable sexual demands. Those same white masters presumed to intervene forcefully and by legal right to "protect" black women against abusive husbands. The power of the master constituted the fundamental condition of slave women's lives, however much it was hedged in by the direct and subtle resistance of the women themselves.

Slave women, like slave men, lived in a world in which no solid or independently guaranteed institutions mediated between their basic relations of gender and the master's power. Under adverse circumstances they did their best to develop a collective sense of community legitimacy to substitute for institutions grounded in law. Their ideal lay somewhere between the whites' notions of domesticity and African notions of tribe and lineage. Both systems predicated fundamental distinctions and appropriate relations between men and women, but they organized those relations in different social forms that expressed their discrete politics and political economies. Slave women forged their own identities as women in their relations with slave men, but they did so under the political and economic domination of their masters. . . .

During the antebellum period, slave women's resistance was likely to be individual rather than collective. Even their forms of individual resistance differed somewhat from those of men, in part because of their reproductive capacities, in part because of Afro-American attitudes toward womanhood, and in part because of the various opportunities offered and denied by white gender conventions. In innumerable ways, from biology to interlocking social relations with slaveholders and with other slaves, women's everyday lives were organized by gender. Both slaves and slaveholders had strong, if different, reasons to view their lives as in some sense organically linked and as bound by mutual obligations and responsibilities. This view, which always consisted of both substance and froth, depended heavily on the recognition of gender relations as the anchor for individual identity. Yet the relations of slavery in the abstract, notably the law of slavery, barely recognized slave women as women, and testy masters and mistresses frequently failed to do so in daily practice. Slaveholders always wrestled with the temptation—to which they frequently succumbed—to view slaves above all as the extensions of their own wills, the instruments of their own responsibilities. When provoked, slave women, who were never deceived on the matter, responded in kind.

Mistresses and slaves lived in tense bonds of conflict-ridden intimacy that frequently exploded into violence on one side or the other. Everyday proximity to mistresses permitted slave women special kinds of psychological resistance, the consequences of which are almost impossible to assess. Impudence and "uppityness," which derived from intimate knowledge of a mistress's weak points, demonstrated a kind of resistance and frequently provoked retaliation out of all proportion to the acts, if not the spirit. Because the mistress lacked the full authority of the master, her relations with her servants could easily lapse into a personal struggle. When servants compounded sauciness and subtle disrespect with a studied cheerful resistance to accomplishing the task at hand, the mistress could rapidly find herself losing control—of herself as well as her servant. "Puttin' on ole massa" must have been, if anything, more trying when practiced by slave women against the mistress. But slave women who worked in the big house were uniquely positioned to resist the message of deference, to undermine the distinctions, and to make the lives of privileged mistresses an unending war of nerves. Withal, it was the mistress, not the servant, who held the whip and who, much more often than not, initiated the violence. . . .

The personal relations between house slaves and the white family could range from love to hatred, but whatever their emotional quality, they were more likely than not to include a high level of intimacy. Mistresses whipped slave women with whom they might have shared beds, whose children they might have delivered or who might have delivered theirs, whose children they might have suckled and who frequently had suckled theirs. Young masters fought with young slave women with whom they had played as children and whom they might already be attempting to seduce. And masters, who embodied the ultimate authority, might have sexual relations with the women they disciplined and who indeed might be their daughters. Not surprisingly, house slaves felt that they had grounds to resist abuses of authority and even to claim a role in determining its legitimate bounds. Whether the tensions were openly acknowledged or not, slave women's lives in the big house constituted a dense pattern of day-to-day resistance that could at any moment explode into violence.

House slaves believed they had a right to a just share of the goods of the household, to which they enjoyed easier access than other members of the slave community. Cooks and others benefited from their positions to supplement their diets and those of families and friends. House servants were also likely to know who was pilfering what around the place. Fannie Dorum bargained with her master that, if he would not hit her anymore, she would tell him who had been stealing all his eggs. No naïf, he queried, "Will you tell me, sure 'nough?" She said she would. "But I never done it." As a rule, house slaves did not look on the lifting of an odd biscuit or cookie or even a helping of meat as a theft, but rather as a perquisite. Slaveholders were much more likely to label small disappearances as thefts, although they were not likely to recognize them as acts of defiance.

Life in the big house also opened opportunities for resistance that could less easily be mistaken. Clara used her position in the big house to search for bullets for her son, who intended to murder his master. He succeeded, and she was convicted with him. Poison was a much more common weapon than bullets, and much more peculiarly women's own. Slaveholders were especially conscious of the threat of poison, although they rarely acknowledged it as a regular feature of their everyday lives. Eliza Magruder noted that a female slave in a neighboring household had tried to poison her mistress and was expected to hang. Betsey, a servant in the Manigault household and "a very wicked woman," was said to have poisoned several children. Mary Chesnut reported the tale of a nurse who killed a child she was nursing. The fears that such tales provoked could lead mistresses into violence against suspected offenders. A slave named Alice brought her sick mistress some water and food, and the mistress got sick to her stomach. "She sez dat Alice done try ter pizen her. Ter sho yo' how sick she wuz, she gits out of de bed, strips dat gal ter de waist an' whips her wid a cowhide till de blood runs down her back. Dat gal's back wuz cut in gashes an' de blood run down ter 'er heels." Thereafter she was chained down until she recovered from her wounds and then "carried off ter Richmond in chains an' sold."

The resistance of house slaves combined features of their identity as women with features of the white gender conventions that assigned them to women's work. Like the resistance of other women, it also embodied a determination to lighten work loads and to reject the worst consequences of enslavement, with no special relation to gender. The resistance of house slaves was, nonetheless, complicated by their personal relations with their mistresses, their masters, and other members of the white family. The resistance of field slaves manifested few of these complications. Like house slaves, field slaves ultimately resisted the master, but in their case his delegate was not the mistress, but an overseer or driver. The overseer, who belonged neither to the white family nor the slave community, was frequently perceived as lacking all claim to legitimate authority. Field women did more than their share to unsettle the overseer's position and to ensure that, on the average, he held his job for no more than three years.

As field workers, women resisted in the same ways as men. Male slaves held no monopoly on the breaking of tools and the challenging and even the murdering of overseers. Even when female slaves worked in the field with other women, they did not work at specifically women's tasks or normally work under the supervision of a woman. Frequently, especially on large plantations, they worked under the supervision of an overseer or a black driver, whom they regarded more as a taskmaster than as a person. Field women fiercely defended their sense of acceptable work loads and violently resisted abuses of power, which for some meant any discipline at all. When anyone started to whip Lily Perry, "I'd bite lak a [rum?] mad dog so dey'd chain my han's." The chains left permanent scars, but the pain did not induce her compliance. "Dey'd also pick me up by de years an' fling me." Once Lily Perry was working around the yard, carrying slops, and, not feeling well, she poured some of the slops out on the ground. The overseer, who observed her, grabbed her up to whip her. "De minute he grabs me I seize on ter his thumb an' I bites hit ter de bone, den he gits mad an' he picks me up an' lifts me higher dan my haid an' flings me down on de steel mat dere in front of de do." She had to be revived with cold water and was sick for a week. Once when Martha Bradley was working in the fields, the overseer "come 'roun and say sumpin' to me he had no bizness say." She took her hoe and "knocked him plum down." Nancy Ward fought with her overseer "for a whole day and stripped him naked as the day he was born.". . .

Running away provided an important safety valve for slave women's frustrations with the demands on their lives. Since women did not figure prominently among the visible fugitives who escaped to the North and wrote of their experiences, it is easy to assume that they were not among the more frequent runaways, but for reasons that had less to do with resolve than with opportunity. Whether as a result of white or black male bias—or more likely a combination of the two—female slaves were unlikely to be trained in carpentry, blacksmithing, masonry, coopering, or other specialized crafts that would lead them to be hired out. Accordingly, they were less likely than men to have an excuse to be abroad alone. The pool of skilled craftsmen, who could not only move about with less attention but who also stood a much better chance of being literate, provided the leadership for the most important slave revolts and also the largest number of fugitives. When Ellen Craft fled to the North with her husband, she dressed as a man. Furthermore, because, under the laws of slavery, children stayed with their mothers (at least until they were sold away from all kin), fathers more often than mothers were forced to run away in order to visit the rest of the family. Women, too, sometimes ran away to visit kin in other households, but slaveholders, for reasons best known to themselves, were much less likely to advertise for them than for men. The advertisements for runaways misrepresent—perhaps to a great degree—the proportion of women to men. We know that innumerable women, who lacked men's opportunities for mobility and who never ran to freedom, regularly ran away to avoid work, to avoid punishment, or simply to have some time to themselves. . . .

At first glance, it is tempting to argue that if, in the case of runaways, southern gender conventions favored slave men over women, they compensated by affording slave women some protection as women, especially as mothers. Slaveholders did permit women greater latitude than men in feigning illness, especially if they claimed to be pregnant, but not necessarily out of solicitude for female delicacy or maternal feeling. Because the condition of slavery was passed on through the mother, all children born to slave women were slaves, no matter what their father's status. No slaveholder could lightly dismiss potential increases to his human property, and most felt themselves obliged to give women who claimed illness related to pregnancy the benefit of the doubt. Slave women perfectly understood their masters' motives and were quick to use the excuse even when they were not pregnant, or to claim unusual discomfort or weakness when they were. The tactic, which did not always work, embodied a marvelous challenge to the master: You want me to reproduce as a woman, treat me as a woman. Most masters did not view their slaves' maternity the way they viewed that of their wives and daughters, but self-interest led many, like George J. Kollock, to go easy on pregnant slave women, especially in their third trimester. This attitude, whatever prompted it, unquestionably contributed to Afro-American slave women's success in bearing enough children to make their people the only self-reproducing slave population in the Western Hemisphere. If a slave woman's resistance in this matter lightened her work, it also contributed to strengthening her people.

Many slave women took pride and joy in motherhood. Deborah White has convincingly argued that for Afro-American women, as for their African foremothers, motherhood was of much greater significance than marriage in a young woman's coming of age and identity. Slaveholders and slaves both acknowledged the special pain of separating mothers and children by sale. Slave children frequently took great pride in their mothers, whom they deeply loved. They also frequently displayed a healthy respect—sometimes fear—for the sharpness of their mothers' tongues and the power of their blows. Slave women inescapably bore children into slavery and had every reason to try to prepare them to survive in the dangerous world that awaited them. They also bore them into a slave community that nurtured its own ideals of relations among human beings. It is next to impossible, and probably presumptuous, to attempt to understand fully how slave women felt about their identities as mothers, but it is safe to assume that those feelings did not necessarily correspond to white models. Mothers throughout the world have loved children without subscribing to a modern Western ideal of motherhood, and loving mothers have defined themselves by more than their identities as mothers.

Anna Baker remembered that, "when I was too little to know anything 'bout it," her mother "run off an lef' us." She did not remember much about her mother from that time, but after the war her mother returned to get them and explained why she had had to go. "It was 'count o' de Nigger overseers. . . . Dey kep' a-tryin' to mess 'roun' wid her an' she wouldn' have nothin' to do wid 'em." Once, when one of the overseers asked her to go to the woods with him, she said she would go ahead and find a nice place, and she "jus kep' a'goin. She swum de river an' run away." She hired herself out to some "folks dat wasnt rich 'nough to have no slaves o' dey own" and who were good to her, and once or twice she slipped back at night to see her children. Her resistance to the sexual abuse she could not safely refuse forced her to desert her children, although she could count on their being fed by the master and reared by the other women of the slave community.

Anna Baker's mother could rely upon the cohesiveness of the slave community to provide a stable world for her children, but she could not tolerate the sexual abuses to herself. Other women, who could live with their own situation but who could not accept what was done to their children, took more drastic measures. Lou Smith's mother told her of a woman who had borne several children, only to see her master sell them when they were one or two years old. "It would break her heart. She never got to keep them." After the birth of her fourth baby, "she just studied all the time about how she would have to give it up," and one day she decided that she just was not going to let her master sell that baby. "She got up and give it something out of a bottle and purty soon it was dead. 'Course didn't nobody tell on her or he'd of beat her nearly to death." Enough slave babies died from a variety of causes that a master would not necessarily recognize infanticide when it occurred. Slave women who slept with their children could unintentionally roll over on them and smother them during the night, and some slaveholders expressed compassion for their loss. Many infants died from natural causes, ranging from what is now called sudden infant death syndrome (SIDS) to the ubiquitous diseases that carried off white children as well. Many others may have died because their mothers were not allowed to nurse them for longer than a year, and they lacked adequate nutrition. Even mothers who were still nursing but who had been returned to their labor in the fields could not always feed their infants enough. When Celia Robinson's mother had a young child, the overseer would tell her it was time to go home to suckle it and she had better be back at her work in fifteen minutes. "Mother said she knowed she could not go home and suckle dat child and git back in 15 minutes so she would go somewhere an' sit down an' pray de child would die."

For women who loved their children, infanticide and even abortion constituted costly forms of resistance. Whether women turned to such desperate measures depended upon a variety of factors that defy generalization, but those who did were, at whatever pain to themselves, resisting from the center of their experience as women. More, they were implicitly calling to account the slaveholders, who protected the sexuality and revered the motherhood of white ladies while denying black women both. From slave women's perspective, the slaveholders' behavior arrogantly assimilated the essence of womanhood to the prerogatives of class and racial status. Slave mothers knew that if their infanticide were discovered, it would be recognized as a crime against their master's property. Perhaps that knowledge led some of the more desperate to feel that, by killing an infant they loved, they would be in some way reclaiming it as their own. Jane, "a mulatto woman, slave," who was indicted for the murder of her infant child, had resisted, at however high a cost to herself. But she had also implicitly acknowledged that the oppression of slavery had, at least in her case, won out over the vigor and vitality of the slave community—and even more, over the slaveholders' cherished paternalistic ideal of the family, white and black.

When slaveholders lived up to their side of the paternalistic compromise, they undercut some aspects of slave women's active resistance. Sarah Wilson had been called Annie until she was eight years old. "My old Mistress' name was Annie and she name me that, and Mammy was afraid to change it until old Mistress died, then she change it." Sarah's mother hated her mistress, but the mistress, perhaps impervious to the woman's feelings, symbolically claimed the woman's child as her own. She also claimed Sarah's half-sister, Lottie, whom she insisted also be called Annie. Sarah's and Lottie's mother changed Lottie's name "in her own mind but she was afraid to say it out loud, a-feared she would get a whipping." When Lottie was sold, her mother told her "to call herself Annie when she was leaving but call herself Lottie when she git over to the Starrs. And she done it too. I seen her after that and she was called Lottie all right." Martha Jackson gave one of her favorite servants a fancy wedding and expected her to name her first daughter Patsy. There was no evidence of special friction between mistress and servant, but we may doubt that Patsy would have been the servant's own first choice. Names held great symbolic significance for slaves, as for slaveholders. Especially under conditions in which families could all too easily be fractured by sales, the choice of a name could provide an important link in the delineation of kin and a statement of an independent identity. To this day, Afro-American women in the deep South make up names for their children that symbolically confirm the bearer's unique identity. Slaveholders considered it a sign of condescension and interdependence to bestow their own names on their slaves' children, but many slaves saw that benevolence as an act of usurpation.

Slaveholders' sexual exploitation of slave women further shredded the illusions of a harmonious white and black family but did not easily permit resistance, especially if the master was the perpetrator. "Plenty of the colored women have children by the white man. She know better than to not do what he say." Young masters presented a more complicated problem. Whites knew as well as blacks that the young men were likely to claim sexual prerogatives with the slave women and frequently sought to remove them from temptation by sending them away to school. When Eliza Washington's mother fought with her young master, she may well have been fending off his sexual advances, which she may have found all the more distasteful for being initiated before an audience of his peers. Overseers and black drivers caused even worse problems by assuming that their positions as delegates of the masters' authority implicitly carried sexual prerogatives. Slave women did not agree with their interpretation and were wont violently to resist advances that they might have been forced to endure from the master himself. Masters, who normally did not encourage the sexual license of others, often proved sympathetic to their outrage and dispatched the presumptuous delegate.

Many southerners privately concurred with the harshest northern critics of slavery that the system suffered from sexual disarray. Slaveholding women in particular found their men's relations with slave women almost impossible to bear. One white lady "slipped in a colored gal's room and cut her baby's head clean off 'cause it belonged to her husband." The husband beat her for her act "and started to kill her, but she begged so I reckon he got to feelin' sorry for her." Most ladies did not resort to such drastic measures, and many husbands never repented of their ways. Annie Young's master was determined to have her aunt. Her aunt ran into the woods, but the master set the bloodhounds on her. When he caught her, "he knocked a hole in her head and she bleed like a hog, and he made her have him." She told her mistress, who told her that she might as well be with him, "'cause he's gonna kill you."

The power of the master constituted the linchpin of slavery as a social system, and no one ever satisfactorily defined its limits. If, as many jurists, echoing Thomas Ruffin, insisted, the power of the master must be absolute, how could it be curtailed in domestic affairs, especially when its victims had no identity as women at law? The supreme court of Alabama conceded the difficulty with respect to punishment: "Absolute obedience, and subordination to the lawful authority of the master, are the duty of the slave. . . . The law cannot enter into strict scrutiny of the precise force employed [by the master], with the view of ascertaining that the chastisement had or had not been reasonable." The law did hold masters accountable for what it defined as wanton murder, but not for accidental deaths and assuredly not for sexual assault. By the late 1850s, some jurists, theologians, and uncommonly conscientious masters were beginning to worry about the total lack of legal protection for slave women as women and were beginning to argue that the rape of slave women should be regarded as a crime. But convention and attitude alike militated against a serious hearing for their views. White male sexual power followed naturally upon white male social power, oppressing both white ladies and black slaves, however unequally, but white ladies often displaced their anger at the husbands who "protected" them onto the slave women whom their husbands' power entitled them to bully.

Slave women's husbands, legally not husbands at all, lacked any power to defend their wives, short of placing their own lives at high risk. Slave women's freedom from the legal domination of their own men ensured that in most instances they would confront the power of their masters alone. The lack of legal guarantees, however, did not preclude slaves from developing intense loyalty to their mates and even a deep commitment to the substance of marriage in the absence of its forms. Annie Tate's grandmother drowned herself "'cause dey sold her husban'." Lily Perry grew up with her husband, Robert, who always tried to defend her. Robert hated to see her beaten and would beg her "not ter let my mouth be so sassy, but I can't help hit." Any number of times he sneaked out to the fields in the evening to carry the slops to the pigs for her, and whenever he could he tried to take her beatings. Once, when the master was beating her, Robert ran up and begged him to "put de whuppin on him 'stead of me. De result was marse whupped us both an' we 'cided ter run away." They did run away, but the master brought them back to yet another whipping and they never tried to run away again. Sallie Carder's father tried to protect his wife from a whipping. The overseer had tied her up and her husband untied her. "De overseer shot and killed him." When Harrod C. Anderson sold the husband of one of his women, she put ground glass in his milk. He found her out in time and made her drink the milk herself, and then gave her an emetic. But he subsequently sold her out of fear that the next time she would succeed.

Slave husbands and wives could vary in their mutual loyalty and devotion, like husbands and wives throughout the world and throughout history, but the absence of legal standing for their marriages confronted them with especially difficult conditions. Men who lacked all external supports for their domination of their women frequently lost them to other men or were faced with the women's more or less open infidelity. Sexual fidelity is not exclusively a modern Western virtue: Many African societies, like medieval Christian and Islamic societies, prized it highly. Slave men fought and even killed other men who had sexual relations with their women. Women also fought and sometimes killed each other over men. The complexities of modern attitudes toward sexuality and the sexual values of other peoples should not prevent us from recognizing that a high level of violence resulted from slave men's inability to exercise the domination over women that most societies have awarded to men.

If struggles among slave women and slave men testified to the oppressive power of masters, they hardly constituted effective resistance to it. The lack of sanction for slave marriages placed an almost unbearable burden on individuals who were forced to defend their personal commitments without the assistance of enforceable conventions. The slave community developed its own conventions, but even those informal collective sanctions were vulnerable to wanton intervention on the part of whites who, whatever their commitment to the decorous behavior and orderly conduct of their people, had little personal stake in their slaves' independent community life. Slaveholders who were committed Christians had strong reasons of conscience as well as of social stability for encouraging monogamy and family life among their slaves, but even they remained torn between their ideals and the economic exigencies that could lead them at any time to break up marriages and families through sale. And even Christian masters dealt with slave women primarily as individuals rather than as socially defined wives, daughters, and mothers.

The churches did better than the masters in supporting slave marriage, but even they remained essentially powerless. By the 1830s they had irrevocably committed themselves to the defense of slavery and could at best deal with individual cases on their own merits, without considering the context from which they derived. Thus a church could censure or expel a slave "husband" who beat his wife, just as it could a white husband, but such discipline remained more symbolic than real. Many slaveholders were committed to converting their slaves to Christianity, both to prove to themselves that they were indeed good Christian masters and mistresses and to encourage their slaves to observe their standards of personal probity. Christian slaves drew upon their own faith to reject the messages of docility and blind obedience and to project a future world in which the last would indeed be first. Their Afro-American Christianity contained the seeds of resistance and in many instances probably helped to spark outright rebellion, but in everyday life it did not offer an unambiguous model of resistance.

Fannie Moore's mother "was trouble in her heart bout de way they treated. Ever night she pray for de Lawd to git her an' her chillun out ob de place." One day in the fields the light descended and she let out a big yell. "Den she sta't singin' an' a shoutin', an' a whoopin' an' a hollowin'." She seemed to plow all the harder. Upon her return, the master's mother asked her what had been going on and reminded her that she was out there to work and if she did not they would have the overseer whip her. "My mammy jes grin all over her black wrinkled face and say: 'I's saved. De Lawd done tell me I's saved. Now I know de Lord will show me de way. I ain't gwine a grieve no more. No matter how much yo' all done beat me an' my chillun de Lawd will show me de way. An' some day we nevah be slaves.'" The mistress got out her cowhide and set to work, but Fannie Moore's mother did not let out a peep and returned to the fields singing. Faith permitted Fannie Moore's mother to endure with equanimity and inner certainty and could, accordingly, be viewed as a source of resistance. But, like Celia Robinson's mother, who prayed for her infant to die, she did not resist in a way that threatened the everyday operation of the system.

Slave women resisted within the system by setting limits to the work they considered tolerable and the punishments they could endure. Afro-American Christianity and the fellowship of the slave community strengthened their internal resistance to slavery by strengthening their sense of identification with their own society and beliefs, by offering them a place in the world and an identity as members of a gender. The sources of their internal resistance helped to undercut the logic of slavery that reduced them to isolated individuals, but it also tended to undercut the more extreme forms of resistance by binding them to a viable community in this world and to the hope of salvation in the next. If the community or the faith failed them, or if the master decisively exceeded the limits of an authority that could begrudgingly be accepted as legitimate, they found themselves once again confronting the master in social and psychological isolation. Women in that situation frequently turned to a violent and contemptuous resistance for which they might pay with their own lives. One of Nancy Bean's aunts "was a mean, fighting woman." Her master, presumably because he could not master her, determined to sell her. "When the bidding started she grabbed a hatchet, laid her hand on a log and chopped it off. Then she throwed the bleeding hand right in her master's face." T. W. Cotton's aunt, Adeline, was another woman who refused to be whipped. One day when she thought that she would be, "she took a rope and tied it to a limb and to her neck and then jumped. Her toes barely touched the ground." Charlotte Foster knew a young girl of about sixteen who said "she'd as leave be dead as to take the beatings her master gave her." One day she simply went "into the woods and eat some poison oak. She died, too."

Resistance was woven into the fabric of slave women's lives and identities. If they defined themselves as wives, mothers, daughters, and sisters within the slave community that offered them positive images of themselves as women, they were also likely to define themselves in opposition to the images of the slaveholders for whom their status as slave ultimately outweighed their identity as woman. The ubiquity of their resistance ensured that its most common forms would be those that followed the patterns of everyday life: shirking, running off, "taking," sassing, defying. The extreme forms of resistance—murder, self-mutilation, infanticide, suicide—were rare. But no understanding of slave women's identities can afford to ignore them, for, if they were abnormal in their occurrence, they nonetheless embodied the core psychological dynamic of all resistance. The extreme forms captured the essence of self-definition: You cannot do that to me, whatever the price I must pay to prevent you.

Slave women normally resisted in forms determined within the household and in direct confrontation with masters, mistresses, and especially overseers. In most cases, they were punished within the same context, as befitted what was most comfortably viewed as a private matter. Murders, poisonings, infanticide, and arson could bring them to the courts, which recognized such acts as attacks against the system and accordingly recognized the slave women's legal standing as a criminal. Richard Mocks remembered a mulatto girl "of fine stature and good looks," who was put on sale. "Of high spirits and determined disposition," she refused to be coerced or forced. While she was awaiting sale, one of the traders took her to his room "to satisfy his bestial nature." During the ensuing struggle, she "grabbed a knife and with it, she sterilized him and from the result of injury he died the next day." She was tried for murder, but with the advent of the war she was taken to Washington and freed.

Arson, another favored form of violent resistance, was guaranteed to provoke the wrath of the law, for arson, even when directed at an individual master, constituted a danger to the whole area. Lee Guidon knew an old woman who set "Stingy Tom's" barn on fire, "and burned thirteen head of horses and mules together." Stingy Tom called the sheriff to try to get her to tell "what white folks put her up to do it. He knowed they all hated him cause he jes' so mean." The woman "never did tell but they hung her anyhow.

There was a big crowd to see it." The courts did not view women accused of arson as mere extensions of their masters' wills: "The Rolling-house was maliciously burnt by a Negro woman of the Defts. [defendant] whereof she was Convicted . . . and Executed for it." The court, which was unwilling to convict the woman's master for the crime, held that he "is not Chargeable for the wilful wrong of his servant."

Slave women resisted their enslavement, as women and as individuals, in all the ways available to them, according to their particular situations and their particular temperaments. Like other women of oppressed groups everywhere, they participated in their people's struggle for national liberation and self-determination. Like other women in comparable struggles, depending upon specific conditions, they were found in almost any role from leadership to armed combat to spying to a variety of less dramatic ones. As in other struggles for national or class liberation, at least some women resisted with no regard for their ascribed gender roles. There was no form of insurrectionary struggle in which some women did not, at some time, engage. Nontheless, with the consolidation of white slaveholding society and the slave community, slave women effectively disappeared from the leadership of formal revolts. That disappearance had nothing to do with the ferocity of their personal opposition to slavery, but it probably had much to do with the emergence of a slave community that naturally viewed the reestablishment of gender relations as the necessary foundation for long-term collective resistance.

The disappearance of women from visible roles in formal revolt does not mean that they did not continue to support those efforts in decisive ways. Enslaved and oppressed peoples, as Frantz Fanon movingly demonstrates in "Algeria Unveiled," have readily taken advantage of the "invisibility" of their women in the interests of a victorious struggle. For the black men who left firsthand accounts of their struggle against slavery, the invisibility of women was essential, because in struggling against oppression they regarded the affirmation of their own independent manhood as central to the argument that they and their people deserved freedom. The records that they constructed constituted an integral part of the struggle itself.

Yet, as Vincent Harding has particularly insisted, the various records of revolts invariably make some mention of churches or funerals or religious gatherings as a backdrop for rebellion. Afro-American religion, including secret black churches and religious meetings and networks, provided a focal point for slave organizations. Those churches and secret religious networks undoubtedly provided the institutional links between acts of individual resistance and collective revolts. Women were not much more prominent as religious than as military leaders, although they occasionally held high positions in the churches, especially in New Orleans and in conjunction with the persistence of voodoo. It is nonetheless difficult to believe that informal—and perhaps formal—associations of women, or sisterhoods, did not extend women's networks into slave religious communities. Especially after the prohibition of separate black churches, such associations would likely have been as secret as the congregations to which they were linked.

Like black men, whose associations took shape so rapidly during Reconstruction, black women probably developed associations under slavery that were rooted in African culture. Such gender groupings are reasonably common in societies in which gender constitutes one of the principal forms of social organization, as it did among many West African peoples, and the same spirit doubtless informed the female community of slaves. It is plausible to assume that the community of female slaves generated some kind of religious sisterhood, however fragile and informal. At the least, slave women indisputably saw themselves as sisters in religion, as essential members of the religious community of slaves. To the extent that the religious community provided the context or underpinnings for slave revolts, the women of that community constituted its backbone—not least because, not being active members of the revolt, they did not risk being cut down with their brothers. They would live to keep the tradition alive.

Slave women participated in discussions of revolts and in shaping the emerging political goals of their people. Daniel Goddard's parents and their friends frequently discussed political matters in his presence. They spoke of the Nat Turner insurrection in Virginia and the Vesey plot in Charleston. "I learned that revolts of slaves in Martinique, Antigua, Santiago, Caracas and Tortigua was known all over the South. Slaves were about as well aware of what was going on, as their masters were," although the masters tried not to share such information with them. The masters had reason to be cautious.

Maria Thompson was present at many discussions in which "de scared slaves would git together and talk about dere freedom. Dey would git together, polish up dere huntin' guns and be ready to start somethin'." The slaves had one main ambition: "to git dere freedom, but de mawsters had better not hear about it." Slave women, none-theless, did their best to make sure that the slaves learned of the masters' discussions. During the war, Elizabeth Russell was still small, "yet I served my people as a secret service agent." She spent her days in the big house to "attend the babies" and "would often pretend to be asleep" in order to overhear "the folk at the big house" talk about the battles "and which side was winning or losing and when the word came that the north had won and the slaves were free, it was I who carried the word to the hundreds of slaves in our section." Though she was only a little child, "God used me as a bearer of good news to my people."

Withal, the common denominator of the innumerable ways in which slave women opposed their own enslavement lay in the indi-vidual will. Normally, that will does not appear naked, but comes wrapped in gender, in race, in class—in the complex of relations that composes any social system. Absolute rejection of slavery results in the stripping away of those wraps, of those components of self as a social being. Slave women's absolute rejection of their own enslave-ment has, at the extreme limit, no history and is not gender specific. The recognizable patterns of slave women's resistance to and of their participation in revolts against slavery as a social system has a history and is gender specific. These patterns of resistance and revolt derive from the interaction of slaves with other slaves, with slaveholders, with nonslaveholding whites, and with free blacks in specific societ-ies.

There is a danger in insisting upon the specific experience of women as women: We can miss the determined struggle of the in-dividual soul and consciousness against reduction to the status of thing. However deeply slave women themselves felt their exploita-tion and vulnerability as women, they also seem to have insisted, in the end, on their oppression as slaves. Despite the extensive com-mentary that has arisen from Judge Thomas Ruffin's celebrated de-cision in *State* v. *Mann* (1824), there has been almost no comment on the sex of the slave who provoked the action that led to the case. Lydia "had committed some small offence, for which the Defendant undertook to chastise her—that while in the act of so doing, the slave ran off, whereupon the Defendant called upon her to stop, which being refused, he shot at and wounded her." The supreme court of North Carolina reversed the conviction of the white man. In Ruffin's words: "The Power of the master must be absolute to render the submission of the slave perfect." Power and submission: The conflict pitted one will against another. Time and again, slave women in their resistance confirmed that they, too, saw the conflict as one between the master's will and their own.

The ultimate resistance lay in the ultimate loneliness—the absolute opposition of power and submission, of one will to another. In that extreme case, gender counted for little. Gender counted increasingly as the vitality and vigor of the slave community and slave culture anchored individuals into a viable world—anchored them as women and as men in relation to other women and other men. The political division of labor by gender that came to characterize Afro-American slaves' resistance to slavery testifies to a growing commitment not merely to escaping from or defying their enslavement as individuals, but to replacing the prevailing social system with a more just one.

United States Slavery in

Comparative Perspective

George M. Fredrickson

THE ORIGINS OF RACIAL SLAVERY IN VIRGINIA AND SOUTH AFRICA

George M. Fredrickson, a historian at Stanford University, presents a significant contrast between the evolution of slavery in Virginia and its emergence in South Africa. He argues that the social and economic pressures for a stable source of exploitable labor in seventeenth-century Virginia encouraged the English to override an earlier reluctance to enslave fellow Christians among the Africans and that they thus proceeded to create a racial caste of hereditary bondsmen. In the Cape colony of southern Africa the Dutch remained uncomfortable with the practice of enslaving people who practiced the same religion as they did, so they strove to maintain a distinct cultural separation between themselves and their African slaves. The establishment of white supremacy in South Africa therefore rested more firmly on a tradition of cultural apartheid than it did in the United States.

According to John C. Hurd, the great mid-nineteenth-century authority on the law of American slavery, heathen Africans imported into the American colonies were from the outset regarded and treated as slaves—despite the lack of positive legislation authorizing chattel servitude—because "the *law of nations* for Christian powers" sanctioned such status for "prisoners in war with heathen and infidel nations." Local legislation was nevertheless required, Hurd contended, first to qualify their status as mere property or merchandise by recognizing that for some purposes they were legal persons, and secondly to justify their continued enslavement after they had been converted to Christianity. International law or the custom of nations may not have been as clear-cut as Hurd believed, but the gist of his argument deserves to be taken seriously. His thesis that original enslavement on religious grounds was followed by local action shifting the basis to ethnic or racial origin has not been accorded much respect by recent historians, mainly because doubts have arisen as to

From *White Supremacy: A Comparative Study in American and South African History*, pp. 76–85 by George M. Fredrickson. Copyright © 1981 by Oxford University Press, Inc. Reprinted by permission.

whether the first blacks to arrive in the colonies were indeed subjected to *de facto* slavery. As a result of what appears to have occurred in Virginia, a belief has grown up that the imposition of lifetime servitude developed only gradually and that the eventual sanctioning of slavery for converts was merely one aspect of the process of legalizing a unique status for blacks that had evolved over several decades.

The facts are fragmentary, but this much at least is definitely known of the situation of blacks in early Virginia: of the relatively small number who arrived in the colony between 1619 and the middle of the century, some were or became free while others were serving for life—at least by the 1640s when cases involving black servitude began to appear in court records. During that decade there were approximately 300 blacks in Virginia, representing about 2.5 percent of a total population of 15,000. The fact that all blacks were not slaves makes it possible that the earliest arrivals, the handful who arrived before the 1630s, were actually considered term rather than lifetime servants, because the notion that slavery was the proper status for imported Africans had not yet taken hold.

But there is another possibility, equally plausible as an interpretation of the local evidence and somewhat more persuasive in the light of international opinion concerning whom it was rightful to enslave. The census and other data of the first decade of black immigration suggest that many of the earliest arrivals had already been baptized. The prevalence of Spanish names among them has led Wesley Frank Craven to speculate that they were "probably native to America" and that "it is possible that some or all of them were Christian," having been previously converted by the Spaniards. It is known that the first twenty, who arrived in 1619, had been captured from the Spanish by a Dutch privateer cruising in the West Indies and that a child born in Virginia to one couple from this group was baptized, while his parents were not, presumably because they had already been converted. In 1624 a case came before the General Court that provides presumptive evidence of the consequence of prior conversion among Africans. A Negro named John Phillip was accorded the status of a free man and allowed to give testimony in a suit because he had been "Christened in *England* 12 years since." It appears very likely, therefore, that the class of blacks who were either free or engaged as servants for a limited term originated not so much from uncertainty about the legitimacy of slavery *per se* as from the operation of the principle that baptized slaves could not be held in perpetual bondage. If, as seems probable, a greater proportion of the larger number who arrived in the 1630s were heathens, then the emergence of lifetime servitude could well have resulted primarily from a shift in the religious status of new arrivals.

If this hypothesis is valid, it bears out John C. Hurd's contention that the introduction of *heathen* slavery into an English colony caused no ideological or legal problem, and one might conclude that recent historians have made too much of the apparent confusion and inconsistency surrounding the status of imported Africans in Virginia before the formal recognition of slavery in the 1660s. No comparable uncertainty seems to have shrouded the initial process of heathen enslavement in other British colonies established in the early seventeenth century. If, as Hurd suggested, heathen slavery could exist for a time without positive legal sanctions, it becomes quite conceivable that all or most of the non-Christian slaves who arrived in Virginia before the era of legislative clarification were held by their masters, as a matter of course, for just as long as their services were desired. This might in some cases have been less than their lifetimes because of the tendency existing in any slave society for masters to manumit slaves whose declining work capabilities have made them no longer worth their keep or whose unusually faithful service is deemed to merit an exceptional reward.

The important decision of the 1660s in Virginia was not that there could be slaves, for there already were, but that converted slaves could thenceforth be held in bondage. Fragmentary evidence suggests that the legislation of 1667 implementing this principle negated an enforceable right, not just a remote legal possibility. In 1644, the General Assembly determined in the case of Manuel, a baptized mulatto who had originally been purchased as a "Slave for Ever," that he was liable only "to serve as other Christians do."* In two later cases for which some records survive—Elizabeth Key's suit of 1655–56 and that of Fernando in 1667—conversion was explicitly used to support a claim for freedom. Although the final dispo-

---

*But the fact that Manuel was not actually freed for twenty-one years may be an indication of ethnic discrimination among Christian servants; for his was a longer obligation than any known to have been imposed on white indentured workers.

sition and grounds for resolution of these cases remain obscure, the fact that they were entertained by the courts and seriously litigated had led Warren Billings to conclude that as late as the 1660s "a nexus existed between an African's religion and his status as a laborer in Virginia. Conversion to Christianity evidently conferred upon blacks a rank higher than that of a slave. If an African retained his native religion, in all likelihood he stayed a slave, but if he converted or were born into slavery and baptized, his conversion or baptism could provide grounds for his release from life servitude." In 1667, the Assembly sought to remedy this situation by proclaiming "that the conferring of baptism doth not alter the condition of a person as to his bondage or freedom." But this first statutory sanction for Christian slavery applied directly only to slaves who had been baptized after they had arrived in the colony; the presumption of freedom for those who were Christians before their importation remained, as shown by a law of 1670 prescribing "that all servants *not* being Christians, imported into the colony by shipping, shall be slaves for life." The loophole of prior conversion was finally closed in 1682 by an enactment making slaves of all those arriving "whose parentage and native country are not Christian at the time of their first purchase . . . by some Christian." From this point on, heathen descent rather than actual heathenism was the legal basis for slavery in Virginia.

Although the language was still that of religious distinctions, the concept of heathen ancestry was a giant step toward making racial differences the foundation of servitude. Winthrop Jordan has cogently described how the equation of whiteness with Christianity and freedom and of blackness with heathenism and slavery gradually took hold in a way that obscured any contrary facts or possibilities. According to the clergyman Morgan Godwyn, who published a book in 1680 advocating increased efforts to Christianize blacks and Indians: "These two words, *Negro* and *Slave*," have "by custom grown Homogeneous and Convertible; even as *Negro* and *Christian, Englishman* and *Heathen,* are by the like corrupt nature and Partiality made *opposites;* thereby as it were implying that the one could not be *Christians,* nor the other *Infidels.*" The legal developments and semantic tendencies that in effect made the disabilities of heathenism inheritable and inextricably associated with blackness laid the groundwork for what I have elsewhere called "societal racism," or the relegation of members of a racial or ethnic group to a status that implies that they are innately inferior, even though there is no explicit ideology on which to base such an assertion.

It would probably confuse cause and effect, however, to view the transition to racial slavery as motivated primarily by color prejudice. There is no doubt that the blackness of Africans was an important part of what made them seem so alien and different to white Virginians. But planters also had very strong economic and social incentives to create a caste of hereditary bondsmen. For Virginia planters, slaves probably became a better long-term investment than servants by 1660. Although limited availability, high prices, and the large initial outlay of capital required meant that only men who already possessed substantial wealth were able to take advantage of the opportunity—while lesser planters had to continue to rely almost exclusively on indentured servants—such a propertied elite could readily use its dominance over colonial assemblies to pass laws protecting its growing economic stake in lifetime bondage. The Maryland law of 1664 requiring all Negroes to serve *"durante vita"* so that they could not claim freedom by professing Christianity quite candidly justified this measure as necessary to protect the property interests of the masters. The Virginia law of three years later had a somewhat different rationale; its alleged intent was to encourage owners to convert their slaves free of any fear that proselytizing would lead to emancipation. But the underlying assumption was clear—masters wanted to keep their slaves in lifetime service, so the law should enable them to do so. In the words of Wilbert Moore, both laws indicated that "there was a conflict between profitable slavery and the spread of Christianity." The fact that Virginia planters continued to resist baptism even after the law was passed may indicate which of the two objectives had the higher priority. Fateful as it may have been for the future of race relations, the original decision to create what amounted to a racially derived status probably arose less from a consciousness of racial privilege than from palpable self-interest on the part of members of a dominant class who had been fortunate enough to acquire slaves to supplement or replace their fluctuating force of indentured servants.

Whatever might have been the situation in Virginia, there was no uncertainty at the Cape [colony] about the initial status of imported heathens. Slavery was already an established institution in the domain of the Dutch East India Company, and nonwhite slaves were present in the colony almost from the beginning. For the Dutch, like the English, the victims of the slave trade had legitimately forfeited their status as persons under the law and custom of nations and become a form of merchandise, which meant that they had only such rights as the authorities of the colonies into which they were introduced were willing to grant them as a matter of expediency. The Dutch had the advantage of having somewhat less need than the English to spell out the full legal conditions of servitude and could make do for extended periods without elaborate slave codes. During the whole period that the Dutch occupied what later became New York, they gave no explicit recognition to the institution in statutory law despite a heavy reliance on slave labor. Pre-existing East Indian statutes could be applied at the Cape, but it remains noteworthy that a comprehensive local slave code was not promulgated for a full century. English colonies moved rapidly to formal legal sanctions when the numbers of slaves warranted such action, because the common law of England made no provision for slavery; the Dutch could be more casual, because the statutory law governing the Netherlands was based directly on Roman law, with its ample precedents for regulating slave status. Although the aspects of Roman law pertaining to slavery were held to be inapplicable to the Netherlands itself, they were customarily applied in the colonies to govern situations for which the statutes made no clear provisions.

If the legal implications of slavery as an institution presented little problem for the Dutch, the question of the status of baptized slaves was even more troublesome than for the English because . . . the Synod of Dort had made it contrary to the official doctrines of the Dutch Reformed Church to hold converted heathens in chattel servitude. The Dutch East India Company and its colonies were in effect barred from following the example of Virginia and Maryland and explicitly legalizing Christian slavery. Religious authorities sometimes wished them to go further and actively enforce the principle of "Christian freedom." In 1681, the Church Council of Batavia advised the Cape government that masters who baptized their slaves were responsible for emancipating them.

In the early years at the Cape, the Company did encourage the baptism of its own slaves and even established schools in which they could be instructed in Protestant Christianity. But there was no clear policy requiring that the converts be manumitted, and the majority of them were not in fact freed. In 1685, High Commissioner van Rheede of the East India Company visited the Cape and left behind a number of instructions concerning the Company's slaves, including some guidelines for the manumission of those who professed Reformed Christianity. Noting that there were a large number of slave children in the Company's lodge who had Dutch fathers, he ordered that these half-castes be raised as Dutch-speaking Christians, taught useful trades, and then emancipated and granted free burgher status when they were grown, boys to be freed at twenty-five and girls at twenty-two. As for the full-blooded slaves of the Company, they were to be considered *eligible* for manumission after thirty years of service if imported or at the age of forty if born at the Cape, provided that they had been converted and spoke Dutch. Although this policy may seem generous in its implications, it fell short of implementing the principle that Christians could not be kept in chattel slavery. The manumission of baptized slaves who had two heathen parents was made a privilege rather than a right, and the eligibility requirements applied only to slaves of the Company and not to those in private hands.

Furthermore, it appears from evidence concerning subsequent manumissions by the Company that van Rheede's plan was never actually put into effect. By the early eighteenth century, the Company was protecting its investment in a servile labor force by responding to all petitions for the emancipation of one of its adult slaves by requiring that another slave be supplied to take the place of the freedman; in the case of children substantial monetary compensation was demanded. In 1708, a restriction was placed on the right of burghers to emancipate their own bondsmen; owners thenceforth had to provide a guarantee that their ex-slaves would not be dependent on the communal poor fund for ten years. There is no indication that the new limitations on emancipation made any exception for baptized slaves. A Dutch Reformed minister then resident at the Cape complained to church authorities in Amsterdam in 1708 that slaves who were church members were being kept in bondage and were subject to being sold or inherited, despite the fact that such practices were contrary to "Christian freedom."

Although the doctrine of "Christian freedom" was not being adhered to in practice, the presumption that baptized slaves had a right to emancipation if they could somehow enforce it persisted throughout the eighteenth century. The inevitable result was that masters saw to it that few of their slaves were formally converted. A German who resided at the Cape in the 1730s later reported that "there is a common and well-grounded belief that Christians must not be held in bondage; hence only such children as are intended for emancipation are baptised." A Swedish scientist visiting the Cape in the 1770s described some psalm-singing slaves who had not been christened, "since by that means, according to the law of the land, they would have obtained their freedom and [their master] would have lost them from his service." Comparable resistance to Christianization persisted among American slaveholders long after the laws had made it clear that their property rights would not be affected; missionaries were seriously impeded in their proselytizing efforts until late in the eighteenth century by fears that slaves would not grasp the distinction between spiritual and temporal equality. At the Cape, where a body of legal and religious precedent was actually on the side of the converted slave seeking to change his or her condition, the intensity of opposition to Christianization can readily be imagined.

This situation in fact had the remarkable effect of encouraging a tolerance for Islam as an alternative slave religion. Malays and other East Indian slaves who brought their faith with them were not only allowed to practice it, but even to proselytize among other non-Christian slaves. Although such toleration was not an official policy, the lack of active persecution and repression must have reflected a sense among the whites that there were some practical advantages in having Muslim slaves. When the British took over the colony, they were shocked at the extent to which the Dutch had allowed Islam to spread in the slave population, and in 1808 the new government called for increased missionary activity in order to counter this tendency. But in 1820, when the first survey was taken of the religious affiliations of the slaves, it was revealed that there were three times as many Muslims as Christians among them. In order to discover how such a thing could have occurred in a Christian colony, a commission listened to the testimony of a Malay priest who described how Islam had found a haven in a Christian slave society by teaching its adherents such religious obligations as obedience to masters and abstinence from alcohol. In the eighteenth century, when there were constant complaints of drunkenness among slaves—as might be expected in a colony which listed wine and brandy among its most important commodities—many masters must have welcomed the services of a teetotalling Muslim. But probably even more important in encouraging the policy of *de facto* tolerance toward the traditional enemies of Christendom was the fact that there could be no question of any obligation to free a Muslim slave.

The Council of the Indies in Batavia, a governing body with jurisdiction over the Cape, finally resolved the issue of the effect of baptism on slave status in 1770 when it issued a regulation that Christian slaves could not be sold or otherwise alienated by their masters. This fell short of requiring their manumission, but it did follow the prescription of the Council of Dort to the extent that it exempted them from the full rigors of chattel servitude. To the degree that this law was enforced at the Cape—and there is some evidence from testamentary documents that it was—it probably confirmed the fears of masters that Christianization would limit their property interests and served as an added discouragement to proselytization. In an effort to allay these fears by stressing that outright emancipation was still not required, a local church council of 1792 made the first explicit statement that had ever come from any official or authoritative body in the Cape to the effect that neither the law nor the Church prevented a master from retaining possession of his baptized slaves. But it was the British administration of 1812 that finally removed all doubt by formally nullifying the 1770 regulation of the Council of the Indies on the grounds that any restriction on the right of a master to dispose of his slaves as he saw fit impeded the progress of Christianity. Enunciating a principle that had long been established in British slave colonies, the Chief Justice wrote to the governor that he could not "deduce from the true principles of our religion why a slave here cannot be a *slave* and at the same time a *Christian*."

In a much slower and more uncertain fashion than in the southern colonies, the criterion for enslavement had thus shifted from heathenism to what could only be racial origin. The latter principle was not made explicit at the end of the process, any more than it had been in the South more than a century earlier, but it was clearly implied by the fact that it was no longer religion *and* race but race alone that was the essential distinguishing mark of the slave class.

It may have been of lasting significance that the official disassociation of heathenism and slavery took so much longer in South Africa than in the South. In the latter instance, early resolution of the issue in favor of hereditary racial slavery helped create favorable conditions for a trend toward the acceptance or encouragement of slave conversion that picked up momentum in the late eighteenth century. This new receptivity to the propagation of the gospel in the quarters was due partly to the rise of a more evangelical form of Christianity after the Great Awakening of the mid-eighteenth century and partly to the fact that an increasing majority of the slaves were American born, making them seem better raw material for baptism than the "outlandish" Africans who had predominated earlier. But what allowed the trend to persist and develop into the more substantial missionary effort of the pre–Civil War era was the growing conviction of slaveholders—and eventually even of the southern evangelical clergymen who had earlier expressed doubts about the compatibility of slavery and Christianity—that assimilation of the whites' religion did not give the blacks any claim to freedom or equality and might in fact make them better slaves by instilling the Pauline doctrine that obedience to masters was a Christian duty.

No such trend of thought developed among slaveholders at the Cape before the British-imposed emancipation of the 1830s, despite the government's active encouragement of the Christianization of slaves. To some extent this difference can be explained by the fact that there was no major evangelical revival among the Dutch settlers. But the continued resistance to mission work, which left most slaves without religion of any kind or secure in their Islamic faith right up to the time they were freed, may also have represented the persistence of patterns of thought inculcated during the century and a half when Christian slavery was under a cloud. It appears that South African masters remained acutely uncomfortable with slaves or other nonwhite dependents who practiced the same religion and thus partook of the same cultural heritage as themselves. Indeed, the kind of "homogeneity" between "white" and "Christian" or "black" and "heathen" that Morgan Godwyn found in late-seventeenth-century Virginia persisted in the discourse of the Afrikaners until late in the nineteenth century. What is more, they made strenuous efforts to see that these linguistic correlations mirrored reality—by neglecting and sometimes vigorously discouraging the propagation of Christianity among their nonwhite dependents. Since they craved a cultural gap as well as a racial one, they preferred to allow color and religion to remain reinforcing aspects of differentness rather than making a clear decision, such as was made in the South, as to which was to have priority. The long delay in the full legitimation of racial slavery may therefore have been one factor making the South African white-supremacist tradition more dependent on cultural pluralism than the American.

Peter Kolchin

AMERICAN SLAVERY AND RUSSIAN SERFDOM

Slaves in the United States and serfs in Russia each sought to establish and follow their own customs. Peter Kolchin of the University of Delaware finds, however, that American slavery was more corrosive of slave autonomy than its counterpart of serfdom was in Russia. Slaves were subject to racism, geographic displacement, and the eventual erosion of African culture in the New World. A minority in the total southern population, they lived on relatively small farms and plantations. In contrast, the Russian serfs composed a majority of the total population and belonged to the same ethnic group as their masters. Serfs worked on large estates, supported themselves, and dwelled in their own ancestral villages. Unlike slaves, serfs usually had little direct contact with their masters. Serfs and slaves were unfree and held to the service of a dominant class, but, Kolchin argues, the different social conditions of their bondage explain the stronger ties of community among serfs.

Reprinted by permission of the publishers from *Unfree Labor: American Slavery and Russian Serfdom*, pp. 195–200, 233–236 by Peter Kolchin, Cambridge, Mass.: The Belknap Press of Harvard University Press, copyright © 1987 by the President and Fellows of Harvard College.

It was one thing for the masters to prescribe the nature of estate management and life but another to put those prescriptions into effect. In both Russia and the American South the bondsmen endeavored to follow their own customs, adhere to their own values, and develop their own style of life apart from—and largely unknown to—their owners. Perceptive observers noted that the bondsmen rarely revealed their feelings to outsiders. "Persons live and die in the midst of Negroes and know comparatively little of their real character," noted South Carolina minister and planter Charles C. Jones. "The Negroes are a distinct class in community, and keep very much to *themselves*. They are one thing before the whites, and another before their own color." Travelers to Russia, like those to the South, saw "cunning" and "deception" as prime traits of the bondsmen's character and attributed it to their desire to keep their lives as free as possible of owner control. "The character of the peasant is a profound abyss, to the bottom of which no eye can pierce," asserted Frenchman Germain de Lagny. "Like the Negro . . . he practices the art of dissimulation to an extent of which it is perfectly impossible to convey an idea." Because absolute regulation of the bondsmen's lives was impossible, slaves and serfs were able, in slave quarters and peasant villages, to lead lives that were at least partially autonomous from the influences of their masters.

The nature and degree of that autonomy, however, differed in the two countries. For a number of reasons the serfs found it easier than the slaves to achieve substantial independence from outside forces, and they were able to forge communal values, customs, and organizations based on centuries of tradition. Although the slaves, like the serfs, developed a culture that differed significantly from that of their owners, they found it more difficult to create their own collective forms and norms, and their communal life was more attenuated. Ultimately, slavery impinged to a greater degree in a more corrosive manner on the independence of American blacks than serfdom did on that of Russian peasants.

Strikingly different environments helped shaped the lives of the Russian and American bondsmen. Most obvious was the contrast between the historical continuity experienced by the former and the discontinuity experienced by the latter. Slaves in the United States, as in the rest of the Americas, were the descendants of Africans uprooted from their homes and forced to live in an alien world, whereas serfs in Russia resided on their ancestral lands. The serfs, unlike the slaves, lived "at home" in a traditional world where customs had emerged over the centuries and changed but slowly.

Any examination of slave life in the American South must consequently begin by taking account of the foreign origins of the slave population. These origins were responsible for the particular complexity associated with the topic of American slave culture, because intertwined with the class dimension—the lives, values, and responses of slaves—is the ethnic dimension resulting from those slaves' distinctive background. Slave culture was at first also African culture; to the extent that slaves had ancient customs handed down from generation to generation, these were, perforce, of African origin. Yet subsequent generations of slaves in America were not themselves Africans but a new people, shaped by their new surroundings. This newness gives rise to a series of questions concerning slave culture: To what extent did the descendants of Africans transmit to their children the ways of their ancestors? What changes did those ways undergo under the influence of the dominant white society? How, in turn, did the dominant whites adapt to African influences? In short, what is the relationship between the culture of southern slaves and their peculiar background?

Although scholars have differed sharply on these questions, there can be no denying the pervasive impact of historical discontinuity on the character of slave life in America. By the second half of the eighteenth century the slave population was already overwhelmingly creole or native rather than African-born, and after the ending of slave imports in 1808 the proportion of first-generation Americans in the slave population faded to insignificance. As a result the language, diet, religion, and most customs of the slaves became "Americanized," although, like other ethnic groups, blacks retained remnants of their traditional culture and in turn helped to shape the dominant culture, influencing a broad range of southern features from pronunciation of English to diet and agriculture. The strongest African survivals occurred in black music, which eventually exerted a powerful influence on American music in general, and in certain folk practices such as medicine and magic. In areas of especially heavy black concentration African influences were sometimes more persistent, and assimilation into the mainstream of American culture was slower and more tenuous; on the sea islands off South Carolina and Georgia, for example, blacks continued into the twentieth century to speak a "Gullah" dialect unintelligible to those unfamiliar with it. On the whole, however, African traditions were less persistent among slaves in the United States than in most of the Caribbean and Brazil, because African-born slaves in the United States quickly became a small and diminishing proportion of the black population, because in the South blacks lacked the numerical preponderance they enjoyed in many other New World slave societies, and because southern slaveowners impinged so greatly on the lives of their people. The forced migration of hundreds of thousands of slaves to the American South thus resulted in a cultural break of major proportions; the Afro-American descendants of early imports were less African in their beliefs and behavior than American.

This discontinuity was evident in numerous social forms. The West African religious orientation, in which people lived in close proximity to gods personifying natural phenomena—trees, rivers, rain—and to spirits of ancestors who if properly propitiated watched over their descendants, was largely lost by the second generation. During the century preceding emancipation white southerners pressed with increasing vigor the conversion and religious instruction of their slaves, and John W. Blassingame has suggested that "the church was the single most important institution for the 'Americanization' of the bondsman." As one recent scholar put it, "in the United States the gods of Africa died." The same was true of traditional polygamous and extended family groupings. But perhaps most basic of all was the transformation of the West Africans' communal life-style. The ancestors of American slaves lived in villages that dominated virtually every aspect of life, from religious ritual to kinship and political relations. Lacking any concept of private property, they worked together, in communal groups, on communal land; tradition linked the individual—who counted for little—to family, clan, and village, and through these to ancestors and spirits. Because "the village was the family writ large," the slave trade to America not only tore apart families but also fragmented the communal identity and consciousness of their members. Africans survived in the United States, but their traditional way of life did not.

Over the course of two and one-half centuries blacks in America developed customs and values different from those of both their African forebears and their white owners. Historical discontinuity interacted with the development of a distinctive Afro-American life-style to render southern slave culture a continually changing phenomenon. Some of its most widely noted attributes were most evident during the early colonial period but lost their salience as the African consciousness receded. Others were relatively late developments: black Christianity, for example, was largely a product of the century before emancipation and reached its apogee only during the last half-century. The slave experience, in short, was as subject to historical change as that of other Americans.

Although remnants of African tradition melded into this Afro-American culture and prevailing white mores strongly influenced it, its basis was the shared experience of blacks in American slavery, and the crucible in which it was forged was the slave quarters. Although blacks were unable to reproduce the African communities of their ancestors, the slave quarters facilitated the emergence of new communal standards and relationships. Although slaves held in very small units almost invariably lived in or near the houses of their owners, plantation hands usually resided in the quarters, a collection of huts grouped together in a semivillage some distance from the dwellings of owner and overseer. This relative isolation afforded millions of slaves a degree of independence and enabled them to enjoy a partially autonomous life-style.

In the quarters slaves prayed and partied, lived and loved, in great measure out of the control—and sight—of whites. As one historian has put it, "While from sunup to sundown the American slave worked for another and was harshly exploited, from sundown to sunup he lived for himself and created the behavioral and institutional basis which prevented him from becoming the absolute victim." To a degree slaveowner paternalism facilitated this independence, by providing the necessary breathing space for slaves to live their own lives as well as by giving them the frequent opportunity to hold dances, barbecues, celebrations, and prayer meetings. About ten days after Charles Ball arrived on his new plantation in South Carolina, his owner arranged a huge feast for the slaves to celebrate completion of the harvest. "I doubt if there was in the world a happier assemblage than ours, on this Saturday evening," Ball wrote later. That night, they celebrated with dancing, singing, and storytelling, and on Sunday afternoon "we had a meeting, at which . . . a man named Jacob . . . sang and prayed"; meanwhile, "great many of the people went out about the plantation, in search of fruits . . . With us, this was a day of uninterrupted happiness." Numerous other blacks had similar recollections. "Whoopee, didn' us have good Sa'dd'y night frolics and jubilees," remembered one. "Some clap and some play de fiddle, and, man, dey danced all night. Cornshucking was 'nother big frolic."

Although slave communal life, for decades virtually ignored by historians, has in recent years received heavy emphasis from a new generation of scholars, the concept of the slave community has remained vague and poorly defined. . . . Of course, the term *community* has several legitimate meanings. Dictionary definitions include the purely physical—"a group of people living in the same locality and under the same government" or "the locality in which they live"—as well as the relational: "the quality of appertaining to all in common," or "society, the social state." Surely, however, it is primarily the latter connotation that is significant to us; all people live in a locality, and to argue that slaves lived in a community in this sense is a truism. The term has historical significance in terms of relations among people and implies some form of social organization regulating shared standards of behavior. As Thomas Bender argues, "Community . . . is best defined as a network of social relations marked by mutuality and emotional bonds." Crucial to this definition is a sense of solidarity—Bender calls it "we-ness"—stemming from common values, perceptions, and interests as well as from a sense of mutual or collective responsibility. The concept of community overlaps but is distinct from that of culture; the bondsmen's communal organizations were both prime examples of their cultural activities and vehicles through which most of those activities were expressed, but at the same time *community* constituted a special cultural form that must be isolated in order to prevent its obscuration and mystification.

When the slave community is seen in this way, an important observation concerns the rudimentary nature of its organization. Although the African community perished with the establishment of slavery in America, it was never fully replaced. The slave quarters functioned as a refuge from white control, but institutionally the slave community remained undeveloped, never assuming the concrete forms and functions that would enable it to serve as a basis around which the slaves could fully organize their lives. . . .

Clearly, the cultural break resulting from the forced migration from Africa to America fundamentally differentiated the experiences of American slaves and Russian serfs. The serfs were held on their home turf, where despite their bondage they could continue in many respects to live and act as their ancestors had; the slaves were torn from their homeland and held in a new continent where inevitably, despite strenuous efforts to preserve old ways, a drastic change in life-style and consciousness ensued. Geographic continuity or discontinuity was the most obvious single influence on the degree of cultural continuity among the bondsmen. In this respect the experience of serfs in Russia differed radically not only from that of slaves in the United States but also from that of slaves in other New World societies. The African diaspora was a fundamental fact of black slavery in the Americas, whereby black slaves became outsiders in white, European-derived societies.

There were a number of other significant causes, however, of the contrasting worlds and world views of the Russian and American bondsmen. Most of these have already been touched on and need only to be brought together, but a couple require slightly more elaboration. It is important to note that unlike the African diaspora these other elements did not separate the experience of Russian serfs from that of all New World slaves; concrete historical experiences differentiated the lives of Russian serfs and southern slaves, but the contrast was not one between slaves and serfs per se. Indeed, with respect to culture and community, Russian and American bondsmen stood at two extremes of a broad spectrum or continuum, on which slaves of other countries were fixed in varying more central locations.

Several demographic factors served to facilitate the development of autonomous communal behavior among the Russian serfs while severely restricting its potentiality among American slaves. Most obvious were the differing population mixes in the two countries. Whereas blacks were a minority in the South as a whole and about one-half of the population in the deep South, peasants constituted the overwhelming majority of Russians; similarly, the serfs were typically held in far larger units than the slaves. As a consequence the serfs had far more opportunity to lead autonomous lives than did the slaves. Among slaves held in very small groups the chance to partake of communal activities was often virtually non-existent, but even among most others simple population ratios meant that they came in contact with whites far more often than most serfs did with noblemen. The internal lives of bondsmen who were widely dispersed among many slaveholders in small units had to be very different from the lives of those who were concentrated among a tiny class of noblemen on large estates.

Even given the southern slaves' numerical disadvantage, an independent black culture could have been reinvigorated by a steady supply of new Africans keeping alive the memory of traditional ways and fostering resistance to European cultural penetration. Precisely this happened in some other New World slave societies. It is therefore significant that the American slave population was largely creole from an early date. In part, this was because alone among major slave societies the United States prohibited the importation of new slaves more than half a century before it abolished slavery, but even more important was the natural population growth that rendered American slaves overwhelmingly creole generations before the end of the slave trade. By the American Revolution only about one-fifth of American slaves were African-born, and during the first half of the nineteenth century the proportion of Africans among southern slaves was insignificant. In contrast to Brazil, Cuba, Haiti, and Jamaica, where traditional African culture was continually buttressed from without, in the United States during the century and a half before emancipation an increasingly creole slave population became more and more divorced from its ancestral roots.

Differences in owner attitudes and behavior strongly reinforced the dichotomy resulting from contrasting demographic patterns in Russia and the United States. The absentee orientation of pomeshchiki [nobles who were granted land by the czar on the condition of their continued loyalty to the czar] allowed most serfs a substantial measure of freedom from direct, day-to-day owner interference; even when serfs had resident owners, those owners usually concerned themselves much less than most American planters with the internal lives of their laborers. The absentee mentality of Russian noblemen thus served to strengthen the autonomy of peasant life. In the United States planter paternalism had the opposite impact: the constant meddling that it engendered in slaves' lives proved destructive of their communal independence. Paternalism not only provided antebellum slaves with one of the world's highest material standards of living; it also subjected them to constant white cultural penetration and thus seriously undermined their cultural autonomy. One might suggest that in a rough sense there was an inverse relationship between the coherence of the masters' civilization and the autonomy of the bondsmen's communal culture: where resident slaveowners took a lively interest in their communities and their property, as southern planters did, that interest tended to have a corrosive impact on the ability of the slaves to maintain their own communal values and customs; where owners tended toward absenteeism, the bondsmen were correspondingly freer to lead their own lives and develop their own separate communal standards. (The process worked the other way as well. Where the bondsmen were in a huge numerical majority and showed strong communal solidarity, their owners found it convenient to put an appropriate distance between themselves and their "brutish" property.)

There was, finally, an economic basis for the serf community that was largely lacking among American slaves: the existence of a secondary, peasant economy. Except for house servants, serfs grew their own food on their landed allotments and were self-supporting; in addition many—especially those on obrok* estates—raised goods for market on "their" land as well as cultivating their owners' fields. Of course, many southern slaves had garden plots whose produce they used to supplement their diets and even to earn pocket money for luxuries, and on the rice estates of coastal South Carolina and Georgia a real although limited slave economy developed as slaves raised and sold their "own" provisions on their "own" time. Nevertheless, the distinction was basic: the slaves received primary sustenance from their masters for whom they worked full-time, and when allowed they supplemented this by cultivating garden plots; the serfs were entirely self-supporting and were increasingly engaged in their own commercial operations. A major function of the commune was to regulate relations inhering in economic independence, from dividing peasant landholdings equitably to adjusting the rent they paid their owners. In short, communal independence rested on economic autonomy. In the slave South, where many planters believed that

---

Obrok was the feudal obligation or quitrent the serf paid in kind—foodstuffs or cash—to the lord for the use of seigneurial land.

allowing slave families to cook their own meals promoted excessive independence, the slave community lacked any corresponding economic function.

Thus, a series of fundamental differences between the experiences of American slaves and Russian serfs served to encourage autonomous communal life and culture among the latter and to restrict them among the former. The slaves were physically torn from their African roots, which grew increasingly remote as they became an almost entirely creole population; they constituted a minority of the southern population, both numerically and in the sense of being outsiders; they lived in relatively small groups on farms and small plantations, where a resident slaveowning class interacted with them on a daily basis, making every effort to limit their independence. The serfs lived on their ancestral lands, where—together with state peasants—they constituted a large majority of the population; they lived isolated from noblemen, whom they rarely saw, on large estates where, so long as they made money for their owners, they were often left free to do what they wanted; they were self-supporting and engaged in a flourishing, market-oriented economy of their own. The two groups were both unfree peoples forced to labor for the wellbeing of a parasitic class, but the environmental conditions of their bondage—conditions that largely determined what kinds of lives they could lead—were in many respects different.

Stanley L. Engerman

SLAVERY AND EMANCIPATION IN COMPARATIVE PERSPECTIVE

The following selection is from Stanley L. Engerman's presidential address in 1986 to the Economic History Association. His concern is the
broad topic of how slavery and emancipation influenced the economic
development of the Americas. He points out that the emergence of free-
wage labor in the northeastern states of the United States during the
nineteenth century was the exception rather than the rule in the Americas, where in 1850 slavery was economically an expansive and productive force. It took military and political power, not economic decline, to
end slavery in the United States. Emancipation and the breakup of the
plantation system were accompanied by a reduction in export crops,
except where contract labor was successfully employed or where a high
population density allowed large-scale production to persist. The contemporary debate over the transition from a slave- to free-labor economy reveals much about nineteenth-century perceptions, which historians can best illuminate, Engerman insists, by employing a variety of
approaches, including economics. Engerman is professor of economics
and history at the University of Rochester.

The view of slavery as the antithesis of progress, with its moral as
well as economic dimensions, is a theme developed and analyzed in
a recent book by David Brion Davis, entitled, with apparent irony,
Slavery and Human Progress. Whether the long and frequent equations of slavery with regression and antislavery with progress is best
regarded as an expression of contemporary belief, or as a nineteenth-
and twentieth-century view, may be an open question, as would be
any correlation of economic and moral progress.

Even without arguments about its economic role, however, the
topic of slavery has long been able to generate significant intellectual
controversy. There remain, for example, heated debates about the
extent to which Greek democracy (usually "a good thing") was

From Stanley L. Engerman, "Slavery and Emancipation in Comparative Perspective: A Look at Some Recent Debates," from *Journal of Economic History*, 46, June
1986, pp. 322–339. Reprinted with the permission of Cambridge University
Press.

linked to the existence of Greek slavery (always "not a good thing"), an issue recently raised for Virginia and (possibly generalized for the entire United States) by Edmund Morgan in his *American Slavery, American Freedom*. And a major debate in the nineteenth century concerned the extent to which the development of Christianity was the crucial factor in the decline of Roman slavery, a debate which, with appropriate transformations, has surfaced anew for the nineteenth-century process of emancipation. Thus controversies about slavery have a long history, and recent debates about the economics of slavery fall within this tradition, with their implications for some of the central views of the western world of the nineteenth and twentieth centuries.

Economic criticisms of slavery have been extensive, some raised as part of the movement against slavery, some recast by subsequent historical interpreters. There were two quite distinct strands in the literature of classical economics concerning slavery, with different implications for understanding the antislavery argument and, more importantly, the political, ideological, and economic circumstances of nineteenth-century emancipation.

First, and most familiar, is the argument that free labor will be more productive than slave labor because of the greater incentives of self-interest. The solution offered by Adam Smith to this early version of what is now called the principal-agent problem is the familiar one of changing property rights assignments—letting people own themselves. The incentive arguments in regard to slavery had actually surfaced much earlier in classical slavery, and were, in the nineteenth century also used in the attack on serfdom in Europe. . . .

There was a second aspect of the economic argument on slavery. Slavery was seen, by some, as one of the stages through which civilization would proceed—a necessary stage but one that would be superseded, somehow, by a more desirable system of freedom with free labor once population density grew sufficient to eliminate the necessity of slave labor. In some arguments, the economic preconditions of slavery were the unusual climatic conditions of those tropical areas where slavery was economically most central, with again the point that slavery was a stage to be gone through until some combination of the appropriate population density, "civilizing" of tropical residents, and a willingness (or ability) of Europeans to live in the tropics, would provide the desired transition to freed labor.

This set of arguments—with slavery as a stage in progressive economic development, but one with a limited productive capacity that might soon be reached—could, of course, reconcile the importance of the economic benefits of slavery in the settlement and expansion of Europeans overseas and for economic developments in Britain and the United States. The implication was that the process by which such benefits were achieved would soon pass and that slavery would come to an end with the next step forward of human progress. One may, of course, ask what the full implications of such "progress" would be. Descriptions, however accurate, of the ending of Roman slavery by a blending of slave and free workers into a serf labor force might suggest that a population-induced movement away from unfree labor may not always be "a good thing."

The role of the land-labor ratio has become familiar in recent work in economic history, following the lucid discussion by Evsey Domar. Actually, as he pointed out, in terms of the relative amounts of land and labor, the point was well-known and described by many early writers and policymakers. They understood that the availability of free land made labor more valuable, as well as permitting an alternative to working for others. There was also agreement on what the ending of free land and a larger population would mean—a reduction in the relative value of labor, leading in one case to a lowering of free labor incomes and, in another, a reduction in the value of slave labor.

A variant of the argument about the impact of increased labor relative to usable land has become familiar in the historiography of United States slavery as the "natural limits" argument—the contention that slavery would run out of land onto which expansion was possible and that it would therefore become unprofitable and "grind to a halt" of its own accord, with voluntary emancipation undertaken peacefully by slaveowners. The analysis of the impact of the frontier in the United States in influencing free-labor institutions and the rewards to free labor also had a long history before Frederick Jackson Turner, including that by many labor leaders throughout the nineteenth century. It, too, provided a variant of a stages view of history, linking present and future conditions in an inevitable process.

The emphasis on the available frontier and the role of labor mobility led many to a rather familiar prediction: that the unusual American conditions would soon be changing because of the "closing of the frontier." Thus the economic and political life of America would be dramatically changed, with a worsening of wage labor's economic position. Certainly it was this expectation that had led to the call for "free land" by laborers throughout the nineteenth century. Thus, for example, while most of the interest in Werner Sombart's 1906 work, *Why Is There No Socialism in the United States?* (really why there was no major U.S. labor movement with a political impact—still the central question for most labor historians, old and new) focuses on his political and economic explanations concerning the nineteenth-century experience, less attention is given to his concluding remarks forecasting a major transformation in the twentieth century. After a brief discussion of census data on land and labor, and following a long quote from Henry George, Sombart concludes: "all the factors that till now have prevented the development of Socialism in the United States are about to disappear or to be converted into their opposite, with the result that in the next generation Socialism in America will very probably experience the greatest possible expansion of its appeal."

As a forecast it was not very good and the same may be said about similar forecasts of the future course of wages. Wage increases in the twentieth century have been greater than those in the nineteenth century. Here, however, I want merely to note that the set of arguments that pointed to the expected economic demise of slavery in the United States—with its stress on land availability—was a prediction based upon a chain of reasoning that was also applied, at the same time, to the case of the economic conditions of free labor.

In the slavery debate, then and now, there were those who accepted the profitability of slavery under certain specified conditions but very clearly laid out the theoretical conditions for its demise—the limited land useful for slave-grown crops as well as the inabilities of slave societies to make those adjustments necessary to offset the absence of land for expansion. As statements of economic theory, such arguments about the demise of slavery, with their specified conditions, are obviously correct. What seems to me, however, to be the central issue is the distinction between the correctness of the theoretical logic and a proper statement of the time span over which such an outcome is to occur.

John Elliott Cairnes, in his classic on *The Slave Power,* for example, used terms such as "in due time," and "gradual but sure process," even quoting the *New British Review* (of 1862) to the effect that once "its [slavery's] doom is sealed . . . the execution of the sentence may seem to be relegated to a very distant day." Indeed much of the argument about the economic (and, also, perhaps the political) factors in the ending of slavery can be described as history in the "future conditional," a very useful exercise but one for which it should be clear exactly what is at issue.

For those United States historians who in the 1920s and 1930s were claiming that the Civil War was an "unnecessary war," the implication was of a rather short horizon before slavery's demise, a timing that still has its adherents, whether explained by political or by economic factors. It is interesting to note, however, that while the theoretical logic had been accepted even in the first part of the nineteenth century, for many a quite different period before decline was anticipated. A notable prediction, in 1858, was that of Abraham Lincoln, who based his argument for the limiting of slavery's expansion (while not interfering with slavery where it already was) on the basic population density point, forecasting a rather longer period before it would be in the South's interests to voluntarily end slavery. He claimed:

> I do not mean that when it takes a turn towards ultimate extinction it will be in a day, nor in a year, nor in two years. I do not suppose that in the most peaceful way ultimate extinction would occur in less than a hundred years at the least; but that it will occur in the best way for both races in God's own good time I have no doubt.

—a remark that apparently drew "Applause" from his audience. There were many abolitionists (as well as slaveowners) who presented a similar argument for the ultimate ending to slavery and, while not specifying the precise timing, were willing to be quite patient in awaiting the peaceful ending of the peculiar institution. There was thus a sense of slavery as a declining economic institution, one on the way out, requiring special conditions for its survival and, therefore, economically, not just morally, a "wave of the past"; though, as noted, the same could be and was said about worker prospects in the "Best Poor Man's Country."

Within recent years, however, there have been some apparent changes in the interpretation of the pattern of slavery's economic development in the United States and elsewhere. Slavery existed in the United States for nearly two-and-one-half centuries, but until very recently most scholarly attention had been given only to its last half-century. But nineteenth-century slavery was a quite different slavery in terms of major crops grown, migration patterns, and geographic location, than that of the preceding two centuries. The nineteenth-century transformation is seen, by some, as an indication of slavery's adjustment capabilities; to others, it is a prime piece of evidence that slavery was incapable of long-term survival and was moving ever closer to its collapse.

Indeed another twist is sometimes given to the North-South differences in nineteenth-century economic structure than that familiar to earlier scholars. Whereas it had been customary to argue that the South had remained in agriculture because of its economic backwardness and lack of productivity, some now seem to be suggesting that it was the southern success in producing agricultural commodities (relative to that in parts of the North) and the greater responsiveness of labor in response to differential economic opportunity within the South that led to the initial development of industry in the Northeast. This is not the place to discuss some of the possible paradoxes of conditions for economic growth, nor what most will agree were the long-run payoffs to the industrial transition in the Northeast, but it should be noted that this view of North-South differences provides a quite different interpretation of the economics and politics of the first two-thirds of the nineteenth century than do earlier views of the economic backwardness of the South.

Slave prices rose dramatically in the nineteenth century (albeit with some fluctuations which, it might be noted, did not seem to threaten the system and often coincided with fluctuations affecting the northern industrial economy), doubling in the 1850s when they reached all-time peaks. At this time the South produced over three-quarters of the world's cotton and was probably responsible for one-half of the world's tobacco exports, in addition to its slave-production of rice, sugar, wheat, and other foodstuffs.

And what was true in the southern states in the seventeenth, eighteenth, and nineteenth centuries was true of the other New World slave powers. Although by the 1830s slavery had ended in the British West Indies, as will be suggested below, there was no indication of overall economic decline preceding its demise. Dramatic expansions occurred throughout the nineteenth century in the other remaining major slave powers, Cuba and Brazil, with sharp increases in the value of slaves (while, unlike the United States during the period, still importing large numbers of slaves from Africa). The expansion of Cuban and Brazilian sugar and coffee production after the 1830s was somewhat of an embarrassment for those who had advocated the emancipation of slaves in the British West Indies to reap the benefits of free labor. It was difficult to use these production and trade data as a clearcut demonstration of the greater productivity of free over slave labor. (Although, of course, many did try and as economists and others can, did come up with interesting and plausible-sounding arguments, as a detailed look at the Sugar Duty debates of the 1840s will demonstrate.) The frequent need to posit "other circumstances are equal" maintained the validity of the theoretical arguments, while leaving open questions of current applicability.

By mid-century, Cuba had increased its sugar production to account for over one-third of the world's cane sugar output. By the 1850s, Brazil's coffee exports were more than double its sugar exports, and Brazil by then accounted for over 50 percent of the world trade in coffee. In both Cuba and Brazil slave prices rose sharply after the 1830s, more than doubled in the 1850s, and as late as the 1870s were above levels of the first half of the nineteenth century.

In Cuba, even with slaves from Africa still being imported in an "illegal" trade, the mid-century plantations, feeling an acute labor shortage, began to import large numbers of contract laborers, with over 125,000 being brought over from China between 1848 and 1874, in addition to several thousand Yucutani from Mexico. In Brazil, as late as 1885, a sophisticated Dutch observer—an indication of his sophistication is that he begins with a table on population per square kilometer by country—commented that there was no nonplantation (free white labor) production of coffee and advocated the ending of slavery, not because it was economically unproductive and dying out, but rather because no white Europeans would come to enter coffee production unless they did not have to compete with slave labor.

It should be remembered, also, that the slave trade from Africa to the Americas remained high throughout the first half of the nineteenth century (as did the slave trade to other destinations). Overall, despite the fact that two major economic powers (the United States and Great Britain) ended their transatlantic slave trades in the first decade of the nineteenth century (and, from all accounts, received very few smuggled slaves) and that most colonies of European powers also presumably ended their trade in slaves in response to British urging, bribes, and attempted naval suppression, on an annual basis in the sixty-seven years of its nineteenth-century operation, about four-fifths the numbers left Africa in the transatlantic slave trade as in the eighteenth century. And, it should be noted that after 1838 there were also tens of thousands of Africans coming into the Caribbean as contract laborers and *engagés* on the British and French islands, and the relations of this movement to the African slave trade became the source of controversy.

Thus, in the middle of the nineteenth century slavery in the Americas was, economically, not yet a decaying institution, inflexible and incapable of adapting to economic change, and inconsistent with modernization and productivity change, within those sectors in which it had its comparative (and absolute) advantages. Slave labor was responsible for much of the world's sugar, cotton, coffee, and tobacco, and slave production of these crops greatly exceeded the production by nominally free labor. And, generally, when crops such as sugar and coffee were being produced by so-called free labor, it was frequently either based upon a form of indentured labor (as in the British and French Caribbean and Indian Ocean colonies after emancipation) or upon extensive governmental controls in areas of high population density and extreme poverty (as in Dutch Java). In the major cases—the United States, Cuba, Brazil, the British, French, and Dutch West Indies, and Puerto Rico—it now seems clear that slavery had not yet ground to a halt economically; rather slavery was expanding and it took political and military action to bring it to a halt.

One might briefly note that there have been some recent reinterpretations in a similar manner of another major form of coerced labor, European serfdom. The past few issues of this journal [*Journal of Economic History*], for example, contain two detailed papers on this topic: one, by Evsey Domar and Mark Machina, indicating (at least tentatively) that "the behavior of serf prices before the Emancipation does not on the whole indicate the end of serfdom in Russia," and "Except for Lithuania, we found no other region where serfdom was coming to an end"; the other, by Richard Rudolph, pointing to the flexibility of economic structure that was possible within Eastern European and Russian serfdom. Political factors have been emphasized by Jerome Blum, in his magisterial discussion of the ending of serfdom, and it is perhaps indicative of the perceptions (as well as the power) of the political elites, that when both slavery and serfdom were ended it was most frequently with some compensation paid—in cash, securities, land, or labor time—to slaveowners and serfowners, presumably as partial payment for their expected economic losses.

By 1888 slavery had ended throughout the Americas, although slavery did continue longer in areas of Asia and Africa. The basic questions of why emancipation did occur and what the crucial factors in its ending were have long been a focus of historical attention. The economics of slavery is central to any understanding of the abolition process, and the recent work on the dynamics of nineteenth-century slavery has pointed to the importance of understanding the major political and ideological aspects of the process. To place attention on the ideological transformations that led to the explicit attack on slavery and to study the political process by which it was ended become more interesting and important once the economics is placed in better perspective.

A look at the history of slave emancipation in the Americas finds it difficult to find any cases of slavery declining economically prior to the imposition of emancipation. In the case most widely debated by historians as the first major legislated ending of the slave trade and of slavery—that of the British ending of their slave trade in 1808 and of slavery in their Caribbean and African colonies in 1834—there now seems a shift in the way that the economic argument is being presented by its advocates. Eric Williams, in his 1944 book on *Capitalism and Slavery,* began the successful overturn of the earlier moralistic and religious views of the abolition process, replacing it by a focus on economic, as well as economically based political, factors. By drawing upon the economic arguments presented by the American scholar, Lowell Ragatz, Williams argued for a post–American Revolution decline in the profitability of the West Indian plantations and a reduced importance of West Indian trade to the British metropolis as critical factors in the success of the antislavery movement. This economic decline argument seemed to make the explanation rather straightforward, and without a moral basis, with Williams's description of economic (and political) factors fitting into the pattern of evolving stages described above.

Recent work by Seymour Drescher, particularly his study of *Econocide,* however, has made any single-minded reliance on economic factors more difficult. Drescher argues for the increasing importance of the British West Indies in British trade in the late eighteenth and early nineteenth centuries, and, as the book's title suggests, claims that it was the political ending of the slave trade and various imposed restrictions on the inter-island transfer of slaves that served to retard the economic expansion of the British West Indies.

The earlier arguments of a declining British West Indian slavery cannot easily explain the continued rise in slave prices from the period of the American Revolution until the 1820s (even when allowance is made for the post-1808 declines in slave population), nor the expansion of British West Indian slave imports in the period between 1780 and its 1808 ending. Price declines, on a persistent basis for some of the islands, do not occur until the 1820s when the final and successful attack on slavery itself began in Parliament. Even in the 1820s, in the more recently acquired and expanding areas of Trinidad and what would become British Guiana, slave prices rose by about 30 to 40 percent, leading to substantial price differentials between these expanding and the other parts of the British Caribbean and suggesting the great importance of earlier decisions limiting the inter-island slave trade.

Perhaps a suggestive indication of what might have happened if the slave trade had not been ended can be seen in the responses in the British West Indies once slavery and, finally, apprenticeship was ended in 1838. Planters sought more labor by getting Colonial Office approval for the "free" migration of contract labor which, after several go-arounds, they were able to obtain but with quite detailed regulations. While some of these new arrivals were to replace the ex-slaves who had left the plantations, particularly in those expanding areas of Trinidad and British Guiana, it is striking that the level of imported labor from Africa, Portuguese Madeira, China, and India remained high throughout the second half of the nineteenth century. The quinquennium with the largest number of arrivals was 1846 to 1850 at an annual average of over 10,000 per year (about three-fifths the level of the last three decades of the British slave trade).

These contract laborers were described either as "free labor" voluntarily coming (as did the British and German indentured migrants to North America in the seventeenth and eighteenth centuries) or else as part of "a new system of slavery," as others argued. In any event, however, it would seem indicative that a continued slave trade would have meant substantially more involuntary migrants to the British West Indies (as the absence of subsequent British suppression policy of the slave trade elsewhere would no doubt have meant for Cuba and Brazil).

It is now suggested that it was the growth of the British economy that made it economically feasible for the British to end slavery, no matter how profitable or how large the trade in the slave-produced commodities. But why something, even if its relative costs were becoming smaller to Britain, should be considered an evil whose ending was necessary, had again become a heated source of debate, and the particular mix of religion, secular morality, and class factors in the British case is now being reexamined (as it is also, for similar reasons, in the United States). Whether the impetus in Britain and elsewhere came from religious elites, political elites, economic elites, artisans, or the working class and why it was perceived in their interests to end slavery is the subject of much recent work. Whatever the outcome of these debates, however, the parliamentary-legislated ending of the slave trade and of slavery [is] no longer seen as clearcut proof of the waning of the British West Indian slave economy nor is the American Civil War outcome taken to be an obvious demonstration of the lack of economic viability of the southern slave economy.

In retrospect, perhaps one of the clearest indications of the nature of slave economies, and of the relation between free and slave labor, can be seen in the developments of these economies after slavery ended and some form of freed labor introduced. Despite differences in crops produced and their technologies, in world market demands, in land-labor ratios, and in political circumstances, some basic similarities do appear in the economic adjustments arising from emancipation and the responses to them throughout the Americas. The economic difficulties of the postbellum South were not unique, for example, in the initial reductions in the production of export crops and in the decline of the plantation sector, nor in the debate about when and why the ex-slaves left the plantation and sought their own land. As with the British Caribbean, the question remains whether the large-scale ex-slave movement off the plantation was immediate, with freedom reflected in a desire to avoid work for their old masters at any cost, or after some delay, as a response to changing wage rates and income possibilities. And, of course, as with the northern farmers and southern yeoman, was the desire for land ownership to limit reliance on the market or, rather, to be able to benefit from market production?

The South was unusual in the continued high level of cotton output. There were considerably more dramatic shifts in the output pattern of other plantation crops, such as sugar and rice, but there was a major shift in the racial composition of those producing that traditional export crop, cotton. While there was some discussion and even a few attempts to attract foreign laborers—Chinese (from California or direct from China) and Italians (who several decades later were to become the basis for the post-emancipation coffee sector in Brazil)—these were not successful and were of limited importance. Rather noteworthy, for a number of questions, was an extensive movement of southern whites on smaller farms into cotton production, a movement whose causes are still debated, given the antebellum yeoman's relatively (and absolutely) smaller role in cotton production.

The southern adjustment process can be placed in better context by a brief overview of what happened elsewhere. The case of Haiti, the second new nation of the Western Hemisphere, is the most dramatic. Before the successful slave uprising Haiti (Saint Domingue as it then was) was perhaps the world's richest plantation area with large-scale production of sugar and coffee. After the Haitian Revolution, sugar output fell away completely, and although some coffee was still exported, the basic plantation economy was replaced by small-scale farms. This occurred despite attempts in the first decades of the nineteenth century to reintroduce a plantation economy, attempts that failed completely. The Haitian example was widely discussed in the British and American debates on slavery and emancipation and in many ways set the contours of subsequent analysis. It was seen by one side as a problem of economic decline that it would be necessary to avoid in the future, and by others as a problem to be explained away—either by attributing the perceived economic decline to special factors in the Haitian case or, in a manner that would reappear (although apparently more as a fallback argument), by contrasting the effects on human welfare with those on measured economic production. The importance of human welfare was of obvious importance, but it did leave some problems, particularly for those who were arguing that the comparative productivity of free and slave labor meant that moral progress would come without any loss—and possibly with an increase—in economic output.

In the British colonies emancipation took place with both cash compensation paid to slaveowners and a compulsory period of so-called labor apprenticeship, with the ex-slaves working for their former owners under regulated conditions. The apprenticeship period was meant to accomplish two ends at the same time. First, it was to provide further compensation to the slaveowners by linking labor to the land to produce export crops for several more years. Second, following the logic of the attack on slavery, it was meant to serve as a period in which to "educate" the ex-slaves into the intricacies of the workings of free-labor markets under controlled conditions.

With some exceptions, after the early ending of apprenticeship there were sharp declines in the production of sugar and coffee, a shrinking of the plantation sector, and a shift to smaller-scale producing units. There were two types of exceptions to these extended declines, for quite different reasons, although both point to the importance of the land-labor ratio in influencing the economic and political outcome.

On the islands of Barbados and Antigua, where population densities were unusually high, there were no post-emancipation declines in sugar production and the plantation system basically continued, albeit with some changes. The Antigua planters knew their economics quite well, and took the "humanitarian" gesture of foregoing a period of apprenticeship, arguing (accurately) that, in effect, it was unnecessary since the ex-slaves would have no choice but to continue to work on the plantations. Barbados, with an even higher population density, did have a period of apprenticeship, but when it ended the plantation system persisted. What is of interest, however, is that Barbados and Antigua were often held up by emancipators and travelers as the example of a successful slave emancipation, showing what was possible for freed labor to accomplish if only the planters behaved properly and if free labor were treated appropriately. A comparison of wage levels and alternatives between Barba-

dos and Antigua and elsewhere in the British Caribbean might, of
course, have put this in a different light.

The other examples of greatly expanded sugar output in the
British colonies are of interest for what they tell us about the behavior of the ex-slaves in the nature of work they desired and their response to wage opportunities, the behavior of planters in their response to changing labor conditions, and about the constraints on
the political process in the inability of the whites to force ex-slaves
back onto the plantation. Most dramatically, the Indian Ocean island
of Mauritius continued the rapid growth of sugar output from the
late slave era, but the plantation labor force was the result of a new
variant of an earlier labor institution, contract labor or indentured
servitude, with migrants drawn from British India. Within one decade of emancipation it is estimated that over 90 percent of the
workers on Mauritian sugar plantations were drawn from India,
most still under contract, with the ex-slaves apparently having
moved into nonexport, peasant-type production. With a somewhat
longer time lag, a similar pattern of adjustment occurred in those
parts of the British Caribbean that had been expanding rapidly earlier in the nineteenth century—Trinidad and British Guiana. When
plantation sugar output achieved new high levels it was, again, not
on the basis of ex-slave labor but rather on the basis of imported
contract laborers from other parts of the world, mainly, after mid-
century, from India. It is estimated that by the 1870s over 70 percent
of the plantation labor force in these two areas was composed of
contract laborers imported after the end of slavery—some still under
contract, some remaining after their contracts had expired, not wish-
ing to return to their countries of origin. The ex-slaves and their
descendants had frequently moved into small-scale peasant-type production—although it still remains uncertain whether material income was foregone or hours of work reduced, as a result of this
choice.

The pattern of plantation output decline, with the importing
of contract labor from elsewhere around the world, characterized
other parts of the Caribbean and, as a possible indication of what
might have happened if the slave trade had not been ended earlier in
the nineteenth century, those areas with newly expanded sugar production in the second half of the nineteenth century—Australia,
South Africa, Peru, Fiji, and Hawaii—all did so on the basis of con-

tract labor drawn from elsewhere in the world including India, China, Japan, the Pacific Islands, the Portuguese islands, and Java, among the major areas of outmigration. It is striking that, as centuries earlier, sugar production seemed to require the drawing in of labor from elsewhere, rather than being based upon the employment of the resident, free, population, with the few previously mentioned exceptions of areas of very high population density.

Similar studies concerning the initial impacts of ending that other form of coerced labor, serfdom, do not seem to be available in the same detail as those for the ending of slavery. There does seem, however, no clearcut evidence of a rapid expansion in the Russian economy immediately following serf emancipation. There is an interesting recent quantitative analysis by John Komlos of the Austrian and Hungarian cases, showing that under conventional presumptions about free versus serf productivity there was no dramatic output increase, but I am not aware of any analysis that tests the impacts on crop mix and labor intensity. Komlos does argue, however, that rates of growth of agricultural output before and after serf emancipation were "virtually indistinguishable" in Hungary and that "the economic importance of the emancipation of the peasantry [and the enlargement of the customs area] is seriously questioned; they do not appear to have been a sufficient or necessary condition for a gradual transformation of the countryside." And the early commercialization of many serf areas raises, at the least, questions about some earlier extreme views of the nature of backwardness of the serf economy.

The various debates prior to, and after, emancipation, particularly in the British case, provide a fascinating glimpse into nineteenth-century views about the creation of a free labor force and the conditions necessary for a free-labor economy. It resembled the discussions, a century or two earlier, that had characterized the English Mercantilists in their descriptions of the "labor problem" (and is again the subject of detailed examination by labor historians in various countries). Indeed much of the subsequent debate, among contemporaries and historians, remains a variant on the clear-cut dichotomy posed by the Mercantilist, James Steuart: "Men were then forced to labour because they were slaves to others; men are now forced to labour because they are slaves to their own wants." Thus there was the concern with civilizing ex-slaves and others to wish to obtain more material goods in their own long-term interests (as well as those of landowners and capitalists). It was reasonable that the individual labor-supply curve would at some point become backward sloping—the key issue was exactly at what level of material goods and labor input that would occur.

Within the British post-emancipation debate, at least in its earlier stages, there was often a surprisingly nonracist aspect reflected in discussions of the conditions for the creation of a free-wage labor force. Attention was given to the contrasts between the British Isles and the West Indies in regard to climate, resources, and population densities. The British and the Irish had become wage earners, it was argued, because of the higher needs imposed by the less favorable climate and resources of the British Isles and, more importantly, the greater population density which precluded alternatives for laborers.

The colonial agent for Grenada, for example, commented in 1816 in his *Thoughts on the Abolition of the Slave Trade:*

> In Europe, where the climate braces the sinews of the inhabitants to toil, and where the unremitting exertions of the poor man will barely suffice for the maintenance of himself and his family—the necessity of daily labour for daily bread, is felt as the law of nature . . . But in tropical climes, where indolence is considered as the greatest of all enjoyments . . . and where the progress of vegetation is so rapid, that the inhabitants may supply themselves with the means of subsistence, by the labour of one day in seven,—how to induce men, who have no artificial wants, to devote themselves to daily toil, is a difficulty almost insurmountable. . . .

And the Colonial Office, in its detailed 1833 discussions of plans for a successful transition to free labor, argued that parts of the West Indies would soon confront the same difficulties as "the Western States of America," "the British North American Provinces," "the colony of the Cape of Good Hope," and "the Australian settlements," where "the facility of procuring land has invariably created a proportionate difficulty in obtaining hired labor."

And similar arguments were made afterwards, in accounting for the pattern of economic change in the West Indies. An advocate of coolie emigration, writing as late as 1861, claimed:

> If the 800,000 West-Indian slaves had been slaves in England, and if they had been liberated in England: necessity would have compelled

them to work, and work hard too, on their own account . . . The free negro in England would have been as much a slave as every English-man who has to earn his living by manual labour. The poor man in this country is theoretically free, but practically he is a bondsman to his daily necessities and the narrowness of his means.

Thus, given the ease thought to exist within tropical areas in meeting the rather limited wants of the population, it was claimed that unless the ex-slaves could be introduced to higher levels of material wants, long-run problems for all were to be expected. The issue of "want creation" persisted among both planters and abolitionists in the British case, although with some important differences. The former were interested only in the expansion of a wage-laboring population, willing to work on plantations. The latter were concerned with demonstrating the higher measured output from free labor—that is what they had promised and it was felt that to demonstrate its accuracy would be important as an empirical proof of the course to be followed by the remaining slave powers. Unlike the planters, however, abolitionists were willing to endorse the idea of small, owner-operated farms producing the export crops, arguing that this was both desirable and possible—propositions requiring more attention in detailing the interplay of technological changes and alternative forms of labor institutions.

More, of course, could be said about the discussions of the transition from slave to freed labor, and the perceptions of people at that time. I think these are interesting in the examinations of the conditions making for a free labor force, which while not denying its potential long-run beneficial aspects, do provide an interesting set of questions and issues with which to examine the evolution of free-wage labor markets in other societies.

In concluding, I want merely to note some broader implications to be drawn from this brief survey of labor institutions, both in regard to substantive questions and in terms of approach to historical problems. One point that emerges is the conflict that seemed to belie any easy, universal equations among moral, social, and economic progress. More general is the implication that for many of the broader concerns of economic historians we can get only so far without a consideration of political, cultural, and ideological factors and, correspondingly, for many of the broader issues of political, cultural, and intellectual history, there remains a major contribution to be made by the study of economic history. This leads to my last point which is, as is traditional, a reflection on method. Debates on methods of historical study (which are frequently really more about what questions are thought interesting to study) often seem to advocate one or another method to the exclusion of others. One of the remarks most quoted by economists and economic historians is that of Adam Smith on the benefits of specialization and the division of labor—a point which it seems to me remains equally applicable in intellectual and scholarly pursuits. That is, there is much to be gained by regarding different approaches and methods as complements, rather than to see them only as substitutes.

VI

Slavery and Society

Drew G. Faust

SLAVE MANAGEMENT

In this selection Drew G. Faust, professor of history at the University of
Pennsylvania, discusses the master-slave relationship. Her case example
is the South Carolina planter and politician James Henry Hammond,
whose effort to shape slaves into a productive, compliant labor force
was frustrated on almost every account. By law all power rested with
Hammond on his large antebellum plantation at Silver Bluff. He tried to
convince the slaves that his dominance over them was benevolent and
that they were inherently inferior, but the blacks resisted, refusing to
affirm Hammond's idealized vision of his despotic sway. Indeed, antagonism characterized the relationship between master and slave at Silver
Bluff.

A dozen miles south of Augusta, Georgia, the Savannah curves
gently, creating two bends that antebellum river captains knew as
Stingy Venus and Hog Crawl Round. Close to the mouth of Boggy
Gut Creek the channel narrows, and decaying wrecks of steamboats
bear witness to the waterway's importance in an era long departed.
Nearby, on the South Carolina shore, a cliff abruptly rises almost
thirty feet above the water. Deposits of mica in the soil give the
promontory a metallic tinge, and the bank and the plantation of
which it was part came as early as colonial times to be called Silver
Bluff.

Located on an easily navigable river between Augusta and Savannah, the site played a prominent role in the early history of the
up-country region. Although the focus of development in both
South Carolina and Georgia remained near the coast until after the
beginning of the nineteenth century, the famous botanist and traveler William Bartram in 1773 found Silver Bluff already "a very celebrated place." In the course of his mid-sixteenth-century explorations, Hernando DeSoto had discovered an Indian village
flourishing on the bluff, and an Irishman, George Galphin, became
the first white settler in the area when he established an Indian trad-

Reprinted by permission of Louisiana State University Press from *James Henry
Hammond and the Old South: A Design For Mastery*, pp. 69–75, 92–96, 103–104
by Drew Gilpin Faust. Copyright © 1982, Louisiana State University Press.

ing post in 1736. By the second half of the eighteenth century, blacks had added their influence to these strains of red and white. A Baptist congregation that flourished at Silver Bluff in the years just before the Revolution claims the distinction of being the first separate black church in America.

With the dawning of the steamboat era and the general expansion of the up-country after the turn of the century, the region began to seem a promising area for investment. In 1814 the wealthy and enterprising Charleston merchant Christopher Fitzsimons bought two thousand acres of rich swamp land adjacent to the river for three thousand dollars, and eight years later he acquired a second tract almost four times larger. Upon Fitzsimons' death in 1825, this remote property became the share of his estate allotted to his youngest child, eleven-year-old Catherine. For the next six years, the girl's two older brothers officially managed the land, in fact abandoning it almost entirely to the neglectful supervision of a resident overseer.

When James Henry Hammond arrived on December 8, 1831, to take possession of the estate his marriage had won him, he carefully noted in his diary 10,800 acres of land, which he valued at $36,100. Of this, only 967 acres, including 150 acres of swamp, were cleared for corn and cotton cultivation; 90 percent of the property remained entirely undeveloped. The land itself was of two main types: the low, boggy, and malarial tracts near the river and the red-clay soils of the wooded plateaus. Silver Bluff, he would later remark, was located "in an [*sic*] pine wilderness."

Through these woods, the plantation livestock ran unrestrained; Hammond estimated that 95 head of cattle, 130 hogs, and 20 sheep foraged in the underbrush for roots, nuts, and shrubbery. The 25 mules needed as work animals were more carefully treated and maintained in plantation barns. In addition to food for stock, Silver Bluff's forests provided valuable firewood and timber. The plantation sawmill produced an annual crop of lumber, part of which was floated downriver to Savannah and the remainder sold as fuel to steamboat captains who stopped at the Bluff landing. In this survey of his property, Hammond recorded as well a gristmill, a cotton gin-house, a blacksmith's shop, and a carpenter's shop. Although Hammond did not bother to list all the estate's structures, he did note in his inventory that the property included a resident owner's dwelling. The undistinguished house was filled with rough and broken furni-

ture and could hardly have seemed adequate to this aspiring aristo-
crat. But Hammond was for the time being preoccupied with other
matters; he was less concerned about personal comforts than about
the economic foundations of his new enterprise, about the labor
force on which the prosperity of his undertaking depended.

After his brief initial survey of land and livestock, Hammond
made a detailed list of the human chattel he now owned, including
each individual's name and age. The 147 slaves of Silver Bluff were
recorded in his inventory in family groups, as perhaps they appeared
on that December day to meet their new master. Hammond had
acquired seventy-four females and seventy-three males, a population
with a median age of twenty-five. He would certainly have noted
that forty-six, nearly a third of these slaves, were not yet fifteen, too
young to be much use in the fields but a good foundation for a
vigorous future labor force. Undoubtedly, too, he observed that
sixty-four of the slaves were between fifteen and forty-five, the prime
work years. These were the individuals upon whom Hammond
would rely to plant, cultivate, and harvest the cotton and corn that
would generate most of his yearly income. Seven slaves were over
sixty-five and would in all likelihood not produce enough to equal
the cost of their maintenance. But they could be used for chores less
demanding than field labor, such as supervising the stables, selling
wood to passing steamboats, or minding slave children whose mothers were at work on the crop. Despite the drain these elderly blacks
represented, Hammond would have seen in the overall composition
of his slave force, with its well-balanced sex ratio and comparative
youth, promise of rapid natural increase, as well as of a high level of
agricultural productivity. Sixty-one workers, he concluded, could be
used in the fields, eight in the sawmill, one in the gristmill, seven on
the wood landing, and one as stock minder.

But neither Hammond's initial census, nor his first cursory examination could reveal what he all too soon realized about his newly
acquired property. His efforts to shape this group of blacks into a
disciplined, productive, and expanding slave force would be challenged and thwarted at nearly every turn. Hammond would be frustrated in his efforts to produce a high yield both of agricultural crops
and of young blacks. His slaves, he would discover, were not only
undisciplined and in "very bad subjection" as a result of careless management, but extraordinarily unhealthy as well.

When Hammond took possession of Silver Bluff, he assumed a role and entered a world largely unfamiliar to him. . . . The new master at Silver Bluff was entirely inexperienced in the management of large numbers of agricultural and domestic workers. The blacks at Silver Bluff, for their part, also confronted a new situation, for they had become accustomed to living without a master in permanent residence. In 1831 Hammond and his slaves alike faced new circumstances. But it was Hammond who was the outsider, moving into a world of established patterns of behavior and interaction in the community at Silver Bluff. By law all power rested with Hammond. But in reality the situation was rather different.

Hammond quickly learned that the mastery of slaves entailed a good deal more than simply directing 147 individual lives, for he had to dominate a complex social order already in existence on the plantation. For the next three decades, he would struggle to control what he called a "system of roguery" among his slaves, a structured and organized pattern of resistance to his desire for total domination. Nevertheless, the young master was determined from the first to brook no challenge to his power. By asserting his control, he would transform Silver Bluff into a profitable enterprise and its slaves into productive workers. Hammond recognized that his effectiveness in creating a docile and tractable labor force depended upon his success in making the blacks entirely subservient to his will not just in the fields, but in every aspect of their lives. To force them to acknowledge their own weakness and his power, he would destroy the autonomy of the slave community and bring its members under his direct and total domination. Over the next several years, he developed a carefully designed plan of physical and psychological control intended to eliminate the foundations of black solidarity. Yet at the same time he sought despotic power over his slave force, Hammond from the first cherished a conception of himself as a beneficient master whose guidance and control represented the best of all possible worlds for the uncivilized and backward people entrusted to him by God. His need both to dominate and to be loved would pose insuperable difficulties within his evolving system of slave management.

Hammond's slaves, so long under the desultory management of absentee owners, were not accustomed to the rigorous demands made by their new master, and they resented and resisted his drive for efficiency. "The negroes are trying me," Hammond observed on more than one occasion in the first weeks after his arrival. Under such circumstances it was hard to maintain his idealized self-image as a benevolent master surrounded by obedient and grateful servants. Instead, Hammond found himself compelled to "subdue" them, and he later recalled an initial "year of severity which cost me infinite pain" before the blacks were "broken in." If it was painful to the young master, it was undoubtedly more so to the slaves, for he resorted to frequent floggings as the most effective representation of his control. Those who performed unsatisfactory labor, left the plantation without permission, or in any other way challenged Hammond's authority were lashed, in a public display of the consequences of refusal to comply with the master's will. Eight slaves slow in returning to work after the Christmas holidays were severely whipped by the overseer. When they appealed to Hammond for sympathy, he responded by ordering them flogged again. Before he could afford to show mercy, Hammond knew he had to impress the slaves with the reality of his power.

Part of this mastery consisted in extending control over the very souls of those he sought to dominate. "Intend to break up negro preaching & negro churches," he proclaimed in his plantation diary. When a slave named Ben Shubrick requested permission to "join the negro Church," Hammond refused it, but made arrangements for him to be admitted to the congregation of which Hammond was himself a member. "Ordered night meetings on the plantation to be discontinued," he noted in his plantation diary only days after his arrival at Silver Bluff. Hammond saw an implicit threat in the assemblies of fervent and devoted slaves who gathered together in praise and worship. In the authority of the black preacher lay a potential challenge to Hammond's own; in the Old Testament chronicles of Moses and the chosen people lay the germs of an ideology of black revolution. Hammond endeavored to replace independent black worship with devotions entirely under white supervision. Carefully instructed white clergymen could emphasize the less incendiary strain within Christian teachings that promoted meekness and docility. To make certain that black religion would not be transformed into a vehicle of slave revolt, Hammond visited each of his new neighbors to request that they follow his example in eliminating the black church on their plantations.

Hammond soon regularized his white-controlled religious exercises by hiring itinerant ministers for Sunday afternoon slave services. Here the speakers undoubtedly emphasized the virtues of obedience to masters terrestrial as well as divine. While the whip served as the most potent symbol of physical domination, the pulpits of the Methodist and Baptist churches erected on the plantation during the 1840s became an embodiment of Hammond's crusade for ideological hegemony.

In the realm of labor, Hammond's desire for omnipotence was expressed in an unceasing pursuit of efficiency. His rigorous management quickly became evident in the fields, where the amount of labor extracted from each slave had a direct—and in Hammond's self-consciously rational eyes, even measurable—effect upon the master's purse. The new owner found his laborers accustomed to task work, a system in which a clearly defined daily job was assigned to each hand. When this duty was completed, the slave's time was his or her own. Hammond regarded such arrangements as distressingly wasteful of the labor potential of his work force, for most of the blacks, he discovered, seemed to have finished their appointed obligations by the midafternoon. Such a system, moreover, undermined not only efficiency but order, for it provided the slave too much autonomy and permitted hours of dangerous independence. The slave, Hammond explained, was motivated to work too rapidly and too carelessly in order to complete a required job. Task labor encouraged the blacks to overexert themselves, with "no rest until 3 or 4 o'clock." In a gang, under constant surveillance of the overseer, "they work moderately from sunrise to sundown stopping an hour for breakfast & 2 for dinner, go home, sleep all night & are ready & strong for another day." Under such a system, "they do much more," Hammond found, "and are not so apt to strain themselves." Despite the workers' clear preference for the task system, Hammond was determined to use only gang labor at Silver Bluff.

While a significant part of Hammond's objection to task labor was its inefficiency, he also feared the independence it gave the laborers, both in the field, where they were free to determine the pace of their work, and during the unsupervised hours after their tasks were completed. Because Hammond wanted above all to make the slaves feel dependent, he correctly viewed encouraging any area of autonomy as counterproductive and even dangerous. As a result, he curtailed many of the privileges the slaves had enjoyed under the Fitzsimons regime, especially those that provided the blacks direct contact with the world outside the plantation. Slaves were forbidden to trade in local stores, to sell the produce of their garden patches to neighbors, to fraternize with the crews of steamboats refueling at the Bluff landing, or to visit town more than once a year. Hammond intended that his slaves have no access to a world outside his omnipotent rule. . . .

Black autonomy and assertiveness challenged Hammond's management in nearly every aspect of plantation life and even intruded into his own household, where, to Hammond's intense displeasure, slaves stole delicacies from his own larder. Pilfering of food and alcohol at Silver Bluff did not consist simply of random acts by slaves seeking to alleviate hunger or compensate for deprivation. Theft assumed wider significance, taking on the characteristics of a contest between master and slave in which the master was by definition always the loser. The prospect of winning the competition may well have provided the slaves with nearly as much satisfaction as did the material fruits of victory; it was clearly a battle for power as well as for the specific goods in question. Although Hammond had begun immediately in 1831 to try to reduce the level of depredations against his hogs, flogging suspected thieves made little impact. Unable to prevent the disappearance of a sizable number of his pigs, he chose to define black theft as a passive "habit" rather than an assertive and powerful challenge to his control. But he recorded with grim satisfaction that the resulting reduction of the meat allowance would serve as just retribution for the slaves' conspiracy against his droves. Theirs would be, he consoled himself, a hollow victory. "The negroes," he noted in 1845, "have for . . . years killed about half my shoats & must now suffer for it." The impact of black theft was perhaps even greater on other plantation products. Hammond was resigned never to harvest his potato crop at all, for the slaves appropriated the entire yield before it was officially even removed from the ground.

Alcohol, however, inspired the most carefully designed system of slave intrigue. When Hammond began to ferment wines from his own vineyards, slaves constantly tapped the bottles, then blamed the disappearance of the liquid on leaks due to faulty corking. But the slave community's most elaborate assault on Hammond's supplies of alcohol went well beyond such crude tactics to bring together a unique conjunction of engineering skill with the power of voodoo. In 1835 Hammond found that several of his slaves had dug tunnels beneath his wine cellar. A female domestic named Urana, Hammond recorded, had employed "root work" and thus "screened" the excavators by her "conjuration." Hammond determinedly "punished all who have had any thing to do with the matter far or near." But his response could not replace the lost wine or compensate for the way the incident challenged the literal and figurative foundations of his plantation order. The force of voodoo lay entirely outside his system of control and defied his efforts to establish cultural dominance. The blacks worked patiently and ingeniously to undermine his power as well as his house.

For most of Hammond's slaves, insubordination served to establish cultural and personal autonomy within the framework of plantation demands. Resistance was a tool of negotiation, a means of extracting concessions from the master to reduce the extent of his claims over black bodies and souls. At Silver Bluff such efforts were directed more at securing necessary support for black community life than at totally overwhelming the master's power. Hammond learned that he could to a certain degree repress, but never eliminate black cultural patterns; his slaves in turn concealed much of their lives so as not to appear directly to challenge their master's hegemony.

But for some Silver Bluff residents there could be no such compromises. Instead of seeking to avoid the domination inherent in slavery, these individuals overtly challenged it, turning to arson and escape as expressions of open rebellion. Throughout the period of his management, Hammond referred to mysterious fires that would break out in the ginhouse on one occasion, the millhouse or plantation hospital on the next. While these presumed acts of sabotage were never linked to specific individuals and only minimally affected the operation of the plantation, running away offered the slave a potentially more effective means of resistance to Hammond's control. Between 1831 and 1855, when he turned most record-keeping over to his sons, Hammond noted fifty-three escape attempts by his slaves. The most striking fact about these runaways is that Hammond recorded no instance of successful flight. Thirty-five percent of the slaves who tried to escape were repeaters, although no slave was recorded as making more than three attempts. A newly purchased slave who made several efforts to escape was sold; those with long-term ties to the Silver Bluff community eventually abandoned the endeavor. The average age of runaways was thirty-three; 84 percent were male; and the median period during which a runaway had been under Hammond's domination was two years.

While the decision to run away might appear to be a rejection by the slave of the ties of black community as well as of the chains of bondage, the way in which escape functioned at Silver Bluff shows it usually operated somewhat differently. Since there were no runaways who achieved permanent freedom and since most escapees did not get far, they remained in a very real sense a part of the slave community they had seemingly fled. Forty-three percent of the runaways at the Bluff left with others. Females, who made up only 16 percent of the total, almost without exception ran with husbands or to join spouses who had already departed. Once slaves escaped they succeeded in remaining at large an average of forty-nine days. Sixty-five percent were captured and the rest returned voluntarily. The distribution of compulsory and voluntary returns over the calendar year indicates that harsh weather was a significant factor in persuading slaves to give themselves up. Seventy-seven percent of those returning in the winter months did so by choice, while in the spring and summer 80 percent were brought back against their will. Weather and work load made summer the runaway season, and more than half of all escape attempts occurred in June, July, and August.

While certain individuals—notably young males, particularly those without family ties—were most likely to become runaways, the slave community as a whole provided them with assistance and support. Hammond himself recognized that runaways often went no farther than the nearby Savannah River swamps, where they survived on food provided by those remaining at home. The ties between the escapees and the community were sufficiently strong that Hammond endeavored to force runaways to return by disciplining the rest of the slave force. On at least one occasion he determined to stop the meat allowance for the entire plantation until the runaways came in. In another instance, he severely flogged four slaves harboring two runaways, hoping to break the personal and communal bonds that made prolonged absences possible.

The isolation of Silver Bluff made real escape almost impossible. Some newly arrived slaves, perhaps recently separated from their families, intended to escape these new surroundings permanently, and such individuals were captured as far as a hundred miles away. The majority of runaways, however, were part of the established community on Hammond's plantation. Recognizing that they would almost certainly fail to escape the chains of bondage forever, they ran either in pursuit of a brief respite from labor or in response to uncontrollable anger. One function of the black community was to support this outlet for frustration and rage by feeding and sheltering runaways either until they were captured or until they were once again able to operate within the system of compromise that served as the basis of interaction between master and slave at Silver Bluff. . . .

To a gathering of neighborhood agriculturists in 1857 Hammond's son Spann succinctly summarized the principles of slave management his father had developed in a quarter century of practical experience in plantation ownership. "Father said," he reported:

> firmness, justness & moderation, in all things, were the fundamental requisites. Inspire a negro with perfect confidence in you & learn him to look to you for support, & he is your slave. A full belly quells dissension & rebellion, but too full a one breeds inordinate laziness. So in clothing, give sufficient to protect from weather, but give neither of too fine stuff, nor too abundant. Never work a negro systematically all he can do. Leave a reserve for emergencies. Their religious training must be of the most moderate sort, avoiding all excitements. Persuasion should substitute severe punishment in getting done as much as possible.

In its mature form, Hammond's managerial strategy sought to undermine the slaves' "system of roguery" by impressing them with both the master's dominance and his legitimacy. While he hoped to persuade the blacks to accept the culture of slavery—with its concomitant ideology of their own inferiority and of his benevolent paternalism—the slaves manipulated, dissimulated, and resisted to avoid affirming their master's definition of their situation. They retained, in a manner only partially visible to Hammond, essential aspects of black communal life and autonomy.

As a slaveowner, as in so many other dimensions of his life, Hammond desired to be both omnipotent and beloved. And he so cherished his illusions about ideal masterhood that he was usually able to forget he was neither kind paternalist nor all-effective manager. One of his greatest "consolations," he explained to a close friend, was to know that "my negroes . . . love & *appreciate* me." Hammond would never learn that domination is incompatible with the mutuality that serves as the foundation of genuine love. With the exigencies of Civil War and the imminence of emancipation, he would be forced to recognize that what he had regarded as devotion from his slaves had been largely a form of manipulation. The image of the benevolent master proved ultimately as empty of meaning for him as it had so long been for his slaves. Hammond had designed and promulgated an ideology through which to control his slaves. But ironically, he as much as they became its prisoner.

Eugene D. Genovese

SLAVE REVOLTS

Slave revolts occurred with greater frequency and success and in wider scope in the Caribbean and Brazil than in North America. Had the oppressive conditions of slavery in North America reduced the slave to a docile "Sambo," incapable of revolt? According to Eugene D. Genovese, a historian who holds multiple appointments at the University of Georgia, Georgia Institute of Technology, and Georgia State University, the explanation lies elsewhere. He argues that unfavorable conditions for insurrection, the establishment of a paternalistic slave system, and the cultural resistance of slaves to white domination worked against armed rebellion, especially by the nineteenth century. Nevertheless, he concludes, the very existence of slave revolts and insurrectionary plots challenged the racist myth of black docility. Professor Genovese won the prestigious Bancroft Prize for *Roll, Jordan, Roll* (1974), from which this selection is taken.

From *Roll, Jordan, Roll: The World the Slaves Made* by Eugene D. Genovese, pp. 3–7, 587–598. Copyright © 1972, 1974 by Eugene D. Genovese. Reprinted by permission of Pantheon Books, a division of Random House, Inc.

The slaves of the Old South, unlike those of the Caribbean and Brazil, did not take up arms often enough or in large enough numbers to forge a revolutionary tradition. The southern slaves' role in shaping an organic master-slave relationship unfolded under objectively unfavorable military and political circumstances that compelled a different course. But those slaves who rejected the dialectic of accommodation and resistance at its root bore witness, by their rebellion, not only to their own personal courage but to the limits of their masters' hegemony. . . .

The significance of the slave revolts in the United States lies neither in their frequency nor in their extent, but in their very existence as the ultimate manifestation of class war under the most unfavorable conditions. The resort to insurrection in the United States, especially when more than merely a violent outburst against vicious local conditions, provides a yardstick with which to measure the smoldering resentment of an enslaved people who normally had to find radically different forms of struggle. A Gabriel Prosser or a Nat Turner presents the opposite limiting case to the slavish personality delineated in Stanley Elkins's celebrated model. The slaves as a class cannot be understood apart from the combination of these two images, for every slave, being flesh and blood, necessarily had within him elements of both. The preponderance of the one over the other in their peculiar and innumerable combinations ultimately depended on the totality of social conditions.

Notwithstanding the occurrence of insurrections in the Old South that command attention, they did not compare in size, frequency, intensity, or general historical significance with those of the Caribbean or South America. The largest slave revolt in the United States took place in Louisiana in 1811 and involved between 300 and 500 slaves; it alone was comparable in size to those of the Caribbean—that is, comparable to the modest ones. Nat Turner had about 70 slaves with him. Gabriel Prosser and Denmark Vesey apparently expected to raise many more but never had the chance. Risings such as those of 25 or so in New York City in 1712 or of 50 to 100 at Stono, South Carolina, in 1739, although impressive in themselves, qualify as minor events in the general history of slave revolts in the Americas.

Consider the magnitude of a few lesser-known eighteenth-century revolts. In the almost successful insurrection of 1733 on the small island of St. John in the Danish West Indies, 150 slaves were directly implicated and so many others simultaneously slaughtered and punished as to suggest the participation of many more. Thirty years later an estimated 2,000 slaves rose in Berbice and claimed the lives of about 200 of the colony's 350 whites. A few years later 100 or so slaves rose once more. During the eighteenth century a series of slave revolts erupted in Venezuela, culminating in one of about 300 at Coro in 1795, and shook Spanish power. In the first half of the nineteenth century slave risings in Cuba, the heir to the ill-fated sugar boom on Saint-Domingue, featured many hundreds of slaves at a time.

Saint-Domingue aside, Jamaica and the Guianas stand out in the history of slave revolts during the eighteenth and nineteenth centuries. The reports and correspondence in the British Colonial Office demonstrate that the authorities frequently found themselves confronting not merely rebellion but large-scale war. Jamaican revolts varied greatly in size but averaged, according to Orlando Patterson, about 400 slave participants. The first serious revolt broke out in 1669 on a plantation in St. Dorothy's Parish. Several took place in the 1690s and marked virtually every year of the decade 1730–1740. Tacky's rebellion in 1760 numbered about 1,000 slaves. During the eighteenth century more than a dozen slave revolts matured in a contradictory relationship to the great maroon wars that threatened the foundations of white power. By the nineteenth century, when the Jamaican slaves moved into revolutionary action, which profoundly influenced the politics of abolition in England, they had a powerful tradition and body of experience to draw upon. Their movement peaked in the great Christmas rising of 1831.

Or consider the Guianas. The first slave revolt on record broke out on a plantation in Essequibo in 1731, when under the Dutch. As usually happened later, slave revolts in the Guianas centered on a single plantation and could be contained, if with difficulty. Between 1731 and the abolition of slavery at least eighteen revolts occurred in Essequibo, Berbice, and Demerara—present-day Guyana—exclusive of abortive risings and protracted and extensive maroon wars. That is, these colonies averaged one significant slave revolt per decade. In 1823 between 10,000 and 20,000 slaves on some fifty plantations rose in Demerara and almost tore it apart. The British finally put a hard core of 700 slaves to flight, but only after 100 were dead, whether more or less than the number subsequently executed remains unclear. In sheer numbers and power the whole record of the slave revolts in the Old South did not equal this drama, much less that of Palmares or Saint-Domingue. Even little Barbados had one turn. On Easter Sunday in 1816 some sixty plantations felt the impact of a general rising that, in the words of one historian, "brought fire and pillage to a great part of the colony."

Brazilian slaves raised a number of major insurrections as well as sustaining guerrilla warfare from runaway or maroon colonies known as *quilombos*. For more than half a century a great *quilombo*, Palmares, waged war against the Dutch and Portuguese and at its peak housed an estimated 20,000 blacks. Some 3,000 blacks subsequently participated in the movement known as the Balaiada. Major risings took place during every century of the Brazilian slave regime.

The period 1807–1835 in Bahia opened with an abortive plot among Hausa and Mandinka blacks and closed with a primarily Yoruba rising. In the interim the Yoruba rose in 1809, the Hausa in 1814, blacks of undetermined origin in 1816, and the Yoruba and Fon in 1826 and 1830. The Bahian revolt of several hundred slaves and free Negroes in 1835 suggests the general conditions that encouraged the revolts of the whole period. Despite British pressure and treaty obligations, Brazil continued to import Africans, whose numbers in Bahia increased steadily. Although these new slaves came from various areas, certain groups, notably the Hausa and Yoruba, clung together in large numbers. Many went to the city of Bahia as skilled workers and craftsmen, where they established ties with free Negroes of similar background and together formed a coherent community with literate and sophisticated leaders. The surrounding plantations, once filled with Angolan-Congolese slaves who had only a tenuous relationship with the urban Guineans, increasingly received Hausa and Yoruba imports.

A comparative analysis of the slave revolts of the New World will have to await an extended analysis at a more appropriate place. But even a brief review of the general conditions which favored the massive risings and maroon activities elsewhere in the Americas will illuminate the nonrevolutionary self-assertion of the slaves of the Old South. Slave revolt flourished particularly where the master-slave relationship had developed more as a matter of business than paternalistically; where economic distress and unusual hardship prevailed with greater frequency and intensity than in the Old South; and where slaveholding units were large—the great plantations of the Caribbean and Brazil averaged 100 to 200 slaves, not the 20 or so that marked the plantations of the South. Revolts occurred in both town and country; on the whole, urban centers, like the great plantation districts, offered especially favorable conditions. Revolts also germinated in areas in which a high ratio of slave to free and black to white prevailed and in which the slaves had had a chance to acquire military experience. The constant warfare that marked the Caribbean and South America forced the regimens to arm black volunteers periodically in return for promises of freedom. The slaves of the Old South lived under an enormously powerful regime with a white majority and did not face the divisions in the ruling class that marked Saint-Domingue, Brazil, and other countries. Southern slaves developed their own religion and turned it to good effect, but they were not able to retain such African religions as Islam or develop heavily African syncretisms capable of calling them to holy war.

The revolts in Jamaica, Surinam, Saint-Domingue, Brazil, and elsewhere accompanied and followed large-scale maroon wars. In a number of cases the maroons prevailed and forced the regimes to sign peace treaties and recognize their autonomy. The relationship between maroons and slaves was complex and by no means always friendly. The peace treaties between maroons and white regimes usually provided for black autonomy in return for military support against slave revolts and for the return of new runaways. But the existence of militarily respected maroon colonies destroyed in a single stroke the more extravagant racist pretensions of the whites and provided a beacon to spirited slaves.

In the South slaves also ran away in groups, tried to organize colonies, and struggled for autonomy. During the colonial period they even scored some local successes, and in the 1830s some blacks merged with the Seminoles to make a heroic stand against white power in Florida. But the rapid development of the southern back country confronted slaves with a formidable white power and reduced possibilities for sustained guerrilla warfare to a minimum. Thus, the slave might know of small groups of desperate holdouts here and there, but he had no example of an autonomous black movement to guide him.

The two big eighteenth-century revolts in New York City and Stono, South Carolina—not really so big since they respectively involved 30 and 100 slaves, at the very most—shared certain of the features noticeable in risings elsewhere in the hemisphere. In both instances the slaves took advantage of white divisions. The whites in New York had remained politically rent and in constant agitation since Leisler's rebellion in 1689. The whites in South Carolina had had constant trouble with the Indians and with black maroons operating in Florida; worse, everyone, black and white, knew that Spain and England hovered on the brink of war and that the Spanish were providing sanctuary for slaves from the British colonies. In both revolts African-born slaves predominated and raised the religious question. In New York the rebels flew an openly anti-Christian banner; in South Carolina Angolan slaves espoused an Afro-Catholicism that drew them to the Spanish while providing autonomous ground of their own. In New York the rebels drew their leadership and perhaps their following from skilled mechanics, craftsmen, and other privileged slaves; in South Carolina the rebels probably did also, although the record is unclear.

Little is known about the revolt in St. John the Baptist Parish, Louisiana, in 1811, although it has pride of place as the biggest in our history. Between 300 and 500 slaves, armed with pikes, hoes, and axes but few firearms, marched on New Orleans with flags flying and drums beating. Haiti still loomed large among these slaves, some of whom had originated there. Free Negroes generally supported the regime and helped crush the revolt, but at least one rebel leader from Saint-Domingue, Charles Deslondes, was a free mulatto. The rebels organized well, dividing themselves into companies commanded by officers, but they quickly collapsed in combat against the well-armed militia and regular troops under the command of Wade Hampton.

Three nineteenth-century revolts, two of them abortive, received the notoriety that that of 1811, despite its scope, did not. Since the United States had only recently annexed Louisiana, events there seemed peripheral and no more than what might be expected from an untamed frontier region. The other revolts, which occurred in the oldest and most stable slaveholding regions, stunned the whole South. Nat Turner raised only about seventy slaves but won fame by killing an unprecedented number of whites. Since the previous plots and risings in Virginia had failed to draw white blood,

Turner's accomplishment stood out all the more. The Gabriel Prosser and Denmark Vesey plots never had their moment but in some ways emerged as more impressive than Turner's.

These three revolts shared certain features. Each had literate leaders drawn from the ranks of privileged slaves: Gabriel Prosser, a blacksmith; Nat Turner, a foreman and exhorter; Denmark Vesey, a free Negro who had bought his own freedom after having worked as a seaman and visited Haiti among other places. The Vesey plot had such leaders as Peter Poyas, a ship's carpenter, as well as a black overseer, house servants, and skilled mechanics. Each revolt had an urban dimension: Gabriel Prosser planned to seize Richmond; Vesey, Charleston; and Nat Turner, the town of Jerusalem. Each matured in the wake of divisions or apparent divisions in the ruling classes. Gabriel Prosser organized his plot when many slaves believed that the United States had gone to war with France, and they counted on French help. The bitter struggle between Federalists and Republicans also created an impression of deeper divisions than in fact existed. Vesey and his literate fellow conspirators had followed the congressional debate over the Missouri Compromise and knew that slavery evoked no enthusiasm in a large part of the country. The Turner revolt erupted after Virginia's tense Constitutional Convention of 1829–1830, from which the representatives of the antislavery western part of the state had gone home bitter at the slaveholding east's continuing stranglehold over state politics.

In some respects, notably religious ideology, the movements diverged. Gabriel Prosser relied on Christian preaching but stressed secular themes and, possibly to his cost, ignored appeals to the folk religion of the "outlandish people"—the African-born slaves and those country slaves of the first generation who remained close to the African origins of their parents. Nat Turner, of all the North American slave-revolt leaders we know much about, came closest to assuming a messianic and apocalyptic stance. Whereas Prosser and Vesey died more or less in silence, Turner talked about himself, his hopes, and his plans. An exhorter, he told us a great deal about himself and his world when T. R. Gray asked, "Do you not find yourself mistaken now?" His terrifying and self-revealing answer: "Was not Christ crucified?" Denmark Vesey offered the most complex response. He appealed to the Bible and invoked Christian sanction for his revolt. He also drew upon the services of Jack Purcell ("Gullah

Jack"), an Angolan who appealed to traditional African beliefs and relied heavily on magic. Contemporaries and historians have suggested that Vesey behaved cynically and used opposite appeals in order to unite creole and African-born slaves. But there is no evidence that such a dichotomy existed. Vesey seems to have come closest to formulating a flexible religious appeal based on the folk religion and both African and classical Christian ideas and appeals. Gabriel Prosser slighted the folk religion; Nat Turner assumed a messianic stance among a people not prone to following messiahs; Denmark Vesey most creatively captured the complex tradition of the people he sought to lead.

The slaves of the United States had always faced hopeless odds. A slave revolt anywhere in the Americas, at any time, had poor prospects and required organizers with extraordinary daring and resourcefulness. In the United States those prospects, minimal during the eighteenth century, declined toward zero during the nineteenth. The slaves of the Old South should not have to answer for their failure to mount more frequent and effective revolts; they should be honored for having tried at all under the most discouraging circumstances.

As time went on those conditions became steadily more discouraging: the hinterland filled up with armed whites; the population ratios swung against the blacks; creoles replaced Africans; and the regime grew in power and cohesion. Each new defeat, each abortive conspiracy, confirmed the slaves in the thought that rebellion meant suicide. Meeting necessity with their own creativity, the slaves built an Afro-American community life in the interstices of the system and laid the foundations for their future as a people. But their very strategy for survival enmeshed them in a web of paternalistic relationships which sustained the slaveholder's regime despite the deep antagonisms it engendered.

The slaves' success in forging a world of their own within a wider world shaped primarily by their oppressors sapped their will to revolt, not so much because they succumbed to the baubles of amelioration as because they themselves were creating conditions worth living in as slaves while simultaneously facing overwhelming power that discouraged frontal attack. The slaves of the Old South could not readily throw up a Toussaint—a revolutionary of measured temperament, scorning fanaticism, coolly studying his terrain, alternating compromise with intransigence. They came close enough with Denmark Vesey, Peter Poyas, and perhaps Gabriel Prosser. Nat Turner, on the other hand, foreshadowed his white counterpart, John Brown—fanatic, millenarian, and possibly mad. If so, the question presents itself: What judgment should be rendered on a society the evils of which reach such proportions that only madmen are sane enough to challenge them? It was no accident that a Nat Turner arose after the despair occasioned by the defeats of 1800, 1811, and 1822.

Should the slave revolts, then, be viewed as increasingly futile, pathetic, or even insane efforts doomed to defeat and historically productive of no better result than the inevitable ensuing repression? Should we say of the slave revolts, as Marc Bloch did of the peasant revolts of medieval France, that they qualified as disorganized outbursts which counted for little or nothing when weighed against the achievements of the peasants in building their village communities? The question, however compelling, must be turned around: What could the slaves have accomplished if they had totally lacked an insurrectionary spirit and if their masters had had no fear of getting their throats cut?

The panic of the slaveholders at the slightest hint of slave insurrection revealed what lay beneath their endless self-congratulations over the supposed docility, contentment, and loyalty of their slaves. Almost every slaveholder claimed to trust his own slaves but to fear his neighbor's. As Ulrich Bonnell Phillips—of all people—wrote:

> A great number of southerners at all times held the firm belief that the negro population was so docile, so little cohesive, and in the main so friendly toward the whites and so contented that a disastrous insurrection by them would be impossible. But on the whole there was much greater anxiety abroad in the land than historians have told of, and its influence in shaping southern policy was much greater than they have appreciated.

The slaveholders simply did not know what to think. Mary Boykin Chesnut read a book on the Sepoy mutiny and then saw a play.

> What a thrill of terror ran through me as those yellow and black brutes came jumping over the parapets! Their faces were like so many of the same sort at home. To be sure, John Brown had failed to fire their

hearts here, and they saw no cause to rise and burn and murder us
all. . . . But how long would they resist the seductive and irresistible
call: "Rise, kill, and be free!"

In 1856, William Proctor Gould of Greene County, Alabama, reacted to news of an insurrection scare and to the execution of alleged
conspirators by warning his own slaves against getting involved.
They denied knowledge of any plot and assured him of their loyalty.

> This may or may not be so—but from nothing I have noticed in their
> conduct can I bring myself to believe that any of them were looking
> forward to a change in their situation. What they might have done if
> there had been an actual outbreak must forever remain unknown to
> us.

The slaveholders sometimes stimulated fears of slave revolt for
political purposes. An occasional scare went a long way toward jus-
tifying measures to suppress political opposition to the regime. Sam
Houston of Texas did not stand alone in accusing the Fire-Eaters of
manufacturing slave plots in order to silence their white opponents.
As Clement Eaton argues, fear of slave revolt enhanced the pressures
for conformity, white unity, and "a profoundly conservative attitude
toward social reforms." Politically moderate slaveholders often denounced, at least privately, "sham" insurrections and vigilante hysteria. But no amount of drumbeating by slaveholding extremists
would have succeeded in whipping up so much panic so often if the
whites had not believed that their slaves had cause to rise and might
find the resources and opportunity.

For the slaves, the revolts, however rare, served a purpose. Revolt and white fear of revolt encouraged not only repression—all
action calls forth reaction, which hardly constitutes an excuse for
inaction—but also amelioration of material conditions. Much more
important, they combatted, in the most decisive way among both
whites and blacks, the racist myth of black docility. T. R. Dew, J. H.
Hammond, and other proslavery writers ironically expressed certainty that their slaves, being creoles, were too "civilized" to rise.
Others scoffed that all blacks were "errant cowards." And Garnett
Andrews of Georgia rubbed it in: "If unfitted for the relation, the
African would—instead of affection, have the greatest hostility to

those under whose immediate rule he serves." Every slave revolt or even aborted plot set limits to these white self-deceptions and to the tendency for the slaves to accept them themselves.

There is little evidence of a revolutionary folk tradition among the southern slaves of the kind that Palmares inspired among the slaves of the Brazilian Northeast or that Rákóczy and Stenka Razin inspired among the peasants of Hungary and Russia. Songs and stories about Gabriel Prosser and Nat Turner did exist, and some tradition has passed down to the present in localities like Southampton County, Virginia. But as the slave narratives suggest, southern slaves as a whole knew little about the great slave rebels. No powerful tradition emerged, perhaps simply because the revolts never achieved an appropriate size or duration. But the rebels did their best, and weak as their effort was, it was a great deal better than nothing.

Those slaves whose disaffection turned into violence and hatred—those who resisted the regime physically—included slaves who made stealing almost a way of life, killed their overseers and masters, fought back against patrollers, burned down plantation buildings, and ran away either to freedom or to the woods for a short while in order to effect some specific end, as well as those who took the ultimate measures and rose in revolt. Class oppression, whether or not reinforced and modified by racism, induces servility and feelings of inferiority in the oppressed. Force alone usually has not sufficed to keep the lower classes in subjugation. Slavishness constitutes the extreme form of the psychology of the oppressed, although we may doubt that it ever appears in pure form. It longs for acceptance by the other, perceived as the epitome of such superior qualities as beauty, goodness, virtue, and above all, power. But the inevitable inability of the lower classes, especially but not uniquely slave classes, to attain that acceptance generates disaffection, hatred, and violence.

The slaves' response to paternalism and their imaginative creation of a partially autonomous religion provided a record of simultaneous accommodation and resistance to slavery. Accommodation itself breathed a critical spirit and disguised subversive actions and often embraced its apparent opposite—resistance. In fact, accommodation might best be understood as a way of accepting what could not be helped without falling prey to the pressures for dehumanization, emasculation, and self-hatred. In particular, the slaves' accommodation to paternalism enabled them to assert rights, which by their very nature not only set limits to their surrender of self but actually constituted an implicit rejection of slavery.

Stark physical resistance did not represent a sharp break with the process of accommodation except in its most extreme forms—running away to freedom and insurrection. Strictly speaking, only insurrection represented political action, which some choose to define as the only genuine resistance since it alone directly challenged the power of the regime. From that point of view, those activities which others call "day-to-day resistance to slavery"—stealing, lying, dissembling, shirking, murder, infanticide, suicide, arson—qualify at best as prepolitical and at worst as apolitical.

These distinctions have only a limited usefulness and quickly lose their force. Such apparently innocuous and apolitical measures as a preacher's sermon on love and dignity or the mutual support offered by husbands and wives played—under the specific conditions of slave life—an indispensable part in providing the groundwork for the most obviously political action, for they contributed to the cohesion and strength of a social class threatened by disintegration and demoralization. But "day-to-day resistance to slavery" generally implied accommodation and made no sense except on the assumption of an accepted status quo the norms of which, as perceived or defined by the slaves, had been violated.

The definition of resistance as political response nonetheless draws attention to a break—a qualitative leap—in the continuum of resistance in accommodation and accommodation in resistance. The slaves who unambiguously chose to fight for or fly to freedom represented a new quality. They remained a small portion of the total, but their significance far transcended their numbers. The maturation of that new quality, so vital to the health and future of the black community, depended upon those less dramatic efforts in the quarters which produced a collective spiritual life.

Eric Foner

SLAVERY AND THE CIVIL WAR

No other event more dramatically reveals slavery's central role in United States history than the Civil War. As the North and South followed different economic and social paths, Eric Foner argues, incompatible value systems that pivoted on the issue of slavery emerged from the 1830s onward. The consequence was that the national political system experienced increased sectional tension. After 1854 little common ground remained for the antagonistic ideologies of the Republican party and most southern slaveholders. The election of Abraham Lincoln to the presidency in 1860 meant to radical southern "fire-eaters" the ultimate extinction of slavery and prompted their states' secession from the Union. The Republicans, with their nationalistic commitment to a Union protecting the rights of free soil, free labor, and free men, refused to allow the South to secede. Although the war initially was fought over the issue of union, slavery became the critical matter in 1862, when President Lincoln delivered his preliminary Emancipation Proclamation. Thereafter, it was clear that Union victory meant an end to slavery. That same year, African-American regiments were formed so that the Union could harness the commitment and courage of people who had known slavery firsthand. Professor Foner, DeWitt Clinton Professor of History at Columbia University, is a scholar of the Civil War and Reconstruction eras.

It has long been an axiom of political science that political parties help to hold together diverse, heterogeneous societies like our own. Since most major parties in American history have tried, in Seymour Lipset's phrase, to "appear as plausible representatives of the whole society," they have been broad coalitions cutting across lines of class, race, religion, and section. And although party competition requires that there be differences between the major parties, these differences usually have not been along sharp ideological lines. In fact, the very diversity of American society has inhibited the formation of ideological parties, for such parties assume the existence of a single line of social division along which a majority of the electorate can be mo-

Eric Foner, *Politics and Ideology in the Age of the Civil War*, pp. 34–53. Oxford University Press, 1980. Reprinted with the permission of the author.

bilized. In a large, heterogeneous society, such a line rarely exists. There are, therefore, strong reasons why, in a two-party system, a major party—or a party aspiring to become "major"—will eschew ideology, for the statement of a coherent ideology will set limits to the groups in the electorate to which the party can hope to appeal. Under most circumstances, in other words, the party's role as a carrier of a coherent ideology will conflict with its role as an electoral machine bent on winning the largest possible number of votes.

For much of the seventy years preceding the Civil War, the American political system functioned as a mechanism for relieving social tensions, ordering group conflict, and integrating the society. The existence of national political parties, increasingly focused on the contest for the Presidency, necessitated alliances between political elites in various sections of the country. A recent study of early American politics notes that "political nationalization was far ahead of economic, cultural, and social nationalization"—that is, that the national political system was itself a major bond of union in a diverse, growing society. But as North and South increasingly took different paths of economic and social development and as, from the 1830s onward, antagonistic value systems and ideologies grounded in the question of slavery emerged in these sections, the political system inevitably came under severe disruptive pressures. Because they brought into play basic values and moral judgments, the competing sectional ideologies could not be defused by the normal processes of political compromise, nor could they be contained within the existing inter-sectional political system. Once parties began to reorient themselves on sectional lines, a fundamental necessity of democratic politics—that each party look upon the other as a legitimate alternative government—was destroyed.

When we consider the causes of the sectional conflict, we must ask ourselves not only why civil war came when it did, but why it did not come sooner. How did a divided nation manage to hold itself together for as long as it did? In part, the answer lies in the unifying effects of inter-sectional political parties. On the level of politics, the coming of the Civil War is the story of the intrusion of sectional ideology into the political system, despite the efforts of political leaders of both parties to keep it out. Once this happened, political competition worked to exacerbate, rather than to solve, social and sectional conflicts. For as Frank Sorauf has explained:

> The party of extensive ideology develops in and reflects the society in which little consensus prevails on basic social values and institutions. It betokens deep social disagreements and conflicts. Indeed, the party of ideology that is also a major, competitive party accompanies a politics of almost total concern. Since its ideology defines political issues as including almost every facet of life, it brings to the political system almost every division, every difference, every conflict of any importance in society.

"Parties in this country," wrote a conservative northern Whig in 1855, "heretofore have helped, not delayed, the slow and difficult growth of a consummated nationality." Rufus Choate was lamenting the passing of a bygone era, a time when "our allies were everywhere . . . there were no Alleghenies nor Mississippi rivers in our politics." Party organization and the nature of political conflict had taken on new and unprecedented forms in the 1850s. It is no accident that the breakup of the last major inter-sectional party preceded by less than a year the breakup of the Union or that the final crisis was precipitated not by any "overt act," but by a presidential election.

From the beginning of national government, of course, differences of opinion over slavery constituted an important obstacle to the formation of a national community. "The great danger to our general government," as Madison remarked at the Constitutional Convention, "is the great southern and northern interests of the continent, being opposed to each other." "The institution of slavery and its consequences," according to him, was the main "line of discrimination" in convention disputes. As far as slavery was concerned, the Constitution amply fulfilled Lord Acton's dictum that it was an effort to avoid settling basic questions. Aside from the Atlantic slave trade, Congress was given no power to regulate slavery in any way—the framers' main intention seems to have been to place slavery completely outside the national political arena. The only basis on which a national politics could exist—the avoidance of sectional issues—was thus defined at the outset.

Although the slavery question was never completely excluded

from political debate in the 1790s, and there was considerable Federalist grumbling about the three-fifths clause of the Constitution after 1800, the first full demonstration of the political possibilities inherent in a sectional attack on slavery occurred in the Missouri controversy of 1819–21. These debates established a number of precedents which forecast the future course of the slavery extension issue in Congress. Most important was the fact that the issue was able for a time to completely obliterate party lines. In the first votes on slavery in Missouri, virtually every northerner, regardless of party, voted against expansion. It was not surprising, of course, that northern Federalists would try to make political capital out of the issue. What was unexpected was that northern Republicans, many of whom were aggrieved by Virginia's long dominance of the Presidency and by the Monroe administration's tariff and internal improvements policies, would unite with the Federalists. As John Quincy Adams observed, the debate "disclosed a secret: it revealed the basis for a new organization of parties. . . . Here was a new party really formed . . . terrible to the whole Union, but portentously terrible to the South." But the final compromise set another important precedent: enough northern Republicans became convinced that the Federalists were making political gains from the debates and that the Union was seriously endangered to break with the sectional bloc and support a compromise which a majority of northern Congressmen—Republicans and Federalists—opposed. As for the Monroe administration, its semiofficial spokesman, the *National Intelligencer,* pleaded for a return to the policy of avoiding sectional issues, even to the extent of refusing to publish letters which dealt in any way with the subject of slavery.

The Missouri controversy and the election of 1824, in which four candidates contested the Presidency, largely drawing support from their home sections, revealed that in absence of two-party competition, sectional loyalties would constitute the lines of political division. No one recognized this more clearly than the architect of the second party system, Martin Van Buren. In his well-known letter to Thomas Ritchie of Virginia, Van Buren explained the need for a revival of national two-party politics on precisely this ground: "Party attachment in former times furnished a complete antidote for sectional prejudices by producing counteracting feelings. It was not until that defense had been broken down that the clamor against Southern Influence and African Slavery could be made effectual in the North." Van Buren and many of his generation of politicians had been genuinely frightened by the threats of disunion which echoed through Congress in 1820; they saw national two-party competition as the alternative to sectional conflict and eventual disunion. Ironically, as Richard McCormick has made clear, the creation of the second party system owed as much to sectionalism as to national loyalties. The South, for example, only developed an organized, competitive Whig party in 1835 and 1836 when it became apparent that Jackson, the southern President, had chosen Van Buren, a northerner, as his successor. Once party divisions had emerged, however, they stuck, and by 1840, for one of the very few times in American history, two truly inter-sectional parties, each united behind a single candidate, competed for the Presidency.

The 1830s witnessed a vast expansion of political loyalties and awareness and the creation of party mechanisms to channel voter participation in politics. But the new mass sense of identification with politics had ominous implications for the sectional antagonisms which the party system sought to suppress. The historian of the Missouri Compromise has observed that "if there had been a civil war in 1819–1821 it would have been between the members of Congress, with the rest of the country looking on in amazement." This is only one example of the intellectual and political isolation of Washington from the general populace which James Young has described in *The Washington Community.* The mass, non-ideological politics of the Jackson era created the desperately needed link between governors and governed. But this very link made possible the emergence of two kinds of sectional agitators: the abolitionists, who stood outside of politics and hoped to force public opinion—and through it, politicians—to confront the slavery issue, and political agitators, who used politics as a way of heightening sectional self-consciousness and antagonism in the populace at large.

Because of the rise of mass politics and the emergence of these sectional agitators, the 1830s was the decade in which long-standing, latent sectional divisions were suddenly activated, and previously unrelated patterns of derogatory sectional imagery began to emerge into full-blown sectional ideology. Many of the anti-slavery arguments which gained wide currency in the 1830s had roots stretching back into the eighteenth century. The idea that slavery degraded white labor and retarded economic development, for example, had been voiced by Benjamin Franklin. After 1800, the Federalists, increasingly localized in New England, had developed a fairly coherent critique, not only of the social and economic effects of slavery, but of what Harrison Gray Otis called the divergence of "manners, habits, customs, principles, and ways of thinking" which separated northerners and southerners. And, during the Missouri debates, almost every economic, political, and moral argument against slavery that would be used in the later sectional debate was voiced. In fact, one recurring argument was not picked up later—the warning of northern Congressmen that the South faced the danger of slave rebellion if steps were not taken toward abolition. (As far as I know, only Thaddeus Stevens of Republican spokesmen in the 1850s would explicitly use this line of argument.)

The similarity between Federalist attacks on the South and later abolitionist and Republican arguments, coupled with the fact that many abolitionists—including Garrison, Phillips, the Tappans, and others—came from Federalist backgrounds, has led James Banner to describe abolitionism as "the Massachusetts Federalist ideology come back to life." Yet there was a long road to be traveled from Harrison Gray Otis to William H. Seward, just as there was from Thomas Jefferson to George Fitzhugh. For one thing, the Federalist distrust of democracy, social competition, and the Jeffersonian cry of "equal rights," their commitment to social inequality, hierarchy, tradition, and order prevented them from pushing their anti-slavery views to their logical conclusion. And New England Federalists were inhibited by the requirements of national party organization and competition from voicing anti-slavery views. In the 1790s, they maintained close ties with southern Federalists, and after 1800 hope of reviving their strength in the South never completely died. Only a party which embraced social mobility and competitive individualism, rejected the permanent subordination of any "rank" in society, and was unburdened by a southern wing could develop a fully coherent anti-slavery ideology.

An equally important reason why the Federalists did not develop a consistent sectional ideology was that the South in the early part of the nineteenth century shared many of the Federalists' reservations about slavery. The growth of an anti-slavery ideology, in other words, depended in large measure on the growth of pro-slav-

ery thought, and, by the same token, it was the abolitionist assault
which brought into being the coherent defense of slavery. The opening years of the 1830s, of course, were ones of crisis for the South.
The emergence of militant abolitionism, Nat Turner's rebellion, the
Virginia debates on slavery, and the nullification crisis suddenly presented assaults to the institution of slavery from within and outside
the South. The reaction was the closing of southern society in defense of slavery, "the most thorough-going repression of free
thought, free speech, and a free press ever witnessed in an American
community." At the same time, southerners increasingly abandoned
their previous, highly qualified defenses of slavery and embarked on
the formulation of the pro-slavery argument. By 1837, as is well
known, John C. Calhoun could thank the abolitionists on precisely
this ground:

> This agitation has produced one happy effect at least; it has compelled
> us at the South to look into the nature and character of this great
> institution, and to correct many false impressions that even we had
> entertained in relation to it. Many in the South once believed that it
> was a moral and political evil; that folly and delusion are gone; we see
> it now in its true light, and regard it as the most safe and stable basis
> for free institutions in the world.

The South, of course, was hardly as united as Calhoun asserted. But the progressive rejection of the Jeffersonian tradition, the
suppression of civil liberties, and the increasing stridency of the defense of slavery all pushed the South further and further out of the
inter-sectional mainstream, setting it increasingly apart from the rest
of the country. Coupled with the Gag Rule and the mobs which
broke up abolitionist presses and meetings, the growth of pro-slavery thought was vital to a new anti-slavery formulation which
emerged in the late 1830s and which had been absent from both the
Federalist attacks on slavery and the Missouri debates—the idea of
the Slave Power. The Slave Power replaced the three-fifths clause as
the symbol of southern power, and it was a far more sophisticated
and complex formulation. Abolitionists could now argue that slavery
was not only morally repugnant, it was incompatible with the basic
democratic values and liberties of white Americans. As one abolitionist declared, "We commenced the present struggle to obtain the

freedom of the slave; we are compelled to continue it to preserve our own." In other words, a process of ideological expansion had begun, fed in large measure by the sequence of response and counterresponse between the competing sectional outlooks. Once this process had begun, it had an internal dynamic which made it extremely difficult to stop. This was especially true because of the emergence of agitators whose avowed purpose was to sharpen sectional conflict, polarize public opinion, and develop sectional ideologies to their logical extremes.

As the 1840s opened, most political leaders still clung to the traditional basis of politics, but the sectional, ideological political agitators formed growing minorities in each section. In the South, there was a small group of outright secessionists and a larger group, led by Calhoun, who were firmly committed to the Union but who viewed sectional organization and self-defense, not the traditional reliance on inter-sectional political parties, as the surest means of protecting southern interests within the Union. In the North, a small radical group gathered in Congress around John Quincy Adams and Congressmen like Joshua Giddings, William Slade, and Seth Gates— men who represented areas of the most intense abolitionist agitation and whose presence confirmed Garrison's belief that, once public opinion was aroused on the slavery issue, politicians would have to follow step. These radicals were determined to force slavery into every congressional debate. They were continually frustrated but never suppressed, and the reelection of Giddings in 1842 after his censure and resignation from the House proved that in some districts party discipline was no longer able to control the slavery issue.

The northern political agitators, both Congressmen and Liberty party leaders, also performed the function of developing and popularizing a political rhetoric, especially focused on fear of the Slave Power, which could be seized upon by traditional politicians and large masses of voters if slavery ever entered the center of political conflict.

In the 1840s, this is precisely what happened. As one politician later recalled, "Slavery upon which by common consent no party issue had been made was then obtruded upon the field of party action." It is significant that John Tyler and John C. Calhoun, the two men most responsible for this intrusion, were political outsiders, men without places in the national party structure. Both of their careers were blocked by the major parties but might be advanced if tied to the slavery question in the form of Texas annexation. Once introduced into politics, slavery was there to stay. The Wilmot Proviso, introduced in 1846, had precisely the same effect as the proposal two decades earlier to restrict slavery in Missouri—it completely fractured the major parties along sectional lines. As in 1820, opposition to the expansion of slavery became the way in which a diverse group of northerners expressed their various resentments against a southern-dominated administration. And, as in 1821, a small group of northern Democrats eventually broke with their section, reaffirmed their primary loyalty to the party, and joined with the South to kill the Proviso in 1847. In the same year, enough southerners rejected Calhoun's call for united sectional action to doom his personal and sectional ambitions.

But the slavery extension debates of the 1840s had far greater effects on the political system than the Missouri controversy had had. Within each party, they created a significant group of sectional politicians—men whose careers were linked to the slavery question and who would therefore resist its exclusion from future politics. And in the North, the 1840s witnessed the expansion of sectional political rhetoric—as more and more northerners became familiar with the "aggressions" of the Slave Power and the need to resist them. At the same time, as anti-slavery ideas expanded, unpopular and divisive elements were weeded out, especially the old alliance of anti-slavery with demands for the rights of free blacks. Opposition to slavery was already coming to focus on its lowest common denominators—free soil, opposition to the Slave Power, and the union.

The political system reacted to the intrusion of the slavery question in the traditional ways. At first, it tried to suppress it. This is the meaning of the famous letters opposing the immediate annexation of Texas issued by Clay and Van Buren on the same spring day in 1844, probably after consultation on the subject. It was an agreement that slavery was too explosive a question for either party to try to take partisan advantage of it. The agreement, of course, was torpedoed by the defeat of Van Buren for the Democratic nomination, a defeat caused in part by the willingness of his Democratic opponents to use the Texas and slavery questions to discredit Van Buren—thereby violating the previously established rules of political conduct. In the North from 1844 onward, both parties, particularly the Whigs, tried to defuse the slavery issue and minimize defection to the Liberty party by adopting anti-southern rhetoric. This tended to prevent defections to third parties, but it had the effect of nurturing and legitimating anti-southern sentiment within the ranks of the major parties themselves. After the 1848 election in which northern Whigs and Democrats vied for title of "free soil" to minimize the impact of the Free Soil party, William H. Seward commented, "Antislavery is at length a respectable element in politics."

Both parties also attempted to devise formulas for compromising the divisive issue. For the Whigs, it was "no territory"—an end to expansion would end the question of the spread of slavery. The Democratic answer, first announced by Vice President Dallas in 1847 and picked up by Lewis Cass, was popular sovereignty or nonintervention: giving to the people of each territory the right to decide on slavery. As has often been pointed out, popular sovereignty was an exceedingly vague and ambiguous doctrine. It was never precisely clear what the powers of a territorial legislature were to be or at what point the question of slavery was to be decided. But politically such ambiguity was essential (and intentional) if popular sovereignty were to serve as a means of settling the slavery issue on the traditional basis—by removing it from national politics and transferring the battleground from Congress to the territories. Popular sovereignty formed one basis of the Compromise of 1850, the last attempt of the political system to expel the disease of sectional ideology by finally settling all the points at which slavery and national politics intersected.

That compromise was possible in 1850 was testimony to the resiliency of the political system and the continuing ability of party loyalty to compete with sectional commitments. But the very method of passage revealed how deeply sectional divisions were embedded in party politics. Because only a small group of Congressmen—mostly northwestern Democrats and southern Whigs—were committed to compromise on every issue, the "omnibus" compromise measure could not pass. The compromise had to be enacted serially with the small compromise bloc, led by Stephen A. Douglas of Illinois, aligned with first one sectional bloc, then the other, to pass the individual measures.

His role in the passage of the compromise announced the emergence of Douglas as the last of the great Unionist, compromising politicians, the heir of Clay, Webster, and other spokesmen for the center. And his career, like Webster's, showed that it was no longer possible to win the confidence of both sections with a combination of extreme nationalism and the calculated suppression of the slavery issue in national politics. Like his predecessors, Douglas called for a policy of "entire silence on the slavery question," and throughout the 1850s, as Robert Johannsen has written, his aim was to restore "order and stability to American politics through the agency of a national, conservative Democratic party." Ultimately, Douglas failed—a traditional career for the Union was simply not possible in the 1850s—but it is equally true that in 1860 he was the only presidential candidate to draw significant support in all parts of the country.

It is, of course, highly ironic that it was Douglas's attempt to extend the principle of popular sovereignty to territory already guaranteed to free labor by the Missouri Compromise which finally shattered the second party system. We can date exactly the final collapse of that system—February 15, 1854—the day a caucus of southern Whig Congressmen and Senators decided to support Douglas's Nebraska bill, despite the fact that they could have united with northern Whigs in opposition both to the repeal of the Missouri Compromise and the revival of sectional agitation. But in spite of the sectionalization of politics which occurred after 1854, Douglas continued his attempt to maintain a national basis of party competition. In fact, from one angle of vision, whether politics was to be national or sectional was the basic issue of the Lincoln-Douglas debates of 1858. The Little Giant presented local autonomy—popular sovereignty for states and territories—as the only "national" solution to the slavery question, while Lincoln attempted to destroy this middle ground and force a single, sectional solution on the entire Union. There is a common critique of Douglas's politics, expressed perhaps most persuasively by Allan Nevins, which argues that, as a man with no moral feelings about slavery, Douglas was incapable of recognizing that this moral issue affected millions of northern voters. This, in my opinion, is a serious misunderstanding of Douglas's politics. What he insisted was not that there was no moral question involved in slavery but that it was not the function of the politician to deal in moral judgments. To Lincoln's prediction that the nation could not exist half slave and half free, Douglas replied that it had so existed for seventy years and could continue to do so if northerners stopped trying to impose their own brand of morality upon the South.

Douglas's insistence on the separation of politics and morality was expressed in his oft-quoted statement that—in his role as a politician—he did not care if the people of a territory voted slavery "up or down." As he explained in his Chicago speech of July 1858, just before the opening of the great debates:

> I deny the right of Congress to force a slave-holding state upon an unwilling people. I deny their right to force a free state upon an unwilling people. I deny their right to force a good thing upon a people who are unwilling to receive it. . . . It is no answer to this argument to say that slavery is an evil and hence should not be tolerated. You must allow the people to decide for themselves whether it is a good or an evil.

When Lincoln, therefore, said the real purpose of popular sovereignty was "to educate and mould public opinion, at least northern public opinion, to not care whether slavery is voted down or up," he was, of course, right. For Douglas recognized that moral categories, being essentially uncompromisable, are unassimilable in politics. The only solution to the slavery issue was local autonomy. Whatever a majority of a state or territory wished to do about slavery was right—or at least should not be tampered with by politicians from other areas. To this, Lincoln's only possible reply was the one formulated in the debates—the will of the majority must be tempered by considerations of morality. Slavery was not, he declared, an "*ordinary*" matter of domestic concern in the states and territories." Because of its essential immorality, it tainted the entire nation, and its disposition in the territories, and eventually in the entire nation, was a matter of national concern to be decided by a national, not a local, majority. As the debates continued, Lincoln increasingly moved to this moral level of the slavery argument: "Everything that emanates from [Douglas] or his coadjutors, carefully excludes the thought that there is anything wrong with slavery. All their arguments, if you will consider them, will be seen to exclude the thought. . . . If you do admit that it is wrong, Judge Douglas can't logically say that he don't care whether a wrong is voted up or down."

In order to press home the moral argument, moreover, Lincoln had to insist throughout the debates on the basic humanity of the black; while Douglas, by the same token, logically had to define blacks as subhuman, or at least, as the Dred Scott decision had insisted, not part of the American "people" included in the Declaration of Independence and the Constitution. Douglas's view of the black, Lincoln declared, conveyed "no vivid impression that the Negro is a human, and consequently has no idea that there can be any moral question in legislating about him." Of course, the standard of morality which Lincoln felt the nation should adopt regarding slavery and the black was the sectional morality of the Republican party.

By 1860, Douglas's local majoritarianism was no more acceptable to southern political leaders than Lincoln's national and moral majoritarianism. The principle of state rights and minority self-determination had always been the first line of defense of slavery from northern interference, but southerners now coupled it with the demand that Congress intervene to establish and guarantee slavery in the territories. The Lecompton fight had clearly demonstrated that southerners would no longer be satisfied with what Douglas hoped the territories would become—free, Democratic states. And the refusal of the Douglas Democrats to accede to southern demands was the culmination of a long history of resentment on the part of northern Democrats, stretching back into the 1840s, at the impossible political dilemma of being caught between increasingly anti-southern constituency pressure and loyalty to an increasingly pro-southern national party. For their part, southern Democrats viewed their northern allies as too weak at home and too tainted with anti-southernism after the Lecompton battle to be relied on to protect southern interests any longer.

As for the Republicans, by the late 1850s they had succeeded in developing a coherent ideology which, despite internal ambiguities and contradictions, incorporated the fundamental values, hopes, and fears of a majority of northerners. . . . It rested on a commitment to the northern social order, founded on the dignity and opportunities of free labor, and to social mobility, enterprise, and "progress." It gloried in the same qualities of northern life—materialism, social fluidity, and the dominance of the self-made man—which twenty years earlier had been the source of widespread anxiety and fear in Jacksonian America. And it defined the South as a backward, stagnant, aristocratic society, totally alien in values and social order to the middle-class capitalism of the North.

Some elements of the Republican ideology had roots stretching back into the eighteenth century. Others, especially the Republican emphasis on the threat of the Slave Power, were relatively new. Northern politics and thought were permeated by the Slave Power idea in the 1850s. The effect can perhaps be gauged by a brief look at the career of the leading Republican spokesman of the 1850s, William H. Seward. As a political child of upstate New York's burned-over district and anti-masonic crusade, Seward had long believed that the Whig party's main political liability was its image as the spokesman of the wealthy and aristocratic. Firmly committed to egalitarian democracy, Seward had attempted to reorient the New York State Whigs into a reformist, egalitarian party, friendly to immigrants and embracing political and economic democracy, but he was always defeated by the party's downstate conservative wing. In the 1840s, he became convinced that the only way for the party to counteract the Democrats' monopoly of the rhetoric of democracy and equality was for the Whigs to embrace anti-slavery as a party platform.

The Slave Power idea gave the Republicans the anti-aristocratic appeal with which men like Seward had long wished to be associated politically. By fusing older anti-slavery arguments with the idea that slavery posed a threat to northern free labor and democratic values, it enabled the Republicans to tap the egalitarian outlook which lay at the heart of northern society. At the same time, it enabled Republicans to present anti-slavery as an essentially conservative reform, an attempt to reestablish the anti-slavery principles of the founding fathers and rescue the federal government from southern usurpation. And, of course, the Slave Power idea had a far greater appeal to northern self-interest than arguments based on the plight of black slaves in the South. As the black abolitionist Frederick Douglass noted, "The cry of Free Men was raised, not for the extension of liberty to the black man, but for the protection of the liberty of the white."

By the late 1850s, it had become a standard part of Republican rhetoric to accuse the Slave Power of a long series of transgressions against northern rights and liberties and to predict that, unless halted by effective political action, the ultimate aim of the conspiracy—the complete subordination of the national government to slavery and the suppression of northern liberties—would be accomplished. Like other conspiracy theories, the Slave Power idea was a way of ordering and interpreting history, assigning clear causes to otherwise inexplicable events, from the Gag Rule to Bleeding Kansas and the Dred Scott decision. It also provided a convenient symbol through which a host of anxieties about the future could be expressed. At the same time, the notion of a black Republican conspiracy to overthrow slavery and southern society had taken hold in the South. These competing conspiratorial outlooks were reflections, not merely of sectional "paranoia," but of the fact that the nation was every day growing apart and into two societies whose ultimate interests were diametrically opposed. The South's fear of black Republicans, despite its exaggerated rhetoric, was based on the realistic assessment that at the heart of Republican aspirations for the nation's future was the restriction and eventual eradication of slavery. And the Slave Power expressed northerners' conviction, not only that slavery was incompatible with basic democratic values, but that to protect slavery, southerners were determined to control the federal government and use it to foster the expansion of slavery. In summary, the Slave Power idea was the ideological glue of the Republican party—it enabled them to elect in 1860 a man conservative enough to sweep to victory in every northern state, yet radical enough to trigger the secession crisis.

Did the election of Lincoln pose any real danger to the institution of slavery? In my view, it is only possible to argue that it did not if one takes a completely static—and therefore ahistorical—view of the slavery issue. The expansion of slavery was not simply an issue; it was a fact. By 1860, over half the slaves lived in areas outside the original slave states. At the same time, however, the South had become a permanent and shrinking minority within the nation. And in the majority section, anti-slavery sentiment had expanded at a phenomenal rate. Within one generation, it had moved from the commitment of a small minority of northerners to the motive force behind a victorious party. That sentiment now demanded the exclusion of slavery from the territories. Who could tell what its demands would be in ten or twenty years? The incoming President had often declared his commitment to the "ultimate extinction" of slavery. In Alton, Illinois, in the heart of the most pro-slavery area of the North, he had condemned Douglas because "he looks to no end of the institution of slavery." A Lincoln administration seemed likely to be only the beginning of a prolonged period of Republican hegemony. And the succession of generally weak, one-term Presidents between 1836 and 1860 did not obscure the great expansion in the potential power of the Presidency which had taken place during the administration of Andrew Jackson. Old Hickory had clearly shown that a strong-willed President, backed by a united political party, had tremendous power to shape the affairs of government and to transform into policy his version of majority will.

What was at stake in 1860, as in the entire sectional conflict, was the character of the nation's future. This was one reason Republicans had placed so much stress on the question of the expansion of slavery. Not only was this the most available issue concerning slavery constitutionally open to them, but it involved the nation's future in the most direct way. In the West, the future was tabula rasa, and the future course of western development would gravely affect the direction of the entire nation. Now that the territorial issue was settled by Lincoln's election, it seemed likely that the slavery controversy would be transferred back into the southern states themselves. Secessionists, as William Freehling has argued, feared that slavery was weak and vulnerable in the border states, even in Virginia. They feared Republican efforts to encourage the formation of Republican organizations in these areas and the renewal of the long-suppressed internal debate on slavery in the South itself. And, lurking behind these anxieties, may have been fear of anti-slavery debate reaching the slave quarters, of an undermining of the masters' authority, and, ultimately, of slave rebellion itself. The slaveholders knew, despite the great economic strength of King Cotton, that the existence of slavery as a local institution in a larger free economy demanded an inter-sectional community consensus, real or enforced. It was this consensus which Lincoln's election seemed to undermine, which is why the secession convention of South Carolina declared, "Experience has proved that slaveholding states cannot be safe in subjection to non-slaveholding states."

More than seventy years before the secession crisis, James Madison had laid down the principles by which a central government and individual and minority liberties could coexist in a large and heterogeneous Union. The very diversity of interests in the nation, he argued in the Federalist papers, was the security for the rights of minorities, for it ensured that no one interest would ever gain control of the government. In the 1830s, John C. Calhoun recognized the danger which abolitionism posed to the South—it threatened to rally the North in the way Madison had said would not happen—in terms of one commitment hostile to the interests of the minority South. Moreover, Calhoun recognized, when a majority interest is organized into an effective political party, it can seize control of all the branches of government, overturning the system of constitutional checks and balances which supposedly protected minority rights. Only the principle of the concurrent majority—a veto which each major interest could exercise over policies directly affecting it— could reestablish this constitutional balance.

At the outset of the abolitionist crusade, Calhoun had been convinced that, while emancipation must be "resisted at all costs," the South should avoid hasty action until it was "certain that it is the real object, not by a few, but by a very large portion of the non-slaveholding states." By 1850, Calhoun was convinced that "Every portion of the North entertains views more or less hostile to slavery." And by 1860, the election returns demonstrated that this anti-slavery sentiment, contrary to Madison's expectations, had united in an interest capable of electing a President, despite the fact that it had not the slightest support from the sectional minority. The character of Lincoln's election, in other words, completely overturned the ground rules which were supposed to govern American politics. The South Carolina secession convention expressed secessionists' reaction when it declared that once the sectional Republican party, founded on hostility to southern values and interests, took over control of the federal government, "the guarantees of the Constitution will then no longer exist."

Thus the South came face to face with a conflict between its loyalty to the nation and loyalty to the South—that is, to slavery, which, more than anything else, made the South distinct. David Potter has pointed out that the principle of majority rule implies the existence of a coherent, clearly recognizable body of which more than half may be legitimately considered as a majority of the whole. For the South to accept majority rule in 1860, in other words, would have been an affirmation of a common nationality with the North. Certainly, it is true that in terms of ethnicity, language, religion—many of the usual components of nationality—Americans, North and South, were still quite close. On the other hand, one important element, community of interest, was not present. And perhaps most important, the preceding decades had witnessed an escalation of distrust—an erosion of the reciprocal currents of good will so essential for national harmony. "We are not one people," declared the New York *Tribune* in 1855. "We are two peoples. We are a people for Freedom and a people for Slavery. Between the two, conflict is inevitable." We can paraphrase John Adams's famous comment on the American Revolution and apply it to the coming of the Civil War—the separation was complete, in the minds of the people, before the war began. In a sense, the Constitution and national political system had failed in the difficult task of creating a nation—only the Civil War itself would accomplish it.

SUGGESTIONS FOR FURTHER READING

The body of historical literature treating slavery is immense. The following suggestions for additional reading and reference identify bibliographic aids and collections of documents, as well as key historiographical debates and crucial topics in the literature on American slavery.

Bibliographies and Reference Works

Two indispensable bibliographic aids to surveying the voluminous writings on slavery are John David Smith, *Black Slavery in the Americas: An Interdisciplinary Bibliography, 1865–1980,* 2 vols. (Westport, Conn., 1982), and Joseph Miller, *Slavery: A Worldwide Bibliography* (White Plains, N.Y., 1985). The former work contains 21,161 entries and is extensively cross-referenced; the latter is annually updated by Miller and others in *Slavery and Abolition: A Journal of Comparative Studies.* See also James S. Olson, *Slave Life in America: A Historiography and Selected Bibliography* (Lanham, Md., 1983). An essential guide to the law and slavery is Paul Finkelman, *Slavery in the Courtroom: An Annotated Bibliography of American Cases* (Washington, D.C., 1985). Bibliographies that remain useful for sources before the early 1970s include James McPherson et al., *Blacks in America: Bibliographic Essays* (Garden City, N.Y., 1971); Elizabeth Miller and Mary L. Fisher, *The Negro in America: A Bibliography* (Cambridge, Mass., 1970); and Peter C. Hogg, *The African Trade and Its Suppression: A Classified and Annotated Bibliography of Books, Pamphlets and Periodical Articles* (London, 1973). A helpful collection of scholarly essays on slavery gleaned from a wide variety of sources is Paul Finkelman, ed., *Articles on American Slavery,* 18 vols. (New York, 1990). An essential reference work describing people, places, and concepts is Randall M. Miller and John D. Smith, eds., *Dictionary of Afro-American Slavery* (New York, 1988). More general references on the African-American experience are Dwight L. Smith, ed., *Afro-American History: A Bibliography* (Santa Barbara, Calif., 1976); W. A. Low and Virgil A. Clift, eds., *Encyclopedia of Black America* (New York, 1981); and Rayford W. Logan and Michael R. Winston, eds., *The Dictionary of American Negro Biography* (New York, 1983).

A number of studies of slavery also include comprehensive bibliographies, as well as important introductions to the subject. John

B. Boles, *Black Southerners, 1619–1869* (Lexington, Ky., 1983), is an excellent synthesis of recent historiography and contains a thorough bibliographic essay. Peter Kolchin, "American Historians and Antebellum Southern Slavery, 1959–1984," in William J. Cooper, Michael F. Holt, and John McCardell, eds., *A Master's Due: Essays in Honor of David Herbert Donald* (Baton Rouge, La., 1985), 87–111; Charles B. Dew, "The Slavery Experience," in John B. Boles and Evelyn Thomas Nolen, eds., *Interpreting Southern History: Historiographical Essays in Honor of Sanford W. Higginbotham* (Baton Rouge, La., 1987), 120–161; and Peter Parish, *Slavery: History and Historians* (New York, 1989) provide significant insights in addition to useful bibliographies. John Hope Franklin and Alfred A. Moss, Jr., *From Slavery to Freedom: A History of Negro Americans,* 6th ed. (New York, 1987), is the standard textbook on black history and contains an extensive bibliography. An anthology with a comprehensive bibliography is Allan Weinstein, Frank O. Gatell, and David Sarasohn, eds., *American Negro Slavery* (New York, 1979).

Documents

In examining how Americans have interpreted slavery and its impact on American life, students should consult published primary materials. Kenneth M. Stampp has edited the extensive microfilm collection, *Records of Ante-Bellum Southern Plantations from the Revolution through the Civil War,* which is available from University Publications of America. Two excellent collections of documents are Michael Mullin, ed., *American Negro Slavery* (New York, 1976), which is particularly strong on the colonial and early national periods, and Willie Lee Rose, *A Documentary History of Slavery in North America* (New York, 1976), which features more than 100 original sources accompanied by instructive annotation. Elizabeth Donnan, *Documents Illustrative of the History of the Slave Trade to America,* 4 vols. (Washington, D.C., 1930–1935), is important for the African diaspora. An informative statewide guide to legal decisions on slavery is Helen T. Catteral, ed., *Judicial Cases Concerning American Slavery and the Negro,* 5 vols. (Washington, D.C., 1926–1937), which should be supplemented by the pamphlet literature in Paul Finkelman, ed., *Slavery, Race and the American Legal System, 1700–1872,* 16 vols. (New York, 1988). Lathan A. Windley, ed., *Runaway Slave*

Advertisements: A Documentary History from the 1730s to 1790, 4 vols. (Westport, Conn., 1983), is valuable for the subject of fugitive slaves.

Three volumes have been published in the ongoing series *Freedom: A Documentary History,* edited by Ira Berlin, Joseph P. Reidy, and Leslie S. Rowland for Cambridge University Press: vol. 1, *The Destruction of Slavery* (Cambridge, Eng., 1986); vol. 2, *The Black Military Experience* (Cambridge, Eng., 1983); and vol. 3, *The Wartime Genesis of Free Labor: The Lower South* (Cambridge, Eng., 1990). Under the general editorship of C. Peter Ripley, three volumes of the *Black Abolitionist Papers* have been published: vol. 1, *The British Isles, 1830–1865* (Chapel Hill, N.C., 1985); vol. 2, *Canada, 1830–1865* (Chapel Hill, N.C., 1987); and vol. 3, *The United States, 1830–1846* (Chapel Hill, N.C., 1991). Broader collections on the black experience, including slavery, that remain helpful are Leslie H. Fishel and Benjamin Quarles, *The Negro American: A Documentary History* (New York, 1970); Eric Foner, *America's Black Past: A Reader in Afro-American History* (New York, 1970); Nathan Huggins et al., eds., *Key Issues in the Afro-American Experience* (New York, 1971); and William Loren Katz, *The American Negro: History and Literature,* 44 vols. (New York, 1968).

Contemporary White Accounts

Insightful contemporary appraisals of plantation slavery written by a sympathetic foreign visitor, Alexis de Tocqueville, may be found in *Democracy in America,* 2 vols. (New York, 1966; originally 1835 and 1840), edited by J. P. Mayer and Max Lerner; and by a critical northerner, Frederick Law Olmsted, in *The Cotton Kingdom* (New York, 1983), edited and with an introduction by Lawrence N. Powell. See also Charles E. Beveridge and Charles C. McLaughlin, eds., *Slavery and the South, 1852–1857,* vol. 2 of *The Papers of Frederick Law Olmsted* (Baltimore, 1981; originally 1861), for a critical assessment of Olmsted's views. Documents on the plantation system during the colonial era are collected in Aubrey C. Land, ed., *Bases of the Plantation Society* (Columbia, S.C., 1969). The planter's view of slavery and the South can be found in C. Vann Woodward, ed., *Mary Chesnut's Civil War* (New York, 1981); Robert M. Myers, ed., *The Children of Pride: A True Story of Georgia and the Civil War* (New Haven, 1972); and Carol Bleser, ed., *Secret and Sacred: The Diaries of James*

Henry Hammond, a Southern Slaveholder (New York, 1988). Drew G. Faust, ed., *The Ideology of Slavery* (Baton Rouge, La., 1981), presents the views of proslavery ideologues. An impassioned indictment of slavery is the abolitionist Theodore Weld's *American Slavery As It Is,* edited by Richard O. Curry and Joanna Cowden (Itasca, Ill., 1972; originally 1839). The oratorio *Slavery Documents,* composed by Donald Sur, draws on Weld's work and other original sources; the Cantata Singers performed the premiere in Boston in 1990.

Contemporary Black Sources

There are numerous published slave autobiographies and narratives. Good interpretive guides are Frances Smith Foster, *The Development of Ante-Bellum Slave Narratives* (Westport, Conn., 1976); Charles T. Davis and Henry Lewis Gates, Jr., eds., *The Slave's Narrative* (New York, 1984); and William L. Andrews, *To Tell a Free Story: The First Century of Afro-American Autobiography, 1760–1865* (Urbana, Ill., 1986). The most famous narrative is by the ex-slave and prominent abolitionist Frederick Douglass, *A Narrative of the Life of Frederick Douglass* (Boston, 1845). The authoritative edition of Douglass's writings is the multivolumed *The Frederick Douglass Papers,* an ongoing project under the general editorship of John Blassingame for Yale University Press. Major biographies of Douglass are Waldo E. Martin, Jr., *The Mind of Frederick Douglass* (Chapel Hill, N.C., 1984); David W. Blight, *Frederick Douglass' Civil War: Keeping Faith in Jubilee* (Baton Rouge, La., 1989); and William S. McFeely, *Frederick Douglass* (New York, 1991).

A number of ex-slave narratives are readily available. Arna Bontemps, *Five Slave Narratives: A Compendium* (New York, 1960), remains a useful collection. Solomon Northup, *Twelve Years a Slave* (Baton Rouge, La., 1968; originally 1853), is an account of an enslaved northern free black; and a history written by a fugitive slave, William Wells Brown, *The Black Man, His Antecedents, His Genius, and His Achievements* (New York, 1863), is worth consulting. Oxford University Press has reprinted a series on the experiences of slave women. See Harriet Jacobs, *Incidents in the Life of a Slave Girl* (New York, 1988; originally 1861); *Collected Black Women's Narratives* (New York, 1988); *Six Women's Slave Narratives* (New York, 1988); and *The Narrative of Sojourner Truth* (New York, 1991; originally 1850).

The most comprehensive collection of slave narratives and interviews with ex-slaves is George P. Rawick's *The American Slave: A Composite Autobiography,* 41 vols. (Westport, Conn., 1972), for which Donald M. Jacobs has edited *The Index to "The American Slave"* (Westport, Conn., 1981). See also John W. Blassingame, ed., *Slave Testimony: Two Centuries of Letters, Speeches, Interviews, and Autobiographies* (Baton Rouge, La., 1977); Randall M. Miller, ed., *"Dear Master": Letters of a Slave Family* (Ithaca, N.Y., 1978); Charles L. Perdue, Jr., Thomas E. Burder, and Robert K. Phillips, eds., *Weevils in the Wheat: Interviews with Virginia Ex-Slaves* (Charlottesville, Va., 1976); Robert S. Starobin, ed., *Blacks in Bondage: Letters of American Slaves* (New York, 1974); and Norman R. Yetman, *Life Under the "Peculiar Institution": Selections from the Slave Narrative Collection* (Huntington, N.Y., 1976). The caveats and opportunities in using black primary sources on slavery are discussed in John W. Blassingame, "Using the Testimony of Ex-Slaves: Approaches and Problems," *Journal of Southern History* 41 (1975), 473–492; David Thomas Bailey, "A Divided Prism: Two Sources of Black Testimony on Slavery," *Journal of Southern History* 46 (1980), 381–404; and Norman R. Yetman, "Ex-Slave Interviews and the Historiography of Slavery," *American Quarterly* 36 (1984), 181–210.

Historiography: From Phillips to Elkins

Much of the historical literature on slavery focuses on the life and economy of the slave plantation. Ulrich B. Phillips, in *American Negro Slavery: A Survey of the Supply, Employment and Control of Negro Labor as Determined by the Plantation Regime* (New York, 1918) and *Life and Labor in the Old South* (Boston, 1929), was the first scholar to use plantation records extensively; he portrayed slavery as a benign social institution that served as a useful training ground for racially inferior and culturally deprived black slaves. His innovative scholarship was thus joined with a commitment to white supremacy. Furthermore, he maintained that slavery was unprofitable and would have died a natural death if the bellicose Republican party had not waged an internecine war. Phillips remained the dominant authority on American slavery for three decades. Two state studies influenced by Phillips are James B. Sellers, *Slavery in Alabama* (Tuscaloosa, Ala., 1950), and Charles B. Sydnor, *Slavery in Mississippi* (New York, 1933).

Outstanding African-American scholars such as W. E. B. Du Bois and Carter G. Woodson countered Phillips's interpretation, even if few whites were listening at the time. Du Bois's major works include *The Suppression of the African Slave-Trade to the United States of America, 1638–1870* (New York, 1896), *The Souls of Black Folk* (New York, 1903), and *Black Reconstruction* (New York, 1935). For a guide to his copious writings, see Herbert Aptheker, *Annotated Bibliography of the Published Writings of W. E. B. Du Bois* (Millwood, N.Y., 1976). Carter G. Woodson wrote and edited more books in the field of black history than any other scholar. In addition to *The Education of the Negro Prior to 1861* (New York, 1915), he helped to establish the Association for the Study of Negro Life and History, Negro History Week, and the *Negro History Bulletin,* and he founded and edited the *Journal of Negro History* from 1916 to 1950.

With changes in the social and scientific attitudes of mid-twentieth-century Americans, Phillips's conclusions became unacceptable, and scholars challenged his findings. In an important essay, "U. B. Phillips and the Plantation Legend," *Journal of Negro History* 29 (1944), Richard Hofstadter charged that Phillips had used an unrepresentative sample of sources and had been racially biased in selecting facts. In 1950 Oscar Handlin and Mary Handlin followed Hofstadter's critique with "Origins of the Southern Labor System," *William and Mary Quarterly* 6 (1950), 199–222, in order to show that slavery resulted from a particular set of historical developments. The refutation of Phillips culminated with Kenneth Stampp's *The Peculiar Institution: Slavery in the Ante-Bellum South* (New York, 1956). Surpassing Phillips in the scope and depth of his research, Stampp portrayed slavery as a harsh, repressive, and profitable system based on whites' exploitation of black labor. Stampp's neoabolitionist indictment of Phillips's argument for white supremacy marked a new wave of racially liberal studies of slavery.

The demolition of Phillips's long-standing authority provided the opportunity for the redirection of the study of slavery, especially with an emphasis on the responses of slaves. In the controversial book *Slavery: A Problem in American Institutional and Intellectual Life* (Chicago, 1959), Stanley Elkins argued that the institution of slavery was more oppressive in the United States than in Latin America and that this "closed" system, analogous to a Nazi concentration camp, reduced the slave to a dependent, childlike "Sambo." Although Elkins's conclusions have not stood the test of subsequent scholarship, his sympathetic focus on the slave's experience as well as innovative use of comparative history and the social sciences spurred a new generation of studies. For the response to Elkins's pivotal book, see Ann J. Lane, ed., *The Debate over Slavery: Stanley Elkins and His Critics* (Urbana, Ill., 1971).

Slave Culture and Slave Community

In the three decades since the publication of Stampp's and Elkins's landmark books, a revolution has occurred in the historiography of slavery. Scholars have focused on the study of slave life and culture in particular, and important differences in interpretation and emphasis have come to light. John W. Blassingame, *The Slave Community: Plantation Life in the Antebellum South* (New York, 1972; rev. ed., 1979), rebutted Elkins's model of "Sambo" with his own argument for the creative responses of slaves to bondage. Blassingame was not without critics; see Al-Tony Gilmore, ed., *Revisiting Blassingame's* The Slave Community: *The Scholars Respond* (Westport, Conn., 1978). The two major books on slave life are Eugene D. Genovese, *Roll, Jordan, Roll: The World the Slaves Made* (New York, 1974), and Herbert H. Gutman, *The Black Family in Slavery and Freedom, 1750–1925* (New York, 1976), both influential works. They differ, however, in the degree to which they attribute cultural autonomy to the slave from the master class, an independence that Gutman stresses more than Genovese. Gutman was an influential pioneer in revising social and labor history with a stress on working-class culture. Neo-Marxist theory has had a major influence on Genovese's work, including *The Political Economy of Slavery: Studies in the Economy and Society of the Slave South* (New York, 1967); *In Red and Black: Marxian Explorations in Southern and Afro-American History* (New York, 1968); *The World the Slaveholders Made: Two Essays in Interpretation* (New York, 1969); *Roll, Jordan, Roll* (New York, 1974); and, with Elizabeth Fox-Genovese, *Fruits of Merchant Capital: Slavery and Bourgeois Property in the Rise and Expansion of Capitalism* (New York, 1983). Criticism of Genovese's theoretical approach is found in Richard H. King, "Marxism and the Slave South," *American Quarterly* 29 (1977), 117–131; Carl N. Degler, *Place over Time: The Continuity of Southern Distinctiveness* (Baton Rouge, La., 1977); and George M. Fredrickson, "The Challenge of Marxism: The Genoveses on Slavery and Merchant Capital," in Fredrickson, *The Arrogance of Race: Historical Perspectives on Slavery, Racism, and Social Inequality* (Middletown, Conn., 1988).

In addition to the pivotal works by Blassingame, Genovese, and Gutman, there has been a wealth of excellent studies on various aspects of slave culture and slave community. These noteworthy works include George P. Rawick, *From Sundown to Sunup: The Making of the Black Community* (Westport, Conn., 1972); Leslie H. Owens, *This Species of Property: Slave Life and Culture in the Old South* (New York, 1976); Dena S. Epstein, *Sinful Tunes and Spirituals: Black Folk Music to the Civil War* (Urbana, Ill., 1977); Lawrence W. Levine, *Black Culture and Black Consciousness: Afro-American Folk Thought from Slavery to Freedom* (New York, 1977); Albert J. Raboteau, *Slave Religion: The Invisible Institution in the Antebellum South* (New York, 1978); John Vlach, *The Afro-American Tradition in Decorative Arts* (Cleveland, 1978); Thomas L. Webber, *Deep Like the Rivers: Education in the Slave Quarter Community, 1831–1865* (New York, 1978); Paul D. Escott, *Slavery Remembered: A Record of Twentieth Century Slave Narratives* (Chapel Hill, N.C., 1979); Peter Kolchin, "Reevaluating the Antebellum Slave Community: A Comparative Perspective," *Journal of American History* 45 (1983), 579–601; Charles Joyner, *Down by the Riverside: A South Carolina Slave Community* (Urbana, Ill., 1984); Michael P. Johnson, "Work, Culture, and the Slave Community: Slave Occupations in the Cotton Belt in 1860," *Labor History* 27 (1986), 325–355; Sterling Stuckey, *Slave Culture: Nationalist Theory and the Foundations of Black America* (New York, 1987); Margaret Creel, *A Peculiar People: Slave Religion and Community-Culture among the Gullahs* (New York, 1988); and Charles Joyner, *Remember Me: Slave Life in Coastal Georgia* (Athens, Ga., 1989).

Slave Life in the Antebellum Period

In addition to studies on slave culture and community, there have been other important works on slave life during the zenith of the plantation system. Albert J. Raboteau's *Slave Religion* stresses the covert nature of the slave's spiritual practices, and John B. Boles, *Religion in Antebellum Kentucky* (Lexington, Ky., 1976), emphasizes the shared religious experience of blacks and whites. See also: Timothy L. Smith, "Slavery and Theology: The Emergence of Black

Christian Consciousness in Nineteenth-Century America," *Church History* 41 (1972), 497–512; Kenneth K. Bailey, "Protestantism and Afro-Americans in the Old South: Another Look," *Journal of Southern History* 41 (1975), 451–472; and Mechal Sobel, *Trabelin' On: The Slave Journey to an Afro-Baptist Faith* (Westport, Conn., 1979).

Herbert Gutman's *The Black Family* has stimulated interest in this topic. Related literature includes Michael J. Cassity, "Slave Families and 'Living Space': A Note on Evidence and Historical Context," *Southern Studies* 17 (1978), 209–215; Charles Wetherell, "Slave Kinship: A Case Study of the South Carolina Good Hope Plantation, 1835–1856," *Journal of Family History* 6 (1981), 294–308; Cheryll Ann Cody, "Naming, Kinship, and Estate Dispersal: Notes on Slave Family Life on a South Carolina Plantation, 1786–1833," *William and Mary Quarterly* 39 (1982), 192–211; Shepard Krech III, "Black Family Organization in the Nineteenth Century: An Ethnological Perspective," *Journal of Interdisciplinary History* 12 (1982), 429–452; John C. Inscoe, "Carolina Slave Names: An Index to Acculturation," *Journal of Southern History* 49 (1983), 527–554; and Cheryll Ann Cody, "There Was No 'Absalom' on the Ball Plantations: Slave-Naming Practices in the South Carolina Low Country, 1720–1865," *American Historical Review* 92 (1987), 563–596. Miscegenation, the issue of slave "breeding," and the interstate slave trade are discussed in James Hugo Johnston, *Race Relations in Virginia and Miscegenation in the South, 1776–1860* (Amherst, Mass., 1970); Richard G. Lowe and Randolph B. Campbell, "The Slave-Breeding Hypothesis: A Demographic Comment on the 'Buying' and 'Selling' States," *Journal of Southern History* 42 (1976), 401–412; Richard H. Steckel, "Miscegenation and the American Slave Schedules," *Journal of Interdisciplinary History* 11 (1980); Joel Williamson, *New People: Miscegenation and Mulattoes in the United States* (New York, 1980); and Michael Tadman, *Speculators and Slaves: Masters, Traders and Slaves in the Old South* (Madison, Wis., 1989).

The health of slaves and their diets has produced a number of specialized essays. Start with Todd L. Savitt, *Medicine and Slavery: The Diseases and Health Care of Blacks in Antebellum Virginia* (Urbana, Ill., 1978), and Kenneth F. Kiple and Virginia Himmelsteib King, *Another Dimension to the Black Diaspora: Diet, Disease, and Racism* (Cambridge, Eng., 1981). See also Richard H. Steckel, "A Peculiar Population: The Nutrition, Health, and Mortality of American Slaves from Childhood to Maturity," *Journal of Economic History* 46 (1986), 721–741.

Not until the mid-1980s was the subject of slave women systematically addressed, though much remains to be done. Elizabeth Fox-Genovese, *Within the Plantation Household: Black and White Women of the Old South* (Chapel Hill, 1988), is the leading work in the field. See also Dorothy Sterling, ed., *We Are Your Sisters: Black Women in the Nineteenth Century* (New York, 1984); Catherine Clinton, "Caught in the Web of the Big House: Women and Slavery," in Walter J. Fraser, Jr., et al., *The Web of Southern Social Relations: Women, Family, and Education* (Athens, Ga., 1985); Minrose C. Gwin, *Black and White Women of the Old South: The Peculiar Sisterhood in American Literature* (Knoxville, Tenn., 1985); Jacqueline Jones, *Labor of Love, Labor of Sorrows: Black Women, Work, and the Family from Slavery to the Present* (New York, 1985); Deborah Gray White, *Ar'n't I a Woman: Female Slaves in the Plantation South* (New York, 1985); Joan Gundersen, "The Double Bonds of Race and Sex," *Journal of Southern History* 52 (1986), 351–372; Suzanne Lebsock, "Complicity and Contention: Women in the Plantation South," *Georgia Historical Quarterly* 74 (1990), 59–83; and Carol Bleser, ed., *In Joy and in Sorrow: Women, Family, and Marriage in the Victorian South, 1830–1900* (New York, 1991). For comparative purposes, see Hilary Mcd. Beckles, *Natural Rebels: A Social History of Enslaved Black Women in Barbados* (New Brunswick, N.J., 1989); Barbara Bush, *Slave Women in Caribbean Society, 1650–1832* (Bloomington, Ind., 1989); and Marietta Morrisey, *Slave Women in the New World: Gender Stratification in the Caribbean* (Lawrence, Kans., 1989). On the black man, an important revision of the "Sambo" stereotype is Bertram Wyatt-Brown, "The Mark of Obedience: Male Slave Psychology in the Old South," *American Historical Review* 93 (1988), 1228–1252. Joseph Boskin, *Sambo: The Rise and Demise of an American Jester* (New York, 1986), explores the image of the servile black in popular culture.

Slave Resistance

The study of slave resistance is another area that has taken on greater sophistication in recent decades. A pioneering study, Herbert Aptheker, *Negro Slave Revolts* (New York, 1943), is a compendium of slave resistance, but the work is marred by a too enthusiastic definition of rebellion. More balanced early assessments are Harvey Wish, "American Slave Insurrections Before 1861," *Journal of Negro History* 22 (1937), and Raymond A. Bauer and Alice H. Bauer, "Day to Day Resistance to Slavery," *Journal of Negro History* 27 (1942), 388–419. Gerald W. Mullin, *Flight and Rebellion: Slave Resistance in Eighteenth Century Virginia* (New York, 1972), is an excellent case study. Eugene D. Genovese, *From Rebellion to Revolution: Afro-American Slave Revolts in the Making of the Modern World* (Baton Rouge, 1979), is a good place to start for current historiography. Genovese explains why servile insurrection occurred less frequently in the United States than elsewhere in the Western Hemisphere. For slave resistance in the Americas, consult C. L. R. James's classic study, *The Black Jacobins: Toussaint L'Ouverture and the San Domingo Revolution* (New York, 1938). For more recent work, see Richard Price, ed., *Maroon Societies: Rebel Slave Communities in the Americas* (Garden City, N.Y., 1973); Michael Craton, *Testing the Chains: Resistance to Slavery in the British West Indies* (Ithaca, N.Y., 1982); D. Barry Gaspar, *Bondsmen and Rebels: A Case Study of Master-Slave Relations in Antigua, with Implications for Colonial British America* (Baltimore, 1985); and David Geggus, "The Enigma of Jamaica in the 1790s: New Light on the Causes of Slave Rebellions," *William and Mary Quarterly* 45 (1987), 274–299.

On the issue of slave resistance in general, see Marion Kilson, "Towards Freedom: An Analysis of Slave Revolts in the United States," *Phylon* 25 (1964), 175–184; George M. Fredrickson and Christopher Lasch, "Resistance to Slavery," *Civil War History* 13 (1967), 315–329; John H. Bracey, Jr., August Meier, and Elliot Rudwick, eds., *American Slavery: The Question of Resistance* (Belmont, Calif., 1971); William C. Suttles, Jr., "African Religious Survivals as Factors in American Slave Revolts," *Journal of Negro History* 41 (1971), 97–104; Kenneth M. Stampp, "Rebels and Sambos: The Search for the Negro's Personality in Slavery," *Journal of Southern History* 37 (1975), 367–392; and Peter Kolchin, "The Process of Confrontation: Patterns of Resistance to Bondage in Nineteenth-Century Russia and the United States," *Journal of Social History* 11 (1978), 457–490.

There are numerous studies on specific acts of slave resistance. For the Stono rebellion of 1739, see Peter H. Wood, *Black Majority: Negroes in Colonial South Carolina from 1670 through the Stono Rebel-*

lion (New York, 1974), and John K. Thornton, "African Dimensions of the Stono Rebellion," *American Historical Review* 96 (1991), 1101–1113. Consult Michael P. Johnson, "Runaway Slaves and the Slave Communities in South Carolina, 1799–1830," *William and Mary Quarterly* 38 (1981), 418–441, for an examination of a later period in the same state. On Gabriel's revolt of 1800, see Gerald W. Mullin, *Flight and Rebellion*; Philip J. Schwarz, "Gabriel's Challenge: Slaves and Crime in Late Eighteenth-Century Virginia," *Virginia Magazine of History and Biography* 90 (1982), 283–309; and Douglas R. Egerton, "Gabriel's Conspiracy and the Election of 1800," *Journal of Southern History* 56 (1990), 191–214. The Vesey plot of 1822 is discussed in Richard C. Wade, "The Vesey Plot: A Reconsideration," *Journal of Southern History* 30 (1964), 143–161; William W. Freehling, *Prelude to Civil War: The Nullification Controversy in South Carolina, 1816–1836* (New York, 1966); and Robert S. Starobin, ed., *Denmark Vesey's Slave Conspiracy of 1822* (Englewood Cliffs, N.J., 1970). Nat Turner's slave insurrection of 1831, the major event of its kind in the Old South, is the subject of Henry Irving Tragle, *The Southampton Slave Revolt of 1831: A Compilation of Source Material* (Amherst, Mass., 1971), and Stephen B. Oates, *The Fires of Jubilee: Nat Turner's Fierce Rebellion* (New York, 1975). Works that deal with purported slave plots include Edwin A. Miles, "The Mississippi Slave Insurrection Scare of 1835," *Journal of Negro History* 42 (1957), 48–60; Jack D. L. Holmes, "The Abortive Slave Revolt at Pointe Coupee, Louisiana," *Louisiana History* 11 (1970), 341–362; Charles B. Dew, "Black Ironworkers and the Slave Insurrection Panic of 1856," *Journal of Southern History* 41 (1975), 321–338; Dan T. Carter, "The Anatomy of Fear: The Christmas Day Insurrection Scare of 1865," *Journal of Southern History* 42 (1976), 345–364; and Thomas J. Davis, *A Rumor of Revolt: The "Great Negro Plot" in Colonial New York* (New York, 1985).

Surveys and Anthologies

Several distinguished surveys and anthologies have appeared recently. Robert Fogel, *Without Consent or Contract: The Rise and Fall of American Slavery* (New York, 1990), is a monumental work, the result of a twenty-four-year project. Based on quantitative analysis, this landmark overview of slavery from the African slave trade through abolition is a work that scholars must now address. There are three companion volumes on technical matters: *Evidence and Methods*, vol. 1; *Technical Papers: Markets and Production* vol. 2; and *Technical Papers: Conditions of Slave Life and Transition to Freedom*, vol. 3. The best short and accessible introductions to slavery and its historiography are John B. Boles, *Black Southerners, 1619–1869*, and Peter J. Parish, *Slavery: History and Historians*. Nathan I. Huggins, *Black Odyssey: The Afro-American Ordeal in Slavery* (New York, 1977), is a novelistic treatment; Vincent Harding, *There Is a River: The Black Struggle for Freedom in America* (New York, 1981), has a polemic tone; and James Oakes, *Slavery and Freedom: An Interpretation of the Old South* (New York, 1990) focuses on the nineteenth-century.

More general surveys of black history with sections on slavery include Philip S. Foner, *History of Black Americans*, 3 vols. to date (Westport, Conn., 1975–); Mary Frances Berry and John W. Blassingame, *Long Memory: The Black Experience in America* (New York, 1982); and John Hope Franklin and Alfred A. Moss, Jr., *From Slavery to Freedom*, 6th ed. Useful collections of essays include Harry P. Owens, ed., *Perspectives and Irony in American Slavery* (Jackson, Miss., 1976); Kenneth M. Stampp, *The Imperiled Union: Essays on the Background of the Civil War* (New York, 1980); Willie Lee Rose, *Slavery and Freedom*, edited by William H. Freehling (New York, 1982); and Robert H. Abzug and Stephen E. Maizlish, eds., *New Perspectives on Race and Slavery in America: Essays in Honor of Kenneth M. Stampp* (Lexington, Ky., 1986).

The Origins of Slavery and the Atlantic Slave Trade

The origins of slavery on mainland North America are linked with developments in Europe, Africa, and the rest of the New World. Basil Davidson, *The Growth of African Civilization: West Africa, 1000–1800* (London, 1865), is a standard text on African history that should be supplemented by the original essays in Suzanne Miers and Igor Kopytoff, eds., *Slavery in Africa: Historical and Anthropological Perspectives* (Madison, Wis., 1974), as well as by Paul E. Lovejoy, *Transformations in Slavery: A History of Slavery in Africa* (Cambridge, Eng., 1983). The first important argument for the survival of African culture in the New World is Melville J. Herskovits, *The Myth of the Negro Past* (New York, 1941). An overview of slavery and abolition throughout the Americas is C. Duncan Rice, *The Rise and Fall of Black Slavery* (New York, 1975), while David Brion Davis, in the Pulitzer Prize–winning study *The Problem of Slavery in Western Culture* (Ithaca, N.Y., 1966), deals with the European perspective. Winthrop Jordan, *White over Black: American Attitudes Toward the Negro, 1590–1812* (Chapel Hill, N.C., 1968), is an intellectual history of the development of white racism in England and North America based on exhaustive research.

The Atlantic slave trade has attracted widespread attention. A pioneering work that is still worth consulting is W. E. B. Du Bois, *The Suppression of the African Slave Trade to the United States of America, 1638–1870* (New York, 1969; originally 1896). Philip D. Curtin, *The Atlantic Slave Trade: A Census* (Madison, Wis., 1969), was instrumental in documenting the rapid rate of natural increase of the slave population in North America since the early eighteenth century, an exception to the demographic pattern of the African diaspora in the rest of the New World. Reassessments of the quantitative data on the Atlantic slave trade are Joseph C. Miller, "Mortality in the Atlantic Slave Trade: Statistical Evidence on Causality," *Journal of Interdisciplinary History* 11 (1981), 385–423; James A. Rawley, *The Transatlantic Slave Trade: A History* (New York, 1981); Paul E. Lovejoy, "The Volume of the Atlantic Slave Trade: A Synthesis," *Journal of African History* 23 (1982), 473–501; Walter E. Minchinton, Celia King, and Peter Waite, eds., *Virginia Slave-Trade Statistics, 1698–1775* (Richmond, Va., 1984); and David Eltis, *Economic Growth and the Ending of the Transatlantic Slave Trade* (New York, 1987). Other important works are Basil Davidson, *Black Mother: The Years of the African Slave Trade* (Boston, 1961); Philip D. Curtin, "Epidemiology and the Slave Trade," *Political Science Quarterly* 83 (1968), 190–216; Ronald L. Takaki, *A Pro-Slavery Crusade: The Agitation to Reopen the African Slave Trade* (New York, 1971); Herbert S. Klein, *The Middle Passage: Comparative Studies in the Atlantic Slave Trade* (Princeton, 1978); Henry A. Gemery and Jan S. Hogendorn, eds., *The Uncommon Market: Essays in the Economic History of the Atlantic Slave Trade* (New York, 1979); Ira Berlin, "The Slave Trade and the Development of Afro-American Society in English Mainland North America, 1619–1775," *Southern Studies* 20 (1981), 122–136; Jay Coughtry, *The Notorious Triangle: Rhode Island and the African Slave Trade, 1700–1807* (Philadelphia, 1981); David Eltis and James Walvin, eds., *The Abolition of the Atlantic Slave Trade: Origins and Effects in Europe, Africa, and the Americas* (Madison, Wis., 1981); David Galenson, *Traders, Planters and Slaves: Market Behavior in Early America* (New York, 1986); Joseph C. Miller, *Way of Death: Merchant Capitalism and the Angolan Slave Trade, 1730–1830* (Madison, Wis., 1988); and Barbara L. Solow, ed., *Slavery and the Rise of the Atlantic System* (Cambridge, Eng., 1991).

British Mainland North America: The Colonial Era

The development of slavery in British mainland North America has produced much creative scholarship. Good starting points are William M. Wiecek, "The Statutory Law of Slavery and Race in the Thirteen Mainland Colonies of British America," *William and Mary Quarterly* 34 (1977), 258–280, and Ira Berlin, "Time, Space and the Evolution of Afro-American Society on British Mainland North America," *American Historical Review* 85 (1980), 44–78, which emphasizes the importance of regional differences over time. Edmund S. Morgan, *American Slavery, American Freedom: The Ordeal of Colonial Virginia* (New York, 1975), is a brilliant analysis of the emergence of slavery in Virginia. A good survey is Donald R. Wright, *African Americans in the Colonial Era: From African Origins Through the American Revolution* (Arlington Heights, Ill., 1990). Other relevant works are: Oscar Handlin and Mary F. Handlin, "Origins of the Southern Labor System"; Carl N. Degler, "Slavery and the Genesis of American Race Prejudice," *Comparative Studies in Society and History* 2 (1959), 49–66; Winthrop D. Jordan, "Modern Tensions and the Origins of American Slavery," *Journal of Southern History* 28 (1962), 18–30; Winthrop Jordan, *White over Black*; Alden T. Vaughan, "Blacks in Virginia: A Note on the First Decade," *William and Mary Quarterly* 29 (1972), 469–478; Timothy H. Breen, "A Changing Labor Force and Race Relations in Virginia, 1670–1710," *Journal of Social History* 6 (1973), 3–25; Joseph Boskin, *Into Slavery: Racial Decisions in the Virginia Colony* (Philadelphia, 1976); and Timothy H. Breen and Stephen Innes, *'Mine Owne Ground': Race and Freedom on Virginia's Easter Shore, 1640–1676* (New York, 1980). On the emergence of slavery in Maryland and the Chesapeake region, see Jonathan L. Albert, "The Origin of Slavery in the United

States—The Maryland Precedent," *American Journal of Legal History* 14 (1970), 189–221; Russell R. Menard, "The Maryland Slave Population, 1658–1730: A Demographic Profile of Blacks in Four Counties," *William and Mary Quarterly* 32 (1975), 29–54; Menard, "From Servants to Slaves: The Transformation of the Chesapeake Labor System," *Southern Studies* 16 (1977), 355–390; Whittington B. Johnson, "The Origin and Nature of African Slavery in Seventeenth-Century Maryland," *Maryland Historical Magazine* 63 (1978), 236–245; Gloria Main, *Tobacco Colony: Life in Early Maryland, 1650–1720* (Princeton, 1982); and Menard, *Economy and Society in Early Colonial Maryland* (New York, 1985). On South Carolina, see Peter H. Wood, *Black Majority: Negroes in Colonial South Carolina from 1670 Through the Stono Rebellion* (New York, 1974), an innovative study of black culture. Consult also M. Eugene Sirmans, "The Legal Status of the Slave in South Carolina, 1670–1740," *Journal of Southern History* 28 (1962), 462–473, and Daniel C. Littlefield, *Rice and Slaves: Ethnicity and the Slave Trade in Colonial South Carolina* (Baton Rouge, La., 1981). For colonial Louisiana, see Gwendolyn M. Hall, *The Creole Slaves of Louisiana: Roots of the Afro-Latin Heritage of the United States* (forthcoming).

The period of colonial slavery during the eighteenth century has a rich literature. An important early work is Thad W. Tate, *The Negro in Eighteenth-Century Williamsburg* (Charlottesville, Va., 1966). The major work for the Chesapeake is Allan Kulikoff, *Tobacco and Slaves: The Development of Southern Cultures in the Chesapeake, 1680–1800* (Chapel Hill, N.C., 1986). Another creative study is Mechal Sobel, *The World They Made Together: Black and White Values in Eighteenth-Century Virginia* (Princeton, 1987), which argues the confluence of African and English cultures. On Georgia, see Betty Wood, *Slavery in Colonial Georgia, 1730–1775* (Athens, Ga., 1984), which can be supplemented by Julia B. Smith, *Slavery and Rice Culture in Low Country Georgia, 1750–1860* (Knoxville, Tenn., 1985). An important essay is Philip D. Morgan, "Work and Culture: The Task System and the World of Low Country Blacks, 1700–1800," *William and Mary Quarterly* 35 (1982), 563–594. Slavery in the colonial period has been featured in special journal issues. See the "Chesapeake Society," *William and Mary Quarterly* 30 (1973); "St. Mary's City Commission Special Issue," *Maryland Historical Magazine* 49 (1974); "Special Issue on Colonial Slavery," *Southern*

Studies 16 (1977); and "Blacks in Early America," *William and Mary Quarterly* 35 (1978).

The Revolutionary Era

On the Revolutionary era, David Brion Davis, *The Problem of Slavery in the Age of Revolution, 1770–1823* (Ithaca, N.Y., 1975), places the paradox of liberty and slavery in the context of Western thought. Davis provides a critique of William W. Freehling, "The Founding Fathers and Slavery," *American Historical Review* 77 (1972), 81–93. In addition to Davis and Freehling on Thomas Jefferson, see William Cohen, "Thomas Jefferson and the Problem of Slavery," *Journal of American History* 41 (1969), 503–526; Robert McColley, *Slavery and Jeffersonian Virginia,* 2d ed. (Urbana, Ill., 1973); and John C. Miller, *The Wolf by the Ears: Thomas Jefferson and Slavery* (New York, 1977). Benjamin M. Quarles, *The Negro in the American Revolution* (Chapel Hill, N.C., 1961), is a concise narrative account of the black experience during the War of Independence. Other current scholarship includes Donald L. Robinson, *Slavery in the Structure of American Politics, 1765–1820* (New York, 1971); Duncan J. Macleod, *Slavery, Race, and the American Revolution* (New York, 1974); Ira Berlin, "The Revolution in Black Life," in Alfred J. Young, ed., *The American Revolution* (De Kalb, Ill., 1976), 349–382; Ellen Gibson Wilson, *The Loyal Blacks* (New York, 1976); F. Nwabueze Okoye, "Chattel Slavery as the Nightmare of the American Revolutionaries," *William and Mary Quarterly* 37 (1980), 3–28; Ira Berlin and Ronald Hoffman, eds., *Slavery and Freedom in the Age of the American Revolution* (Charlottesville, Va., 1983); Sylvia R. Frey, "Between Slavery and Freedom: Virginia Blacks in the American Revolution," *Journal of Southern History* 49 (1983), 375–398; Sidney Kaplan and Emma N. Kaplan, *The Black Presence in the Era of the American Revolution* (Amherst, Mass., 1989); Frey, *Water from the Rock: Black Resistance in a Revolutionary Age* (Princeton, 1991); and Gary B. Nash, *Race and Revolution* (Madison, Wis., 1991). For the second war with Britain, see Frank A. Cassell, "Slaves of the Chesapeake Bay Area and the War of 1812," *Journal of Negro History* 57 (1972), 144–155.

The Economics of Slavery in the Old South

The expansion of slavery in the United States during the nineteenth century has attracted extensive historiography. The best starting point for slavery in the Old South is Eugene Genovese's *Roll, Jordan, Roll,* which combines provocative insights on a variety of topics with immense scholarship and a lively writing style. Genovese has revised his earlier assessment in *The Political Economy of Slavery* that slavery was precapitalist and now sees slavery as in but not of transatlantic capitalism. Kenneth Stampp in *The Peculiar Institution* concluded that antebellum slavery was profitable, but important clarification of the economic issue came in the works of Alfred H. Conrad and John R. Meyer, "The Economics of Slavery in the Ante Bellum South," *Journal of Political Economy* 66 (1958), 95–130; Conrad and Meyer, *The Economics of Slavery and Other Studies in Econometric History* (Chicago, 1964); Harold D. Woodman, "The Profitability of Slavery: A Historical Perennial," *Journal of Southern History* 29 (1963), 303–325; Otto H. Olsen, "Historians and the Extent of Slaveownership in the Southern United States," *Civil War History* 18 (1972), 101–116; and Gavin Wright, "New and Old Views on the Economics of Slavery," *Journal of Economic History* 33 (1973), 452–466.

A pivotal book on the cliometrics of slavery is Robert W. Fogel and Stanley L. Engerman, *Time on the Cross:* vol. 1, *The Economics of American Negro Slavery,* and the technical companion, vol. 2, *Evidence and Methods* (Boston, 1974). The fanfare that accompanied *Time on the Cross* was quickly drowned out by a chorus of critics who pointed to the abuse of statistics and some questionable conclusions. The critics include: Herbert G. Gutman, *Slavery and the Numbers Game: A Critique of* Time on the Cross (Urbana, Ill., 1975); Thomas L. Haskell, "The True and Tragical History of *Time on the Cross,*" *New York Review of Books* 2 (1975), 33–39; and Paul A. David et al., *Reckoning with Slavery: A Critical Study in the Quantitative History of American Negro Slavery* (New York, 1976). Robert W. Fogel, *Without Consent or Contract,* is in part a rebuttal to these critics. The outstanding econometric study on slavery is Gavin Wright, *The Political Economy of the Cotton South: Households, Markets and Wealth in the Nineteenth Century* (New York, 1978), which disputes the thesis that slavery was a precapitalist institution. Fred Bateman and Thomas Weiss, *A Deplorable Scarcity: The Failure of Industrialization in the Slave Economy* (Chapel Hill, N.C., 1981), challenge Genovese's claim that slavery retarded the southern factory system. They see the South's failure in an inferior transportation system. See also William N. Parker, ed., *The Structure of the Cotton Economy of the Antebellum*

South (Washington, D.C., 1970); Philip D. Morgan, "Work and Culture: The Task System and the World of Lowcountry Blacks, 1700–1880," *William and Mary Quarterly* 39 (1982), 563–599; Laurence Shore, *Southern Capitalists: The Ideological Leadership of an Elite, 1832–1885* (Chapel Hill, N.C., 1986); and Peter Coclanis, *The Shadow of a Dream: Economic Life and Death in the South Carolina Low Country, 1670–1920* (New York, 1989).

Slavery and the Plantation System in the Old South

Slavery and plantation life is the subject of Edgar T. Thompson, *Plantation Societies, Race Relations, and the South: The Regimentation of Populations* (Durham, N.C., 1975). A number of local studies have appeared: Julia Floyd Smith, *Slavery and Plantation Growth in Antebellum Florida, 1821–1860* (Gainesville, Fla., 1973); Randolph B. Campbell, *A Southern Community in Crisis: Harrison County, Texas, 1850–1880* (Austin, Tex., 1983); John S. Otto, *Cannon's Point Plantation, 1794–1860: Living Conditions and Status Patterns in the Old South* (Orlando, Fla., 1984); Orville V. Burton, *In My Father's House Are Many Mansions: Family and Community in Edgefield, South Carolina* (Chapel Hill, N.C., 1985); Barbara Jeanne Fields, *Slavery and Freedom on the Middle Ground: Maryland During the Nineteenth Century* (New Haven, Conn., 1985); Julia Floyd Smith, *Slavery and Rice Culture in Low Country Georgia, 1750–1860* (Knoxville, Tenn., 1985); Theodore Rosengarten, *Tombee: Portrait of a Cotton Planter* (New York, 1986); John Hebron Moore, *The Emergence of the Cotton Kingdom in the Old Southwest: Mississippi, 1770–1860* (Baton Rouge, La., 1988); and Randolph B. Campbell, *An Empire for Slavery: The Peculiar Institution in Texas, 1821–1865* (Baton Rouge, La., 1989). Two collections of local studies are Elinor Miller and Eugene D. Genovese, eds., *Plantation, Town and Country: Essays on the Local History of American Slave Society* (Urbana, Ill., 1974); and Orville V. Burton and Robert C. McMath, eds., *Class, Conflict and Consensus: Antebellum Southern Community Studies* (Westport, Conn., 1982).

On the planter class, southern politics, and white society, see William Freehling, *The Road to Disunion*, vol. 1: *Secessionists at Bay, 1776–1854* (New York, 1990). Important scholarly studies on the proslavery argument are Bertram Wyatt-Brown, "Modernizing Southern Slavery: The Proslavery Argument Reinterpreted," in J. Morgan Kousser and James M. McPherson, eds., *Race, Region and*

Reconstruction: Essays in Honor of C. Vann Woodward (New York, 1982), 27–49, and Larry E. Tise, *Proslavery: A History of the Defense of Slavery in America, 1701–1840* (Athens, Ga., 1988). The forthcoming book by Elizabeth Fox-Genovese and Eugene D. Genovese, *The Mind of the Master Class: The Life and Thought of Southern Slaveholders,* should be a major addition to the literature. Important studies are John McCardell, *The Idea of a Southern Nation: Southern Nationalists and Southern Nationalism, 1830–1860* (New York, 1979); Bertram Wyatt-Brown, *Southern Honor: Ethics and Behavior in the Old South* (New York, 1982); Drew G. Faust, *James Henry Hammond and the Old South: A Design for Mastery* (Baton Rouge, La., 1982); James B. Oakes, *The Ruling Race: A History of American Slaveholders* (New York, 1982); William J. Cooper, *Liberty and Slavery: Southern Politics to 1860* (New York, 1983); Bruce Collins, *White Society in the Antebellum South* (London, 1985); Kenneth S. Greenberg, *Master and Statesman: The Political Culture of American Slavery* (Baltimore, 1985); J. William Harris, *Plain Folk and Gentry in a Slave Society: White Liberty and Black Slavery in Augusta's Hinterlands* (Middletown, Conn., 1985); and Steven M. Stowe, *Intimacy and Power in the Old South: Ritual in the Lives of the Planters* (Baltimore, 1990). See also Lacy K. Ford, "Republican Ideology in a Slave Society: The Political Economy of John C. Calhoun," *Journal of Southern History* 54 (1988), 405–424. Black and white bosses on the plantation are the topic of William K. Scarborough, *The Overseer: Plantation Management in the Old South* (Baton Rouge, La., 1966), and William L. Van Deburg, *The Slave Drivers: Black Agricultural Labor Supervisors* (Westport, Conn., 1979).

Diversity Within Antebellum Slavery

Slavery and race affected more than just the southern plantation. Ira Berlin, *Slaves Without Masters: The Free Negro in the Antebellum South* (New York, 1974), and Leonard P. Curry, *The Free Black in Urban America, 1800–1850: The Shadow of a Dream* (Chicago, 1981), explore a crucial area in social relations. An important state study is Marina Wikramanayake, *A World in Shadow: The Free Black in Antebellum South Carolina* (Columbia, S.C., 1973). The journal *Southern Studies* devoted all of the volume 21 (1982) issue to the topic of free blacks. Recent articles on free blacks are Rowland Berthoff, "Conventional Mentality: Free Blacks, Women, and Business

Corporations as Unequal Persons, 1820–1870," *Journal of American History* 76 (1989), 753–784, and W. Jeffrey Bolster, "'To Feel Like a Man': Black Seamen in the Northern States, 1800–1860," *Journal of American History* 76 (1990), 1173–1199. The exceptional case of black slavemasters and property owners is the subject of Michael P. Johnson and James L. Roark, *Black Masters: A Free Family of Color in the Old South* (New York, 1984); Larry Koger, *Black Slaveowners: Free Black Slave Masters in South Carolina* (Jefferson, N.C., 1985); David O. Whitten, *Andrew Durnford: A Black Sugar Planter in Antebellum Louisiana* (Natchitoches, La., 1987); Loren Schweninger, "Prosperous Blacks in the South, 1790–1880," *American Historical Review* 95 (1990), 31–56; and Schweninger, *Black Property Owners in the South, 1790–1915* (Urbana, Ill., 1990). See also Schweninger's "The Free Slave Phenomenon: James P. Thomas and the Black Community in Ante-Bellum Nashville," *Civil War History* 22 (1976), 293–307, and "The Underside of Slavery: The Internal Economy, Self-Hire, and Quasi-Freedom in Virginia, 1780–1865," *Slavery and Abolition* 12 (1991), 1–22. A related essay is Juliet E. K. Walker, "Racism, Slavery, and Free Enterprise: Black Entrepreneurship in the United States Before the Civil War," *Business History Review* 60 (1988), 343–382. The major books surveying urban slavery are: Richard C. Wade, *Slavery in the Cities: The South, 1820–1860* (New York, 1970), and Claudia Golden, *Urban Slavery in the American South, 1820–1860: A Quantitative History* (Chicago, 1976). Two good case studies of New Orleans are Roger A. Fischer, "Racial Segregation in Ante Bellum New Orleans," *American Historical Review* 74 (1969), 926–937, and John W. Blassingame, *Black New Orleans, 1860–1880* (Chicago, 1973).

Robert S. Starobin, *Industrial Slavery in the Old South* (New York, 1970), is the best overview of the nonagricultural exploitation of slave labor. Charles B. Dew has written widely on industrial slavery, including *Ironmaker to the Confederacy: Joseph R. Anderson and the Tredegar Iron Works* (New Haven, Conn., 1966); "Disciplining Slave Iron Workers in the Antebellum South," *American Historical Review* 79 (1974); "David Ross and the Oxford Iron Works: A Study of Industrial Slavery in the Early Nineteenth Century South," *William and Mary Quarterly* 31 (1974), 189–224; and "Sam Williams, Forgeman: The Life of an Industrial Slave in the Old South," in J. Morgan Kousser and James M. McPherson, eds., *Race, Region and Reconstruction: Essays in Honor of C. Vann Woodward* (New York, 1982). See also Ernest McPherson Lander, Jr., *The Textile Industry in Antebellum South Carolina* (Baton Rouge, La., 1969); Ronald L. Lewis, *Coal, Iron, and Slaves: Industrial Slavery in Maryland and Virginia* (Westport, Conn., 1979); and Fred Bateman and Thomas Weiss, *A Deplorable Scarcity: The Failure of Industrialization in the Slave Economy* (Chapel Hill, 1981).

Slavery and the Law

The legal status of the slave and free black has been prominent in recent historiography. Recommended books are: Don E. Fehrenbacher, *The Dred Scott Case: Its Significance in American Law and Politics* (New York, 1978); A. Leon Higginbotham, Jr., *In the Matter of Color: Race and the American Legal Process, The Colonial Period* (New York, 1978); Michael Stephen Hindus, *Prison and Plantation: Crime, Justice, and Authority in Massachusetts and South Carolina, 1767–1878* (Chapel Hill, 1980); Paul Finkelman, *An Imperfect Union: Slavery, Federalism, and Comity* (Chapel Hill, N.C., 1981); Mark Tushnet, *The American Law of Slavery, 1810–1860: Considerations of Humanity and Interest* (Princeton, 1981); Alison Goodyear Freehling, *Drift Toward Dissolution: The Virginia Slavery Debate of 1831–1832* (Baton Rouge, La., 1982); Edward L. Ayers, *Vengeance and Justice: Crime and Punishment in the Nineteenth-Century American South* (New York, 1984); Kermit L. Hall, ed., *The Law of American Slavery* (New York, 1987), which has reprinted a number of important essays; Philip J. Schwarz, *Twice Condemned: Slaves and the Criminal Laws of Virginia, 1705–1865* (Baton Rouge, La., 1988); Don E. Fehrenbacher, *Constitutions and Constitutionalism in the Slaveholding South* (Athens, Ga., 1989); Kermit L. Hall and James W. Ely, eds., *An Uncertain Tradition: Constitutionalism and the History of the South* (Athens, Ga., 1990); and Donald G. Nieman, *Promises to Keep: African-Americans and the Constitutional Order, 1776–1989* (New York, 1990).

Among numerous articles on legal matters, see William M. Wiecek, "The Statutory Law of Slavery and Race in the Thirteen Mainland Colonies of British America," *William and Mary Quarterly* 34 (1977), 258–280; Wiecek, "Slavery and Abolition Before the United States Supreme Court, 1820–1860," *Journal of American History* 65 (1978), 34–59; Daniel J. Flanigan, "Criminal Procedure in Slave Trials in the Antebellum South," *Journal of Southern History* 40 (1974), 537–564; A. E. Keir Nash, "The Texas Supreme Court and Trial Rights of Blacks, 1845–1860," *Journal of American History* 58 (1971), 622–642; Don Higginbotham and William S. Price, Jr., "Was It Murder for a White Man to Kill a Slave? Chief Justice Martin Howard Condemns the Peculiar Institution in North Carolina," *William and Mary Quarterly* 36 (1979), 593–601; and Paul Finkelman, "Slavery and the Northwest Ordinance: A Study in Ambiguity," *Journal of the Early Republic* 6 (1986), 343–370.

The Native Americans and Slavery

The relationship between several Native American tribes and slavery as well as black participation in the Seminole Wars has become an established field of interest. The major monographs are Kenneth W. Porter, *The Negro on the American Frontier* (New York, 1971); Rudia Halliburton, Jr., *Red over Black: Black Slavery Among the Cherokee Indians* (Westport, Conn., 1977); Daniel F. Littlefield, Jr., *Africans and Seminoles: From Removal to Emancipation* (Westport, Conn., 1977); Littlefield, Jr., *Africans and Creeks: From the Colonial Period to the Civil War* (Westport, Conn., 1979); and Theda Perdue, *Slavery and the Evolution of Cherokee Society, 1540–1866* (Knoxville, Tenn., 1979).

Slavery and Freedom in the North

Studies of northern slavery and free blacks are: Arthur Zilversmit, *The First Emancipation: The Abolition of Slavery in the North* (Chicago, 1967); Edgar J. McManus, *Black Bondage in the North* (Syracuse, N.Y., 1973); William D. Piersen, *Black Yankees: The Development of an Afro-American Subculture in Eighteenth Century New England* (Amherst, Mass., 1988); Shane White, "'We Dwell in Safety and Pursue Our Honest Callings': Free Blacks in New York City, 1783–1810," *Journal of American History* 75 (1988), 445–470; and Gary B. Nash and Jean R. Soderlund, *Freedom by Degrees: Emancipation and Its Aftermath in Pennsylvania* (New York, 1990). Leon Litwack, *North of Slavery: The Negro in the Free States, 1790–1860* (Chicago, 1961); Eric Foner, *Free Soil, Free Labor, Free Men* (New York, 1970); Eugene H. Berwanger, *The Frontier Against Slavery: Western Anti-Negro Prejudice and the Slavery Extension Controversy* (Urbana, Ill., 1971); Robert W. Johannsen, *Lincoln, the South, and*

Slavery: The Political Dimension (Baton Rouge, 1990); and David Zarefsky, *Lincoln, Douglas, and Slavery: In the Crucible of Public Debate* (Chicago, 1990), all probe the racial attitudes of northerners. Racism is explored further in George M. Fredrickson, *The Black Image in the White Mind: The Debate on Afro-American Character and Density, 1817–1914* (New York, 1971).

The historiography of abolitionism is long; good introductions to it are James B. Stewart, *Holy Warriors: Abolitionists and American Slavery* (New York, 1976), and Merton L. Dillon, *Slavery Attacked: Southern Slaves and Their Allies* (Baton Rouge, La., 1990). On black abolitionism, see Benjamin Quarles, *Black Abolitionists* (New York, 1970); Jane H. Pease and William H. Pease, *They Who Would Be Free: Blacks Search for Freedom, 1830–1861* (New York, 1974); and R. J. M. Blackett, *Building an Anti-Slavery Wall: Black Americans in the Atlantic Abolitionist Movement, 1830–1860* (Baton Rouge, La., 1983). A related essay is Leon F. Litwack, "The Abolitionist Dilemma: The Antislavery Movement and the Northern Negro," *New England Quarterly* 34 (1961), 50–73. For the formation of a political party that contained significant antislavery sentiment, see William E. Gienapp, *The Origins of the Republican Party, 1852–1856* (New York, 1987).

The Civil War and Reconstruction

The Civil War and Reconstruction were incomplete revolutions for the slave and freedman. Excellent introductions to the Civil War and Reconstruction are James M. McPherson, *Battle Cry of Freedom: The Era of Civil War* (New York, 1988), which won the Pulitzer Prize, and Eric Foner, *Reconstruction: America's Unfinished Revolution, 1863–1877* (New York, 1988), also a prize-winning book. For the events leading to war, see David M. Potter, *The Impending Crisis: 1848–1861* (New York, 1976), and Richard H. Sewell, *A House Divided: Sectionalism and Civil War, 1848–1865* (Baltimore, 1988). Students should note that Foner's *Nothing but Freedom: Emancipation and Its Legacy* (Baton Rouge, La., 1983) compares emancipation in the United States with the experience in Haiti and the British Caribbean. A pioneering work that foreshadowed current interpretations of Reconstruction is W. E. B. Du Bois, *Black Reconstruction: An Essay Toward a History of the Part Which Black Folk Played in the Attempt to Reconstruct Democracy in America* (New York, 1969; originally 1935). Important books that deal with the transition from slavery to freedom are: Bell I. Wiley, *Southern Negroes, 1861–1865* (New Haven, Conn., 1938); James M. McPherson, *The Struggle for Equality: Abolitionists and the Negro in the Civil War and Reconstruction* (Princeton, 1964); Louis S. Gerteis, *From Contraband to Freedman: Federal Policy Toward Southern Blacks, 1861–1865* (Westport, Conn., 1973); Roger L. Ransom and Richard Sutch, *One Kind of Freedom: The Economic Consequences of Emancipation* (Cambridge, Eng., 1977); Daniel A. Novak, *The Wheel of Servitude: Black Forced Labor After Slavery* (Lexington, Ky., 1978); Leon Litwack, *Been in the Storm So Long! The Aftermath of Slavery* (New York, 1979); Eric Foner, *Politics and Ideology in the Age of the Civil War* (New York, 1980); Gerald D. Jaynes, *Branches Without Roots: The Genesis of the Black Working Class in the American South, 1862–1882* (New York, 1986); John C. Inscoe, *Mountain Masters, Slavery and the Sectional Crisis in Western North Carolina* (Knoxville, Tenn., 1989); and Roger Ransom, *Conflict and Compromise: The Political Economy of Slavery, Emancipation, and the American Civil War* (New York, 1989).

Much of the most sophisticated work on the black experience during the Civil War and Reconstruction has been done on the state and local level. See: Willie Lee Rose, *Rehearsal for Reconstruction: The Port Royal Experiment* (Indianapolis, 1964); Joel Williamson, *After Slavery: The Negro in South Carolina During Reconstruction, 1861–1877* (Chapel Hill, N.C., 1965); Peter Kolchin, *First Freedom: The Response of Alabama's Blacks to Emancipation and Reconstruction* (Westport, Conn., 1972); C. Peter Ripley, *Slaves and Freedmen in Civil War Louisiana* (Baton Rouge, La., 1976); Michael Wayne, *The Reshaping of Plantation Society: The Natchez District, 1860–1890* (Baton Rouge, La., 1983); Victor B. Howard, *Black Liberation in Kentucky: Emancipation and Freedom in Kentucky, 1862–1884* (Lexington, Ky., 1983); Clarence L. Mohr, *On the Threshold of Freedom: Masters and Slaves in Civil War Georgia* (Athens, Ga., 1986); and Wayne K. Durril, *War of Another Kind: A Southern Community in the Great Rebellion* (New York, 1990).

Black military participation during the Civil War is the subject of Benjamin M. Quarles, *The Negro in the Civil War* (Boston, 1953), and Dudley T. Cornish, *The Sable Arm: Negro Troops in the Union Army, 1861–1865* (New York, 1966). Black soldiers and white officers are discussed in Joseph T. Glatthaar, *Forged in Battle: The Civil War Alliance of Black Soldiers and White Officers* (New York, 1989), as well as the movie *Glory* (1989), directed by Edward Zwick. *Glory* portrays the 54th Massachusetts Volunteer Infantry, an African-American unit led by a white colonel, Robert Gould Shaw. The television series on the Public Broadcasting System, *The Civil War* (1989), by Kenneth Burns, depicts black life as part of its overview of the Civil War based largely on the use of contemporary documents. The legacy of racism is the subject of Barbara Jeanne Fields, "Slavery, Race and Ideology in the United States of America," *New Left Review* (May–June 1990), 95–118.

Comparative Slavery

There is an abundance of scholarship comparing slave systems. An essential reference is *Slavery and Abolition: A Journal of Comparative Studies*, a quarterly published in London that covers slave and post-slave societies, from the ancient period to the present. It is concerned with the abolition of slavery as well as the legacy of slavery. The outstanding overview of slavery on a worldwide perspective is Orlando Patterson, *Slavery and Social Death: A Comparative Study* (Cambridge, Mass., 1982). Patterson's *Freedom in the Making of Western Culture*, vol. 1 (New York, 1991), which won a National Book Award, makes the argument that only in the West did the antithesis of slavery give rise to a distinctive love of freedom. David Brion Davis in two award-winning studies, *The Problem of Slavery in Western Culture* (Ithaca, N.Y., 1966) and *The Problem of Slavery in the Age of Revolution* (Ithaca, N.Y., 1975), analyzes attitudes toward slavery in Western culture, a subject he broadened in *Slavery and Human Progress* (New York, 1984). Other important books on slavery in the New World are Frank Tannenbaum, *Slave and Citizen: The Negro in the Americas* (New York, 1946); Harmannus Hoetink, *Slavery and Race Relations in the Americas: Comparative Notes on Their Nature and Nexus* (New York, 1973); Robert Brent Toplin, *Slavery and Race Relations in Latin America* (Westport, Conn., 1974); C. Duncan Rice, *The Rise and Fall of Black Slavery* (New York, 1975); Herbert S. Klein, *The Middle Passage: Comparative Studies in the Atlantic Slave Trade* (Princeton, 1978); Robin Blackburn, *The Overthrow of Colonial Slavery, 1776–1848* (London, 1988); Alan Watson, *Slave Law in the Americas* (Athens, Ga., 1990); and Philip Curtin,

The Rise and Fall of the Plantation Complex: Essays in Atlantic History (New York, 1990). Stanley L. Engerman, "Slavery and Emancipation in Comparative Perspective: A Look at Some Recent Debates," *Journal of Economic History* 46 (1986), surveys the historiographic battles. Ira Berlin and Philip D. Morgan have edited an entire issue of *Slavery and Abolition,* 12 (1991), on "The Slaves' Economy: Independent Production by Slaves in the Americas."

Historians have also focused on comparisons of specific regions. Herbert S. Klein, *Slavery in the Americas: A Comparative Study of Cuba and Virginia* (Chicago, 1967); Carl N. Degler, *Neither Black Nor White: Slavery and Race Relations in Brazil* (New York, 1971); George M. Fredrickson, *White Supremacy: A Comparative Study in American and South African History* (New York, 1981); Peter Kolchin, *Unfree Labor: American Slavery and Russian Serfdom* (Cambridge, Mass., 1987); and Michael Mullin, *Africa in America: Slave Acculturation and Resistance in the American South and the British Caribbean, 1736–1831* (Urbana, Ill., 1992), are essential books. Significant essays are: Carl N. Degler, "Slavery in Brazil and the United States: An Essay in Comparative History," *American Historical Review* 75 (1970), 1004–1028; Richard R. Beeman, "Labor Forces and Race Relations: A Comparative View of the Colonization of Brazil and Virginia," *Political Science Quarterly* 86 (1971), 609–636; Richard S. Dunn, "A Tale of Two Plantations: Slave Life at Mesopotamia in Jamaica and Mount Airy in Virginia, 1799–1828," *William and Mary Quarterly* 34 (1977), 32–65; Shearer Davis Bowman, "Antebellum Planters and Vormarz Junkers in Comparative Perspective," *American Historical Review* 85 (1980), 779–808; Ian F. Hancock, "Gullah and Barbadian—Origins and Relationships," *American Speech* 60 (1980), 17–35; Peter Kolchin, "In Defense of Servitude: American Proslavery and Russian Proserfdom Arguments, 1760–1860," *American Historical Review* 85 (1980), 809–827; Stuart B. Schwartz, "Patterns of Slaveholding in the Americas: New Evidence from Brazil," *American Historical Review* 87 (1982), 55–86; Peter Kolchin, "Reevaluating the Antebellum Slave Community: A Comparative Perspective," *Journal of American History* 70 (1983), 579–601; and Daniel C. Littlefield, "Continuity and Change in Slave Culture, South Carolina and the West Indies," *Southern Studies* 26 (1987), 202–216. Two articles written on the centennial anniversary of Brazilian abolition are Rebecca J. Scott, "Exploring the Meaning of Freedom: Postemancipation Societies in Comparative Perspective," *Hispanic American Historical Review* 68 (1988), and Seymour Drescher, "Brazilian Abolition in Comparative Perspective," *Hispanic American Historical Review* 66 (1988), 429–460.

Other influential studies on slavery in the New World include: Gwendolyn M. Hall, *Social Control in Slave Plantation Societies: A Comparison of St. Domingue and Cuba* (Baltimore, 1971); Richard B. Sheridan, *Sugar and Slavery: An Economic History of the British West Indies, 1623–1775* (Baltimore, 1971); Richard S. Dunn, *Sugar and Slaves: The Rise of the Planter Class in the English West Indies, 1624–1713* (Chapel Hill, N.C., 1972); Sidney W. Mintz, *Caribbean Transformations* (Chicago, 1974); Kenneth F. Kiple, *Blacks in Colonial Cuba, 1774–1899* (Gainesville, Fla., 1976); Manuel M. Fraginals, *The Sugarmill: The Socioeconomic Complex of Sugar in Cuba, 1760–1860* (New York, 1976); Barry Higman, *Slave Populations of the British Caribbean, 1807–1834* (Baltimore, 1984); Sidney W. Mintz, *Sweetness and Power: The Place of Sugar in Modern History* (New York, 1985); Francisco A. Scarano, *Sugar and Slavery in Puerto Rico: The Plantation Economy of Ponce, 1800–1850* (Madison, Wis., 1985); Stuart B. Schwartz, *Sugar Plantations in the Formation of Brazilian Society: Bahia, 1550–1835* (Cambridge, Eng., 1985); Rebecca J. Scott, *Slave Emancipation in Cuba: The Transition to Free Labor, 1860–1899* (Princeton, 1985); Mary C. Karasch, *Slave Life in Rio de Janeiro, 1808–1850* (Princeton, 1987); Robert L. Paquette, *Sugar Is Made with Blood: The Conspiracy of La Escalera and the Conflict Between Empires over Slavery in Cuba* (Middletown, Conn., 1988); J. R. Ward, *British West Indian Slavery, 1750–1834: The Process of Amelioration* (New York, 1988); Hilary Mcd. Beckles, *White Servitude and Black Slavery in Barbados, 1627–1715* (Knoxville, Tenn., 1989); and Dale W. Tomich, *Slavery in the Circuit of Sugar: Martinique and the World Economy, 1830–1848* (Baltimore, 1990). Collections of essays are: Laura Foner and Eugene D. Genovese, eds., *Slavery in the New World: A Reader in Comparative History* (Englewood Cliffs, N.J., 1969), and Stanley L. Engerman and Eugene D. Genovese, eds., *Race and Slavery in the Western Hemisphere: Quantitative Studies* (Princeton, 1975). Gary Okihiro, ed., *In Resis-*

tance: Studies in African, Caribbean and Afro-American History (Amherst, Mass., 1986), is the outgrowth of a symposium honoring the fortieth anniversary of Herbert Aptheker's *American Negro Slave Revolts* (New York, 1943). The pioneering study by Eric Williams, *Capitalism and Slavery* (New York, 1944), is the subject of Barbara L. Solow and Stanley L. Engerman, eds., *British Capitalism and Caribbean Slavery: The Legacy of Eric Williams* (New York, 1987).